REVOLUTION,
REFORM, AND
SOCIAL JUSTICE

REVOLUTION,

REFORM, AND

SOCIAL JUSTICE

*Studies in the Theory
and Practice of Marxism*

BASIL BLACKWELL • OXFORD

Library of Congress Catalog Card Number: 74-21610
ISBN: 0-631-17640-3

Manufactured in the United States of America

First published in the United Kingdom
by Basil Blackwell, Oxford, 1976

ACKNOWLEDGMENTS

For permission to reprint material previously published in article form, I make grateful acknowledgement to the following publishers and periodicals.

Chapter One — From *Marxist Ideology in the Contemporary World*, edited by M. Drachkovitch, published for the Hoover Institution on War, Revolution and Peace, Stanford University by Frederick A. Praeger, New York and London, 1966.

Chapters Two and Three — *Journal of the History of Ideas,* Vol. XXIX, No. 1, Jan-March 1968, and Vol. XXXIV, No. 2, April-June, 1973

Chapter Five — *Quadrant,* Spring 1973

Chapter Six — *Survey,* No. 66, January 1968

Chapter Seven — *The Problems of Communism,* 1957

Chapter Eight — *Encounter Magazine,* December 1974

Chapter Nine — From *Peaceful Change in Modern Society,* Stanford University: Hoover Institution Press, 1971

Chapter Ten — *The Humanist,* Fall 1967

Chapter Eleven — *Saturday Review,* Vol. 41, May 17, 1958

Chapter Twelve — Raleigh School of Liberal Arts of North Carolina State University, 1968

To
Milorad,
Miro,
Bogdan and Nina
and other fighters for human freedom
at home and abroad

CONTENTS

vii

INTRODUCTION

These studies in the theory and practice of Marxism and related themes are primarily chapters in the history of ideas. They are not however without relevance to the prospects of survival of democratic societies in the critical final quarter of the twentieth century.

It is not likely that during this period the democratic societies of the Western world, by which I mean in the first instance England and the United States, will be overthrown from without. Even if they remain virtual islands in a multicolored sea of totalitarianism, the balance of weapons of terror and the mutual hostility of the Communist superpowers, will insure their relative security. There will always remain the danger that in a world in which the proliferation of nuclear weapons has not been halted by an international authority some maniacal dictator or group of terrorists may launch an attack that will trigger a holocaust. Short of such contingencies, which can be guarded against but never completely eliminated, the democratic societies can survive in however modified a form. The necessities of defence, even if they impose a far greater austerity than any so far experienced, do not entail the sacrifice of the basically democratic character of the free nations.

The downfall of the major democracies will come about, if at all, from within, and not necessarily in a violent fashion. This will occur in one of two related ways—either as a consequence of cumulative failures to solve their pressing domestic problems or of an estrangement from the basic values that hold a society together. So long, however, so the latter has not become the pervasive and dominant mood of a society, the failure to solve problems will lead to continued efforts to make life still viable by redoubled efforts to reform within the existing political system.

It is when the cement of loyalty to a free society is dissolved that the greatest danger to its survival manifests itself. This loyalty need not be blind. Although its agglutinative character rests on habit, it also depends on awareness of historical achievement in the slow long march from the unfreedoms and evils of the past, and especially upon the insight into the social and political alternatives to existing society. The absence of this awareness and insight becomes fateful in an era like our own where the sudden death of cultures has become possible. For a short period of time a people may risk its survival in defense of its freedom. However as the atmosphere of crisis is prolonged, doubts arise, directly related to the erosion of basic loyalties, whether the stakes are worth the risks. The malaise of influential intellectual élites and opinion-makers festers, and uncertainty develops among their constituencies whether there is any essential difference between the basic institutions of Western free societies and those of their totalitarian enemies. The imperfections of such societies, in the absence of historical perspective, the occasional and sometimes dramatic lapses from their own ideals, the very measures taken to defend themselves from the violence and subversion by extremist groups, are all taken as evidence of the narrowing gap or the absence of any significant gap, between the patterns of life of ordinary men and women in democratic and communist cultures.

As the will to resist communist aggression weakens, any defence that carries with it risk of widespread death or destruction seems pointless, indeed a form of paranoia. At such a time the convergence theory, a corollary of the latest form of "vulgar" Marxism, will have triumphed.

Under different names and varied emphases this is the view according to which the imperatives of industrial society, whether in the United States or the Soviet Union or for that matter anywhere else, necessarily impose the same organizational and political constraints upon all. Presumably, according to this theory, if Hitler had not carried Nazi Germany into World War II and the Japanese military Zen Buddhist command had not launched the attack on Pearl Harbor, their highly industrialized economies in time would have restored in the one case, and introduced in the other, political and cultural freedoms similar to those found in the democracies with whom they warred. Oddly enough the theory of convergence was rarely, if ever, invoked to predict the development of Fascist countries. Only where the future of Communist Russia is considered has it come into play. The reason is probably that the explicit declaration "ideology is not the relevant force," often heard when the United States and the Soviet Union are compared, could hardly be uttered in discussing the Fascist countries without palpable absurdity. With respect to Communist countries the denial that technology is all important does not, of course, entail the belief that ideology is all important or even that Communist behavior at any particular place and time is predictable on the basis of ideology *alone*. Because ideology is not everything, it is not nothing, a proposition that holds for almost all societies. But for Communist countries ideology is far from nothing. It is often a decisive factor, neglect of which by those whom Communist nations oppose may result in disaster—to those who neglect it.

There have been variations in the way the convergence theory has been applied. During the years when the pitch of terror in the Soviet Union was somewhat reduced the emphasis was on the magnitude of the progress made toward liberalization—a progress considered irreversible. When, however, persecution of dissidents was resumed and confinement to insane asylums in stubborn cases substituted for execution in the cellars of the Lubianka, the United States would be pictured as moving toward a garrison state, and episodic violations of human rights within its borders magnified into signs of the permanent eclipse of freedom.

It is interesting to observe that since Communist China, after its abortive "great leap" toward industrialization, has been proceeding at a very moderate pace in building up its heavy industries, the convergence theory has not yet been widely cited to predict the future political and cultural development of China which currently is in a Stalinist mold. If anything, the personality cult of Mao transcends in its mindless conformity that of Stalin. Embarrassed by the chorus of unanimity on all matters, large or small, on which the rulers of China have taken a stand, their American admirers, as Patrick Moynihan has observed, have been more eager to speak of the absence of flies within China than of the absence of freedom. They have assured us, when the system of pervasive mind control has been brought to their attention, that far from being imposed on the Chinese people it is in deepest accord with their historical genius. One can welcome this admission that technology is not always decisive and still question the easy judgment that a people really want a regime they had no voice or vote in selecting. On the few occasions when inhabitants on the Chinese mainland have been given some opportunity of choice, as when the Chinese prisoners of war in Korea were given the opportunity to return to their homes or choose the bitter bread of exile or when the bamboo curtain to Hong Kong was lifted for a few days, there was no more evidence that the Chinese masses freely supported their Chinese Communist regime than the masses in any other Communist nation supported their Communist regimes.

That Communist ideology by itself is not always decisive in determining Communist political behavior is conclusively established by the Soviet-Sino rift. It is obvious that here neither the mode of economic production which is common nor their common acceptance of the principles of Marxism, in however distorted a form, as interpreted by Lenin and Stalin, can account for their bitter antagonism. The intensity of the antagonism has not only generated armed conflicts but resulted in threats by the Soviet Union to resort to nuclear weapons if Communist China forcibly sought to rectify borders or regain territory yielded to Czarist Russia in the nineteenth century. Once more nationalism or the national interest has proved stronger than any rational interest in peace.

Granted all this it would still be injudicious to assume that these nationalistic conflicts are irresolvable and that the rift between the two great Communist powers will never be healed. When Tito was excommunicated by the Kremlin he was called a Fascist and characterized in even more unsavory fashion than the leaders of the Chinese Communist party. But subsequently he was considered a Communist brother-in-arms. The dispute between the Kremlin and Peking is also a factional Communist dispute over the leadership of the world Communist movement and the most effective strategy of achieving a world Communist order. The fratricidal, if one-sided, struggle between Stalin and Trotsky, both professing Marxist and Leninist orthodoxy, was over the applications of a common ideology to domestic and international problems. Because they differed on how best to achieve Communist victory is no reason to infer that this goal was necessarily subordinate or peripheral in their political behavior. Even the wars of religion in past centuries were never purely ideological —as shifting alliances showed—but they cannot be understood without references to the religious faith of the ruling élites.

Regardless of the role of ideological factors in the Sino-Soviet conflict, even if we assume that they are minimal, it would be dangerous to believe that they count for as little in the relations between these Communist powers and the non-Communist powers. For one thing the existence of Communist parties and groups in many countries of the world acting in concert with Moscow or Peking respectively would be hard to explain without reference to their ideological kinship and allegiances. Polycentric communism means not the demise of Communist ideology but rather a polycentric ideology more complicated than the monolithic ideology of the past but not less effective. Secondly the programmatic declarations of the Communist high command from Lenin to Breznov and Mao leave little doubt that "coexistence" is merely a tactic in the underlying strategy of world domination. There has been no modification of the central doctrines of the Communist creed except on one important point, namely, the manner in which the inevitable and final victory of the Communist system will be brought about. Lenin believed that this would be a consequence of war. His successors have realized that in the age of nuclear weapons, a conflict on the order envisaged by Lenin whould be disastrous for everyone. Consequently for them the inevitable victory is to be brought about by all means short of all-out or total war. This still leaves open the possibility of the judicious use of force, threats, wars of "national liberation" and the deployment of a whole arsenal of weapons of subversion. A tenacious dogmatism about their ends combined with remarkable flexibility and opportunism about their means has characterized Communist behavior. It has led to profound changes in the map of the world.

However one assesses the relative strength of the plural interacting factors that determine the future, the ideological faiths of the historical protagonists will play a significant part. And if this is true, then the knowledge of these faiths or ignorance about them will also be of importance. Regardless, then, of the scientific or objective validity of the fighting faiths of our time, a wise and prudent political policy requires more than a bowing acquaintance with them. This holds true not only for the intelligent citizens of democratic countries but especially for those in positions of leadership in or out of government. Keynes may have overstated the truth when he observed that ideas rule the world but it is incontestable that the world cannot be ruled or understood without ideas. It is my hope that some of the chapters of this book will contribute to their understanding.

                                                          Sidney Hook

REVOLUTION,
REFORM, AND
SOCIAL JUSTICE

CHAPTER ONE

From "Scientific Socialism" to Mythology

1. THE SECOND COMING OF KARL MARX

The intellectual historian of the future will be challenged by a striking phenomenon of the latter half of the twentieth century —the second coming of Karl Marx. In this second coming he appears not in the dusty frock coat of the economist, as the learned author of *Capital,* nor as a benevolent reformer whose beard has been trimmed by the Fabian Webbs and other tribunes of the welfare state, nor as the revolutionary *sans-culotte,* the inspired pamphleteer of the *Communist Manifesto.* He comes robed as a philosopher and moral prophet with glad tidings about human freedom valid beyond the narrow circles of class, party, or faction. In his train flock not the industrial workers of the world but the literary intellectuals of the capital cities of the world, not the proletariat, extended to embrace all wage earners, but many elements of the professoriat, not the socially disinherited but the

1

psychologically alienated, not the hungry and poverty stricken youth of the slums but a varied assortment of artist and writers, idealistic young men and women in search of a cause, some square, some beat, and some Zen.

Almost fifty years ago when I offered the first undergraduate course in the United States in the philosophy of Karl Marx, it was considered by many colleagues as a pedagogical eccentricity reflecting a desire to exploit the results of rather arcane results in the field of post-Hegelian speculation. Among leading intellectual circles within and without the university, Marx was regarded primarily as chief of the jealously worshipped deities of the Soviet Union, and Marxism as the esoteric cult of the commissars of the Kremlin and their devotees at home and abroad. Even in the depths of the economic depression of the 1930s when at long last Marx's prediction of the collapse of the capitalism system seemed about to be confirmed there were only feeble efforts to restate and expand his views. These were primarily politically motivated and had little effect on scholarly research and intellectual interest in the universities of the Western world. The social movements of protest and reform were largely uninfluenced by Marxism. Even those who became sympathetic to the Soviet Union, after Hitler's accession to power (unaware of the role of Stalinist theory and practice in that accession), were indifferent to the ideas of Marx as developed in his writings.

Since the death of Stalin, and particularly since Khrushchev's "revelations" at the Twentieth Congress of the CPSU, Soviet Communism has suffered a political eclipse in cultural and left-wing circles in the West. Yet at no time in the intellectual history of the West have so many members of the intellectual classes evinced so strong an interest in the ideas of Marx or considered themselves "Marxists of a sort." The divisions in the Communist camp and the consequent rise of polycentrism, the removal of Stalin from the Communist pantheon, the new varieties of "revisionism," and the growing interest in the early writings of Marx have generated a climate of opinion in which it is no longer paradoxical to contrast Marxism with contemporary communism.

Even in the academies and universities of the West, in the field of scholarship and historical research, there has been a remarkable surge of interest in the ideas of Marx and Marxism. A generation or two ago, with some noteworthy exceptions among the universities of England, France, and the United States, Marxism was treated, when not ignored, as a movement of the intellectual underworld. Today the picture is impressively different. The course of study in the social sciences and the humanities almost everywhere takes note of ideas and approaches characterized as "Marxist," whatever the validity of the textual support offered in justification of the epithet. Almost every thinker of note feels called upon to define his position in relation to the claims of Marxism. In other words, Marxism has become part of the recognized cultural and historical tradition of the West, which is not surprising in view of the fact that so much has happened to the world in the name of Marxism.

By and large, the recent treatment of Marx in the academy has been sympathetic even if critical of his doctrines, when literally construed. The savage criticisms of Bertrand Russell, of Leopold Schwarzschild, of numerous Catholic writers like McGovern who lumped Marx with Lenin and Stalin as cats of a like breed, are not so much in evidence. There is still an occasional splenetic outburst from the ideologues of "pure" free enterprise. And even they sometimes accord him a respect they begrudge those who, they fancy, are his confused followers. Whether because it is now believed that there must be something to a view of the world and society and human salvation which has stirred more human beings to action, and even sacrifice, than has Christianity, whether because the bitterest enemies of Marx and Marxism have also been enemies of the liberal and democratic tradition, the most frequent of contemporary judgments of Marxism has been "there is a considerable measure of truth in it." Hardly much more could be said of the central ideas of any great figure in the history of thought, and much less was said by Marx of some of his great contemporaries. After all, is there not "a considerable measure of truth" in an observation Bagehot somewhere makes that to illustrate or call attention to a principle "you must exaggerate much and omit much"?

Nonetheless it is surprising how mild and generous some of the recent critical judgments have been on Marx by those who are avowedly non-Marxist. Even Christian philosophers of history, despite the ferocity of Marx's critique of all religion, like Arnold Toynbee, Paul Tillich, Reinhold Niebuhr, and Herbert Butterfield, have paid him great homage not merely because of the quality of prophetic zeal and moral indignation in his writings but on the strength of his historical insight and doctrines. Butterfield, for example, writes: "The Marxists have contributed more to the historical scholarship of all of us than the non-Marxists like to confess." [1] He regards Marx's historical materialism as constituting a remarkable and permanent contribution to our understanding of history because "it hugs the ground so closely," although some might regard this as a narrow perspective from which to grasp things shaping up on the horizon. And then it turns out that for Butterfield, Marx's materialism, considered merely as a *realistic* approach to the conditions under which and the motives out of which men act, is perfectly assimilable to the synoptic view of those who see the finger of God in history.

Among the reasons for the comparatively sympathetic judgment of Marx's theory of history among non-Marxist historians, despite the fact that massive historical phenomena like fascism and even communism as social systems, are hard to account for in its terms, is Engels's restatement of it. By admitting a reciprocity among all social factors, which was part of his Hegelian heritage, and recognizing a plurality of causes, Engels shattered the imposing, yet simplistic, monism of some of Marx's earlier formulations of the doctrine. V. G. Simkhovitch, the Russian-American economic historian who fancied himself, in one of his phases, as the American Bernstein, used to complain that Engels's letters to Bloch, Mehring, Starkenberg, and others spoiled the game for the critics of Marxism by watering down Marx's original doctrine with common sense imbibed from the English scene. For on Engels's version, the "primacy" of the economic factor, its determination in the last analysis of historical events and tendencies, is at best a statistical judgment, although in his pro-

1. Herbert Butterfield, *Christianity and History* (Cambridge and New York: Scribner's, 1950), p. 60.

grammatic zeal Engels himself did not see this. And since no one has actually worked out a theory of measurement assigning different weights to different factors in specific situations, and then assessed all the "relevant" specific situations which enter into the pattern of history, it became possible for avowed Marxists to defend the validity of Marx's theory "on the whole" and "in the last analysis" even if it failed to explain any particular set of events; and for non-Marxists to acknowledge that as a heuristic method it was very useful. It opened up new fields of inquiry and sometimes led to valid conclusions. Instead of becoming *the* scientific method of history, the Marxist approach became an integral part of the scientific resources of inquiry into history, since every historian professing to write a credible account of a period had to look for, and pay attention to if he found, the existing economic class interests and their influence on events. But therewith Marxism as a philosophy of history and as the theory and practice of social revolution became irrelevant to the specific inquiries of the working historian. As a philosophy of history, it became a method of *making* history, an ideology of a group or a political party speaking on its own authority in the name of a class, allegedly on behalf of all mankind. Today the paradoxical fact is that although Marxism as a method of *understanding* history has disintegrated as a system of ideas, even among Marxists, some Marxist ideas have been inflated out of all proportion to their significance by some non-Marxists.

We are dealing with a complex phenomenon which invites Engels's pluralistic approach. Among the main reasons, it seems to me, for the hazy and rather lazy affirmative judgments on Marx's theories in some quarters is the dual attraction exercised on intellectuals by political power, on the one hand, and by the humanistic values in the professed ideals of Marx, on the other. To some, the very existence of the Soviet Union and Communist China and their growing strength presages, if not the ultimate victory of communism as a world social system, at least its permanence. This is a powerful ground for reconciling themselves to its official theory or ideology—"to see something in it"—an attitude almost required by the imperative necessity of political coexistence. There is, so to speak, a social analogue to Newtonian "action at a distance" (a phrase Sartre uses to explain the attraction the proletariat has for intellectuals) exerted by a new constellation of social forces which has achieved a sufficient stability to make unlikely any basic change.[2] The ideology of such a system is as much to be regarded and "respected," not believed of course, as the theology of an established church in a society of plural religious faiths. To others, more fine-grained, who are still mindful of the living costs of established tyranny without having lost their memory of its past infamies, the humanistic ideals of Marx still have a strong appeal. The betrayal of these ideals is explained by the fact that the leaders in the Kremlin were Russian and those in Peking Chinese before either were Communist which, if true, constitutes another grave difficulty for Marxism.

It is curious to observe the rationalization offered by those who despite their professed belief that historical results are the test of historical ideals and movements hold on to their doctrinal allegiances even when grim historical events have undermined their organizational loyalties. Some explain the terror of Stalinism, more pervasive in its cultural effects than even the profit-motive in the West, as due to the cult of personality or Russian backwardness and the heritage of Czarism or other variations of the Russian soul, without realizing that the very effort at such explanation signifies their abandonment of Marx's principle of historical materialism in its canonic form. Others, on the contrary, insist that what happened in the Soviet Union *confirms* the

2. A classic expression of this attitude is to be found in G. S. Fraser's review of Diana Trilling's *Claremont Essays*. He writes: "The Soviet system has had virtue enough to stay alive in the world for forty-seven years and I wondered whether, in her rigorous need to judge, Mrs. Trilling has made allowance enough for the basic virtue—a certain coherence and toughness—that must be allowed to all systems and attitudes that have the mere power of persisting." *Partisan Review* (Winter 1965), p. 132. Would Mr. Fraser attribute the same "basic virtue" to Franco's regime which has also survived? On this view the tougher the tyranny, the longer the persistence, the greater the virtue. Would Hitler have redeemed himself and his system had he triumphed and survived?

validity of historical materialism because the economic unreadiness of Russia made a régime of terror a foregone conclusion as the only way in which a substitute for primitive accumulation under capitalism could be achieved. This falsely assumes that there were no alternatives. And even if this were granted, it fails to explain why if, in the light of the principles of historical materialism, the possibility of socialism in the Soviet Union was doomed, that world-shaking effort was ever attempted. What explains the failure, does not explain the *attempt*. And without the attempt, what a different world it would be! And to span the gamut of absurdity, one should preserve for posterity the proud avowal of an unreconstructed English Marxist (Jack Lindsay) who, although morally reprobating the epoch of Stalin, tells us that he "accepts it all" because, among other reasons, of the great liberations of the spirit which were then achieved—"the liberations that now make possible the ending of the Stalinist epoch." This is very much like praising Hitler because without him there would have been no heroism on the part of the Resistance.

Another source of the renewal and rediscovery of Marx is the natural intellectual evolution of those who develop new social views. I have observed this process for forty years. Members of the academy and university in democratic countries become critical of the social and economic order, or become aroused and frightened by certain events on the international scene. If the development of their views is toward socialism, they often tend to reinterpret Marx in such a way as to bring his thought in line with their antecedent intellectual and philosophical commitments. The oddest syntheses result. I have known professors and graduate students, suddenly stirred into a passion of social protest by some current evil, who have convinced themselves after shortly reading Marx that he was *au fond* a phenomenologist, an existentialist, a positivist, a Spinozist, a Kantian, a Freudian, a Bergsonian, an anticipator of Samuel Alexander (all they had in common were their ethnic origin and beard!)—and, of course, an Hegelian. There are some Catholic writers who rather cautiously suggest that, despite Marx's atheism, Aristotle and Aquinas would not have disowned him. Some Protestants, and not merely pro-Soviet figures like Karl Barth and Niemöller, declare that Marx is essentially a more religious man than many of his religious critics. Such reinterpretations are familiar in the history of thought and subjectively completely sincere. For all that, they sometimes are patently ridiculous, like the attempts of some English scientists converted to communism in the heyday of Stalin to read the theory of relativity and other discoveries of modern physics out of Marx's and Engels's unpublished manuscripts.[3] But they create familiar difficulties of exposition and criticism exacerbated in this case by the passion with which almost every distinguished convert to socialism and peace creates his own Marx.

The psychological compulsion to avow one's Marxism may have been intensified by the intellectual *auto-da-fé* conducted against the few individuals who were willing to support the Socialist, sometimes even the Communist, program of social change but insisted on jettisoning the useless ballast of Marxism in order to make faster progress. They were regarded no matter what their subjective intentions as "objectively" agents of the existing Establishment whose role was to throw the working class off its revolutionary course. And, indeed, the term "socialism" had become so degraded by irresponsible use that it was possible for some totalitarians to declare that Marxism must die in order that Socialism must live.

2. THE CASE OF C. WRIGHT MILLS

That attitudes toward Marxist doctrines are often inspired by considerations which have little to do with their truth and falsity is perhaps best illustrated not so much by non-Marxists, sympathetic in their evaluation of Marx as a fighter for freedom and social progress, as by some writers, truculent if not influential, who proudly avow themselves to be Marxists. In the United States perhaps the best known among them is the late C. Wright Mills.

---

3. See my critique of J. D. Bernal, J. B. S. Haldane, Hyman Levy et al., in my *Reason, Social Myths and Democracy* (New York, 1940), p. 220 ff.

In a comprehensive volume on *The Marxists* [4] which consists of exposition, readings in, and commentary upon, the chief figures in the Marxist tradition, Mills is caustic and scornful of liberalism and social-democracy. He distinguishes three types of Marxists—the vulgar, the sophisticated, and just "plain." Vulgar Marxists "seize upon certain ideological features of Marx's political philosophy and identify these parts with the whole." Sophisticated Marxists "refine and qualify the doctrines to a point where they cannot be confirmed or disconfirmed." Plain Marxists "work in Marx's own tradition." The exemplars of the first two schools are not named but Mills identifies *himself* as a plain Marxist. He enumerates among the fellow-members of this class Gramsci, Rosa Luxemburg, Lukács, Strachey, Sartre, and Isaac Deutscher.

The family of Marxist doctrines whether vulgar, sophisticated, or just plain are related to each other by their derivation from classic Marxism. Mills proceeds to list the seventeen "most important conceptions and propositions of classic Marxism"—all of them buttressed by quotations from Marx on whom he lavishes extravagant praise for the remarkable coherence of his thought. But then in an extraordinary critical assessment of these seventeen important conceptions and propositions, all of them, with one single exception, are declared "false" or "unclear" or "unprecise" or "misleading" or "unfruitful" or "careless" or "confused" or "quite clearly wrong." The single proposition (No. 11) which is regarded as true is dismissed as a truism. It states: *"The opportunity for revolution exists only when objective conditions and subjective readiness coincide."* And with respect to this truism, Mills cannot forbear pointing out that objective conditions and subjective readiness have never coincided in any advanced capitalist society, even during the depths of the world's worst depression. The cumulative effect of Mills's criticisms, largely culled without acknowledgment from criticisms made long before him, is so devastating that were it not for his tone of moral earnestness

4. C. Wright Mills, *The Marxists* (Penguin, 1963; New York, Bell Publishers, 1962), pp. 96 ff.

one would suspect that in calling himself "a plain Marxist," he was perpetrating an intellectual spoof.

There is hardly a single notion of Marx which is not severely called into question by Mills—his theory of class, class interest, historical causation, state, political power, economic development, even the newly refurbished notion of alienation. Mills strains wherever he can to give Marx credit by employing emotively overcharged terms but the reader sees easily through the stratagem. Thus, concerning Marx's theory of alienation, he says: "At any rate, to say the least [in criticism] the condition in which Marx left the conception of alienation is quite incomplete, and brilliantly ambiguous." Similarly, of the Marxist model of history he says it is "brilliantly constructed," but it is valid only "for one phase of one society"—in other words, it is either no model at all or inadequate to all history which is past or future to Marx's present. The actual things Mills writes about Marx's treatment of the theme of alienation leave the reader with a much stronger impression of Marx's ambiguity and inadequacy than of his brilliance.

As if this wholesale repudiation of Marx's theories, doctrines and hypotheses were not enough, Mills goes on to reject Marx's *model* of society and history. And this, after telling us that "what is great and alive" about Marx is his model. Mills indicts Marx strongly for his "metaphysics of labor" and for violating the principle of historical specificity, the tying down of social abstractions to a specific historical period, which was supposed to be central to Marx's method. Indeed, despite his hearty backslapping of Marx, Mills offers nothing to support his judgment of him as a great thinker. Expletives aside, Mills's criticisms could be used by schools devoted to the propagation of *anti*-Marxism. If this is what a plain Marxist makes of Marx—one truism out of seventeen important propositions!—what can someone who is not a Marxist of any variety make of him? It is as if Mills were calling himself a Marxist in order to shock or embarrass his colleagues—which was needless, since most of them, I daresay, give Marx a higher batting average with respect to his important propositions and predictions than does Mills.

After all this, Mills tells his readers that although all of Marx's work is false, inadequate, or misleading (except for a single truism) Marx's *method* "is a signal and lasting contribution to the best sociological way of reflection and inquiry available." Apparently Mills does not judge a method by its fruits! He is fearfully vague, however, about what distinguishes Marx's method. It is *not* the dialectical method about which he has harsh words. Nor is it the so-called principle of historical specificity, first mentioned by Karl Korsch.[5] The principle of historical specificity is not so much a method as an approach which de-limits the scope and context of an inquiry into a social phenomenon. Since whatever exists is individual, this approach notes carefully the historical situation in which it is found, and is cautious about extending any conclusions reached to apparently similar phenomena in other historical eras. Thus, if we are investigating the political and economic life of our times, we may reach certain generalizations or "laws" about the character of class-struggles or the development of the economy. Unless we make it explicit that we are restricting ourselves to capitalist society, we may go astray by extrapolating our findings to other societies. What holds for economic behavior in one type of society or in one historical epoch may not hold for other epochs. So when we discourse about man in economics and psychology, and then talk about man *qua* man, we may be unconsciously identifying man with bourgeois man. To assume that all human beings would behave like Robinson Crusoe is to assume that the eighteenth-century Englishman is the eternal type of man.

It is obvious, however, that this is not a method of inquiry but a restriction of subject matter plus a commonplace caution. It is perfectly legitimate to inquire into the social laws or the development of all societies. It all depends upon our problem and our intellectual concerns. We may be interested in the analysis of value in a commodity-producing society. We may also be interested in the analysis of value in all societies in which there are scarce resources. Just as there are certain biological laws and

5. Karl Korsch, *Karl Marx* (New York, 1938).

principles of organization that hold for all animals, including *human* animals, so there *may* be certain social laws and principles that obtain in all societies. Some Marxists may not be interested in such inquiries but they are as legitimate as other inquiries with a more restricted time span. Further, it can easily be shown that without the use of general concepts or categories which apply to more than the specific subject matter or historical event under analysis, no warranted conclusion of any kind could be reached. A "law" that applies to an individual presupposes the possibility of the existence of *other* individuals of the same type or class, indifferent to the space-time differentia of the individual case from which we take our point of departure.

Marx himself clearly does *not* accept the principle of historical specificity in formulating some of his propositions. He tells us in the *Communist Manifesto* that "All history is the history of class struggles." And in the preface to *A Contribution to the Critique of Political Economy*, he states conclusions which presumably hold for *all* class societies—capitalist, feudal, slave, Asiatic.

It remains, therefore, mystifying on theoretical grounds why Mills insisted upon his "Marxism," whatever the biographical explanation of the fact may be. For essentially his affirmation of Marxism is a programmatic declaration of allegiance, an expression of solidarity for "the new world" extending from China and Russia to Cuba. Mills's rejection of the world of liberalism in all its variants is clear and sharp. But his socialism, he defines negatively by what it is *not*—it is not Leninism, not Stalinism, not Maoism, not Castroism, although it is unmistakably of the same family.

Himself an individualist with a keen if monochromatic vision for power conflicts and aware that they cannot all be reduced to economic class conflicts, he expresses much more hostility to classical liberalism and its ideals of individual freedom (which as far as the United States goes he dismisses merely as "empty rhetoric"), as well as to social-democratic variants and extensions of the ideals of freedom, than to the ideals of classical Marxism. Stalin is treated as the convenient scapegoat to explain the degradation of man and culture in the Soviet Union. Although he formally allows that it is an open question whether Soviet communism will ultimately realize the humanist and democratic heritage of Marx, he leaves the reader with little doubt that he both hopes and believes that it will. Nonetheless, the mass of negative evidence is so strong that Mills cannot summon up the will to believe them. His espousal of socialism has nothing to do with what Marx and Engels called "scientific socialism." It is based on a pre-Marxist, simplistic moralism, a commendable opposition to poverty and exploitation which, as far as his own analysis of moral questions goes, unfortunately sparse and shallow, possesses the same validity as if Marx had never written a line.

The very grounds on which Mills rejects liberalism both as an ideology and as rhetoric indicate how far he is from the historical Marx. First, liberalism "has become practical, flexible, realistic, pragmatic . . . and not at all Utopian." And second, as a consequence it has "become irrelevant to political positions having moral contents." This moral standpoint, proudly impractical, inflexible, unrealistic, and unpragmatic, has less in common with Marx than with the millenary, eschatological traditions of primitive socialism.

3. SARTRE, HEIDEGGER, MERLEAU-PONTY, ALTHUSSER

The case of C. Wright Mills is an extreme illustration of a fetishistic response to Marxist terms and symbols but in lesser degree the same phenomenon can be observed among many other self-characterized Marxists. Some are "revolutionists" without a doctrine or cause except the gospel that the *status quo,* politically, economically and culturally, high, low and middle brow, is in an advanced state of putrescence. Particularly loathsome to them are the programs and movements of social reform.

In England, which has always been less doctrinaire in its socialism than the Continent or even the United States, and because of the Fabians, who have always been indifferent, if not hostile, to Marxism, the opposition to the *status quo* has not unfurled ideological banners. The "new left," or what remains of it, is violently opposed to specific measures like nuclear armament and to attempts to moderate the scope of the socialization plank in the program of the Labour Party or to the perversion of culture by the commercial values of capitalism. But it has left strictly alone the corpus of Marx's work. With the exception of positions expressed in the youthful *Economic-Philosophical Manuscripts,* and especially its key passages on alienation, it has made only half-hearted attempts to defend Marx's historical analyses and predictions.

On emotional grounds, it is much more doctrinaire in its judgments on foreign policy. Despite the repressions of the Hungarian freedom-fighters, Khrushchev's revelations about the kind of régime under Stalin which Kingsley Martin and others had staunchly defended, large numbers among the non-Communist left in England feel much more sympathetic to their "fellow-socialists" in the Kremlin and even in Peking than to their anti-Communist "fellow workers" in the American Labor movement.

A singularly eloquent example of a non-communist socialist who to the end of his life pleaded for a united front between socialists and communists against the United States is the late G. D. H. Cole. He admits without blinking the "innumerable purges and liquidations," "the imprisonment and maltreatment of millions of citizens in 'slave labor camps,' " the extirpation of intellectual, cultural, and political freedom, and the other charges in the formidable indictment democratic socialists have leveled against communism. He admits the betrayal of the Hungarian Revolution and the barbarous excesses against the Hungarian workers. But he remains adamant in his conviction that communism is a progressive phenomenon on a world scale and must be supported by socialists who remain critical of communist manners. The explanation of G. D. H. Cole's position, as well as of his judgment that despite their terror and suffering, "the Russian and Chinese revolutions are the greatest achievements of the modern world," is to be found in his fetishism of "the mode of production." [6]

6. See his *World Socialism Restated* (London, 1957), and more particularly *The New Statesman and Nation,* January 12 and April 20, 1957.

Perhaps the most celebrated recent case of conversion to Marxism is that of Jean-Paul Sartre. In his previous writings, despite his career as a political fellow-traveler of communism, Sartre made no attempt to link his existentialist philosophy to the doctrine of Marxism. If anything he was more hostile to Marxian materialism or naturalism, because of its slighting of the principle of subjectivity, than to traditional idealism, of which this principle was an offshoot.

Despite his words to the contrary, Sartre in a sense has remained a consistent existentialist, consistent in his inconsistency. In some French quarters, it was expected after Khrushchev had delivered his speech at the Twentieth Congress of the CPSU, revealing the horrors of Stalin's terrorist régime which Sartre had so ardently defended against its critics, that Sartre, as an appropriate act of existential atonement, would hang himself. Instead he wrote his gigantic *Critique de la raison dialectique* (1960). In it he not only avows himself a Marxist, implying that he is the only genuine one in the world, but declares that Marxism "is the philosophy of our epoch," the only one which grasps history as "the concrete synthesis of a moving, dialectical totality." Rejecting the official communist interpretation of Marxism as an aberration due to Stalinist perversions—concerning most of which he had remained silent or supported until Stalin's dethronement—he nonetheless agrees with Roger Garaudy, the former French Stalinist whom he otherwise cites as a typical offender against the true spirit of Marxism, about the scope of Marxism.

> Marxism constitutes today the only system of co-ordinates which permits the placing and defining of thought in any domain whatsoever, from political economy to physics [*sic!*], from history to morality. (p. 30)

And as if to leave no doubt about his orthodoxy, he quotes Engels with approval that it is the mode of economic production which

Also my "Moral Judgment and Historical Ambiguity," *Problems of Communism* (July–August 1957).

"in the last analysis" (as if there were any such!) determines *every* aspect of culture, the omnipresent red thread that is the clue to the pattern which runs through and unites the details. The matter, insists Sartre, is far more complex than either Garaudy or Engels suspects but for all the complexity, the monistic emphasis is predominant. Dualism is socially reactionary and pluralism reformist.

What Sartre wishes to do is to make the existentialist approach ancillary to Marxism, to emancipate the latter from mechanistic reductions of cultural phenomena to economic equations of the first degree, to abolish its terrorism of dogma which refuses to differentiate between the events and characters it lumps together too easily under the rubric of Marxist explanation. "Existentialism desires to restore the specificity of the *historical* event; it seeks to restore its function and multiple dimensions." Sartre sees correctly that in the Stalinist world, the event has become "an edifying myth." But in his own reconstruction of Marxism, the event can never refute or disconfirm the Marxist position for the latter is defined not as an empirical hypothesis but as an *a priori universal method* of showing how the totality of social life is organized and expressed in every particular event, in every particular individual. His criticisms of the schematic interpretations of cultural and political phenomena by the Communists are trenchant and justified, but what he substitutes for them is a Hegelianized version of Marxism in which a mythical, idealized working class takes the place of the Spirit, and in which the activity of the working class, whose mission is to make the world more reasonable and men more human and free, is focused in the idealized political "group" which for Sartre, despite the weakness of the vessel, is still the Communist Party.

What Sartre is really doing in his *Critique de la raison dialectique* is disguised in terms of technical philosophical doctrine. He rejects the whole notion of abstract truth and the theory of abstract universals as necessarily unjust to the particular and the singular, and what he calls "the profundity of the lived."

For example, if the theory of historical materialism tries to explain the work and achievement of Flaubert and Baudelaire in terms of economic conditions or class or any other Marxist category, in the nature of the case the differences between them cannot be accounted for by common causal conditions. This ignores the whole project or creation which eventuates in entirely different works. Sainte-Beuve had already made the same kind of objection to Taine and other monistic philosophics of history and civilization without denying the limited usefulness of their approach. (*Nouveaux Lundis,* VIII, 1864.)

Sartre's criticisms are certainly valid with respect to much of the reductionist interpretations of vulgar Marxism. The relative autonomy, the activity and transformative effects of human knowledge had been stressed long before him by the American pragmatists, especially John Dewey, without mythology. It is not necessary, of course, to reject the notion of an abstract universal if it is recognized that an individual may be determined—*not* created, *not* exhausted—by a plural number of relatively independent factors or conditions of unequal weight. These factors or conditions do not lie inertly side by side but operate in interacting historical clusters. No matter how detailed an account be of a life circumscribed by circumstance and social space, it cannot in the same terms do justice to the chemistry and biology of talent and genius whose vision expresses the "magic" of personality. But this pluralistic approach is emphatically condemned by Sartre because it prevents us from understanding a thing, an event, a human being in its "dialectical totality." True comprehension of anything, especially of the human and historical, Sartre insists, can be reached only by seeing it as an aspect or part of a concrete universal. What is true of the part is true of the concrete universal of which it is a part; it, too, is a moment or aspect of another concrete universal of greater comprehensiveness until we reach the one great social and cultural process, the dialectical totality, which constitutes the history of our time.

Sartre's procedure, its difference from traditional Marxism and its own weakness, may be illustrated by his own example in the first part of his *Critique de la raison dialectique,* devoted to a consideration of his method. Engels had been guilty of the absurdity of assuming that if Napoleon or any other great historical figure had not lived, someone else would have done Napoleon's work. This is intelligible only if we deny genuine greatness to individuals, *i.e.*, that no man is indispensable for any task, that someone else, in case of death or accident, could have and necessarily *would* have done the hero's work, or fall back upon a mystical dialectic of nature to establish a bond between human genes, the cosmos, and the social-historical process. In Engels's view, if the human need is strong enough apparently a favorable mutation in the germ-plasm sparks into life to accommodate it.

Sartre does not reject this Marxist ploy but dismisses it as a commonplace that does not go far enough. It is irrelevant to establish that lacking Napoleon someone else would have had to appear to liquidate, and at the same time consolidate, the Revolution by a military dictatorship. He demands that the necessity of *this* Napoleon, the one and only, who actually appeared, be explained, and the necessity of *this* bourgeoisie, *this* revolution, *this* train of events to which he responded as he did, be explained in the same way. In fact, he demands that the web of necessity be woven around every event which had historical significance.

Sartre's pattern of "concrete totalization," despite his denial, is nothing but the Hegelian *Begriff* for which the contingent, the pluralistic, the chance event, reflects only our ignorance. The untenability of Sartre's view becomes evident when we ask whether *this* Columbus was necessary for the discovery of America in *this* historical era. To which the answer obviously is "No" since America was, and would have been, discovered by others. Of course, Napoleon made things happen as they did but had he been killed by a shell which killed other artillerymen, who would have made or sent another Napoleon—the world spirit or the dialectic in nature? Or do they guarantee that nothing will befall Napoleon until his task is finished? Had Napoleon been killed, Sartre would have demanded that the necessity of *this* death at *this* time be shown.

Engels had the merit of trying to explain historical events by tendencies and laws which remove some of the apparent contingencies in history. Sartre really wants to re-live them. Substituting his own sense of dramatic compulsion, he wants to picture events as if they had the same kind of necessity as the events of a story. In most historical situations, the critical mind can discern several alternatives of varying degrees of probability. Rarely can one say that what took place was necessary no matter what had been done to forestall it or bring it about. In the past Sartre would have had us believe that almost anything could have happened in history. Now he seems committed to the belief that almost everything in history had to happen as it did. To be sure, we sometimes can predict the occurrence of a specific event, although not its totality of qualities and relations, on the basis of general laws and given initial conditions. But these initial conditions are themselves not rationally necessary since the explanation of their occurrence presupposes other initial conditions, and so on.

Sartre starts from the concrete, specific, existential fact, impressionistically perceived yet often with considerable insight. But by the time he incorporates it into the totality of social and historical relations whose development is history, despite Sartre the individuality of the event or person is lost.

It is a highly moot question whether social or historical knowledge can be achieved in this fashion. But what is obvious is that the consequence of this approach makes explanation tantamount to justification. The given, as well as the result of its development, in the end turns out to be dialectically necessary. They could not be other than what they are. Freedom is no longer to be found in an act of *choice* between genuine possibilities. It is found in the action or practice by which history itself, so to speak, takes note of, or is conscious of, itself. For Sartre, it is only in the practice of Marxism that freedom can be found. History is not the self-activity of the Hegelian Spirit which develops by inner fission and opposition; nor is it the interplay of interests, ideas, and personality as the pluralistic critics of Hegel contend; it is the *practice* of human beings, expressed in their daily work, a work that until now had led to self-estrangement and alienation instead of self-fulfillment. The liberating force in history for Sartre is the proletariat to which he was originally drawn, he confesses, not by reading Marx but by its very existence, its struggles, its incarnation of Marxist practice.

What is truly amazing in Sartre's book is what he reads into Marx's conception of praxis and class. The "group" is made central to the understanding of society and the making of history, the individual is dissolved into the "group" (actually hypostatized into the ideal Party) which speaks in the name of the proletariat, whom it educates and defends by Terror. Sartre admits that the "dictatorship of the proletariat" is a myth, that it never existed in the Soviet Union or elsewhere, and that by its very nature no group like the proletariat, since it is not a hyper-organism, can exercise a dictatorship. (This would make nonsense of the phrase "dictatorship of the bourgeoisie," too.) He frankly admits that the government of the Soviet Union from the very outset was a dictatorship of the Communist Party. He spares us the verbal legerdemain by which Bolshevik-Leninists tried to explain this away. Terror is exalted as the necessary instrument by which men are made whole and human again after being de-humanized by the processes of "alienation" and "serialization." It is *not* attributed to backward political and cultural traditions.

> Historic experience of the countries in which Communists took power has revealed undeniably that the first stage of socialist society in construction—to consider it from the still abstract view of power—cannot be anything else than the indissoluble aggregation of bureaucracy, the Terror, and the cult of personality. (p. 630)

In other words what some explanations for the Soviet system of terror, like those of E. H. Carr, have attributed to the specific, backward, barbarous conditions of Russian history, Sartre generalizes as universal and necessary in the long march to the classless society. Bolshevism in its Leninist and Stalinist forms is not national but international. In consequence the entire work has been aptly dubbed by one critic "The Metaphysics of Stalinism." [7]

Sartre is not alone in regarding the theme of alienation as central to Marxism and interpreting Marxist doctrines as principles directed to exposing and overcoming alienation. He remains unique in the Stalinist grotesquerie to which he has carried his interpretation. But what has impressed him has also impressed one of his philosophical masters. Just as Sartre regards Marxism as "the philosophy of our epoch," as the best means of overcoming alienation, so Martin Heidegger regards "the Marxist view of history as superior to all other views," [8] because of Marx's prescience in discerning the facets of alienation in the experience of modern man. What for Marx was a youthful insight, derived from and shared with others, and subsequently fleshed out into a sociological criticism of contemporary culture, is transformed by Heidegger into a metaphysics of homelessness beyond all social remedies, in some respects profounder than that of Husserl and Sartre.[9]

A Marxist thinker influenced by both Husserl and Sartre and who developed from writing sophisticated apologies for Stalinism to fresh criticisms of the mystical abstractions of Marxism is

7. Lionel Abel, *Dissent*, Spring 1961, p. 137 ff.

8. Martin Heidegger, *Platon's Lehre von der Wahrheit* (Berne: A. Francke, 1947). p. 87

9. "Homelessness has become a world fate. That is why it is necessary to think this Fate through the history of being. What Marx in an essential and significant sense had recognised in Hegel as the alienation *(Entfremdung)* of man reaches back with its roots into the homelessness of contemporary man. This is called forth from the fate of being in the form of metaphysics, is strengthened by it, and at the same time concealed from it as homelessness. Because Marx experiences alienation as reaching into an essential dimension of history, the Marxist conception of history is superior to all others. Since neither Husserl nor, as far as I can see, Sartre recognises the essentiality of the historical in being, neither phenomenology nor existentialism enters into that dimension within which a fruitful dialogue with Marxism is possible." *loc. cit.*

Maurice Merleau-Ponty. In his *Humanisme et Terreur,* although he is careful not to profess an orthodox Marxism, he regards the cruel and barbarous Moscow Trials as *objectively* justified even though subjectively the accused were not guilty of what they were charged.

According to this view, it is only dotting the *i*'s, after Bukharin's political line turned out to be mistaken, to tax him with murder and arson, for the "politician defines himself not by what he does himself but by the forces on which he relies," [10] in this case allegedly the internal and foreign enemies of the régime. Even if, by definition, one postulates that differences with the Communist Party constitute an error, the assumption that errors are to be judged as political crimes logically entails the view that sooner or later, since men are fallible, *all* may be charged with crimes or that one individual, the Leader, is politically infallible.

This smacks of the political logic of totalitarianism, but Merleau-Ponty denies it on the ground that such a judgment over-looks the fact that Marxism based itself on "the theory of proletariat" —*not* on the theory of the citizen—as a universal class, the carrier of all human value. "The power of the proletariat is the power of humanity" and any action which contributes to its victory is valid or politically true. It is false that the Communists do not believe in objective truth. It is only necessary to understand that in a class society the truth in political affairs must be a class-truth, and a party-truth. "It is not chance," he writes, "nor I suppose a romantic prejudice that the chief newspaper of the USSR carries the name *Pravda."* (p. 132)

Nor is it chance that in his conclusions Merleau-Ponty calls upon intellectuals "to recall Marxists to their humanist inspiration and the democracies to their fundamental hypocrisy." He asserts that anticommunism, indeed *any* criticism of the Soviet Union which does not relate the relevant facts to the whole complex of difficulties which the Soviet Union faces, "should be considered an act of war." Violent criticism of the democratic West, on the other hand, was an act in defense of peace. In a discussion I had with Merleau-Ponty in Paris in 1948 I was able to

10. *Humanisme et Terreur* (Paris: Gallimard, 1947), p. 57.

confirm the incredibly naïve character of his judgments concerning Stalin, the Soviet Union, and the Communist movement.

A few years later, in consequence of the Korean War and the train of events it set up, and in specific criticism of Sartre's articles on "The Communists and the War" in which Sartre identifies the cause of the French working-class with the Communist Party, with the Soviet Union and its strategy of peace, Merleau-Ponty refused to sign the blank check of faith in the Communist Party implied by Sartre's position. He not only renounces Sartre's "ultra-Bolshevism" as a repudiation of the Marxist dialectic and a substitution for it of a "philosophy of absolute creation in the unknown," he reluctantly admits that neither contemporary capitalism, nor contemporary socialism can be understood in terms of traditional Marxism. In the epilogue to his *Les Aventures de la dialectique*, Merleau-Ponty denies that he has betrayed the revolution, denies that he is an apologist for the *status quo*, and appeals vaguely for a new criticism and a program of new action. He remains despite himself very much of a Marxist in his thinking, really helpless before the historical reality which his Marxism did not enable him to anticipate, finally repelled by the practices of the "Marxist" Communist State, and bewildered by the transmutation doctrinal Marxism has undergone at the hands of intellectuals who still believe that the proletariat and the party of the proletariat, although they may be mistaken, can do no wrong.

The third figure in the trinity of French contemporary professional philosophers who have espoused Marxism is Louis Althusser. He differentiates himself from Sartre and Merleau-Ponty by proudly avowing his doctrinal and political Marxist orthodoxy as defined by the French Communist Party of which he is a leading member. Sartre and Merleau-Ponty, although often apologists for the Communist Party, were inclined to be critical of its philosophical orthodoxy, its claims to have objective, scientific knowledge of history, and its consequent disregard of the element of subjectivity, personal decision and moral choice.

For Althusser this philosophical orthodoxy of the Party is its virtue because it expresses the truth. His views are conveniently assembled in a volume *Pour Marx*, now available in English translation,[11] a series of essays written during the 1960s on various aspects of Marxism.

The author discloses in the special preface to his English readers that his ideas are directed toward two fronts. The first is "to draw a line of demarcation" between Marxist theory, properly understood as a scientific and objective body of knowledge, and "empiricism and its variants," which the author interprets, for reasons not altogether clear, as a form of subjectivism. Empiricism threatens Marxism by its pluralism which is incompatible with every kind of organic unity, and consequently by its reliance upon piecemeal evidence to test theories. The object of the second "intervention" is sharply to distinguish between Marxist science and philosophy, on the one hand, and recent reinterpretations of Marxism which present it not as an economic-historical theory but as "a philosophy of man" or a "Humanism" essentially moral and psychological, holding out the promise of final liberation to human beings from all institutions that alienate them from their essential being. This is an attempt to vindicate the Marx of *Capital* against a flock of new interpreters who find the true Marx in his early writings, especially those entitled *The Economic and Philosophical Manuscripts* (1844).

With respect to the second intervention Louis Althusser's position seems to me to be quite justifiable, and even refreshing in view of the many fashionable attempts to show that Marx was a Marxist when he was still a Young Hegelian and Feuerbachian. But the grounds which Althusser offers for his position are needlessly obscure. Nowhere does he state clearly the scholarly evidence which bears on the purely historical question whether reading the mature Marx into the young Marx or the young Marx into the mature Marx is tenable. This evidence, as we shall see in some detail in the next section, is very weighty and cannot be overridden by the occasional references to "alienation *(Entfrem-dung)*" in the later manuscripts of Marx. For it is clear that in the *Economic and Philosophical Manuscripts* Marx had not yet

11. Louis Althusser, *For Marx*. Translated by Ben Brewster (New York: Vintage Books, 1972).

developed his theory of historical materialism. Without an acceptance of historical materialism, belief in Marxism would be comparable to an avowal of Catholicism without a belief in Christianity. Indeed the view expressed in these early writings that private property is caused by alienation is as far from historical materialism as anything can be. Since the latter doctrine entails the view that human nature is historically and culturally determined, to speak of man's *essential* nature as a universal unhistorical norm against which *historical* man at any given time is to be judged, is flatly incompatible with anything that deserves the name of Marxism. "My analytical method does not start from Man but from the economically given social period," wrote Marx in 1879. To make of Marxism primarily an ethical doctrine rather than a scientific social and economic theory is not only to ignore the fact that the ethical approach was common coin among the Feuerbachians and "True Socialists," as well as other critics of industrialism, but that Marx expressly criticized the attempt to organize a revolutionary movement based on ethical socialism. However, the validity of Marx's criticism of ethical socialism —and the adequacy of his own views on ethics—is another question.

Althusser's differentiation between the young and mature Marx, although quite defensible, appears to me to be based not so much on the evidence as on political piety toward the views of Marx which obtain in the Russian and French Communist parties. Althusser's reading of Marx is not only obscure but highhanded and circular to boot. He does not recognize the possibility of an objective, scholarly, and valid interpretation of the meaning of Marx's texts *independently* of whether or not one accepts the truth of Marxism. He contends that "the pre-condition of a reading of Marx" is an *acceptance of* the Marxist view of the relation between theories and history. "The application of Marxist theory to Marx himself appears to be the absolute pre-condition of an understanding of Marx" (p. 38). This is very much as if one were to claim that one could not possibly understand Catholicism or a Catholic thinker unless one were a Catholic oneself.

Indeed, it is even more absurd. For although a Catholic might claim that there is an infallible authority that can lay down in cases of conflict the true Catholic doctrine, there is no canonic authority, as yet, on the true Marxist approach which will finally pronounce on the meaning of Marx. One need no more be a Platonist to understand Plato than a Marxist to understand Marx. This is rejected as uninspired, commonsensical, undialectical thought by Althusser. Marx and Marx alone grasped the way in which philosophy " 'represents' the class struggles in the realm of *Theory*, hence philosophy is neither science nor a pure theory . . . but a *political practice of intervention* in the realm of theory" (p. 256). It follows from this (although Althusser seems too abashed to draw the explicit conclusion) that one must be a Marxist of the right persuasion not only to understand Marx but also to understand every other philosopher. This is reminiscent of the Soviet Stalinist doctrine of the 1930s (Rudas and Mitin) that one must be a member of the Communist Party following the correct political line, as laid down by the Politbureau, in order to understand dialectical materialism.

In his attempt to vindicate Marxism from criticisms made by positivist and empirical critics who argue that if "the proof of the pudding is in the eating" (Engels), history has made a shambles of the theory of historical materialism, Althusser goes to heroic lengths. In his essay on "Contradiction and Overdetermination" he grapples with the charge that the Russian October Revolution constitutes if anything, a disproof of the view that the mode of economic production determines the political and cultural superstructure of a society. He valiantly defends Lenin's contention that if capitalism is considered as a world system it breaks down at its "weakest link," Czarist semifeudal Russia constituting its weakest link. He denies that the revolutionary situation and outcome in Russia were really exceptions to the historical materialist rule. On the contrary, they clarify and confirm the rule. On his analysis the Russian Revolution was the inescapable outcome of a vast and intense accumulation of "contradictions." Far from being a historical fluke, a disconfirming instance of the overriding causal importance of the mode of economic production, in Alth-

usser's view the Bolshevik triumph was "over-determined."
Given the conjuncture of all the contradictions, it could not, so to
speak, *not be*. I shall examine this analysis in a moment but before
doing so it is instructive to observe that Althusser ignores some
obvious difficulties in the Leninist emendation, or revision, of
Marx that he here so uncritically accepts.

First, if capitalism is considered as a world economic system,
and if it is true, as Marx insisted, that no social order ever disappears until all its productive forces have been developed, then the
tremendous expansion of the forces of production during the last
fifty years is evidence that capitalism as a world system had *not*
broken down, and that attempts to seize power in a backward
country, potentially capable of great capitalist expansion, could
not be justified on the basis of historical materialism.

Secondly, capitalism was already a world system during the
days of Marx and Engels, and both repeatedly asserted that the
socialist revolution would come in the industrially and politically
advanced countries of the West. They would have dismissed as
"revolutionary adventurism" attempts to introduce socialism in
any country in independence of its economic presuppositions.

Third, there is no way, if the economic factor is not given
preponderance, to determine *in advance of the outcome* which
country actually is the weakest link. If the revolution by a peculiar
conjuncture of circumstances had succeeded in Spain, or Turkey,
or any other industrially backward country, *that* would have been
evidence of its being the weakest link. The conclusion that Russia
was in actuality the weakest link follows only from the fact that
the Bolsheviks triumphed. It is not a discovery but a tautology,
formulated after the fact.

Finally, and most decisive, even granting Althusser every
methodological freedom to revise Marx, he can at best only establish that capitalism will break down at its weakest link. He
cannot plausibly assert that according to Marx's doctrine of historical materialism *socialism can be built up and developed* at that
link in the absence of all its economic presuppositions. But Althusser emphatically asserts that socialism and the classless society
do exist in the Soviet Union. If so, does it not seem as if Althusser

has not only revised but abandoned Marx despite his protestations of orthodoxy? Regardless of this, one has a right to require of any Marxist scholar who maintains that a socialist economy exists in the Soviet Union, an explanation of why it does not constitute a disproof of the cardinal doctrine of historical materialism as a universal historical generalization. For here we have a clear case of politics determining the economic substructure, not vice versa. At any rate Althusser does not indicate what empirical evidence he is prepared to accept as indicating the invalidity of the doctrine of historical materialism. Is it refutable at all? He can hardly believe it to be true *a priori*.

One wonders about this, however, when his analysis of the Bolshevik victory of October 1917 is examined. According to Althusser this victory was determined by all the "contradictions" present, economic and others. But no attempt is made to derive the presence of all the other contradictions from the "basic" economic one. Indeed the view that they are so derivable is dismissed as a simple and illegitimate inversion of Hegel. How, then, explain the actual historical upshot of the operation of all the structural and superstructural forms, together with the specific events and personalities, involved?

Even as a heuristic approach it is useless to the historian—for all it tells him is that events are related to some other events, not how they are related.

For all his objections to the Hegelianizing of Marx, Althusser himself lapses into a kind of vulgar Hegelianism—to save himself from acknowledging that causal attributions to the mode of economic production, although illuminating many aspects of political and social life (including the range of alternatives open to man) fall far short of explaining the specific choices made among them as well as the relatively autonomous developments that emerge independently of them. And this not only in the spheres of culture but in politics and history as well. Nor is Althusser the only expositor of Marxism who is guilty of this methodological backsliding. It is apparent in Lukács, the later Sartre, and a shoal of lesser commentators.

Too sophisticated to follow Engels in his crude references to "the ultimate" factor as revealed "in the last analysis," to circumvent the plain evidence that the *proximate* causes of some major events have often little to do with the mode of economic production, they substitute the systematic totality of social relationships (Lukács and Sartre) together with the relationships of physical nature (Althusser) to account for the specific phenomenon in question. The result, when not unintelligible verbiage, is often a far-fetched and arbitrary correlation. It has no more explanatory significance for specific events and structures than the invocation of God's Will or Wisdom. It assumes the presence of a dialectically organized totality in which the phenomenon in question is embedded. It never shows that such an all-inclusive totality is required to make sense of what is found, and especially to predict what will occur. It is wise only *after* the event. Aside from its failure to pass the test of any genuinely scientific theory, it fails to explain (if this view is fathered on Marx) in what sense Marx can be considered a materialist and an historical materialist. To Hegelianize Marx is only a little less absurd than to Christianize him as the St. Louis "Maoist-Jesuit" group has done.

Every undogmatic historian is aware of the multitude of contingent events that entered into the victory of the Bolshevik revolution. Lenin hardly expected, a short year before the February revolution, that his party would seize power, and that after the seizure of power it would remain in power. Even Leon Trotsky acknowledged (albeit reluctantly) that without Lenin there would have been no October. Before April 1917 the leaders of the Bolshevik Party were supporting Kerensky.[12]

Althusser is aware of the unique and exceptional collocation of forces, "contradictions" and events that resulted, despite their "radical heterogeneity," in the Russian Revolution. But not all his

12. The extent to which Lenin was responsible not only for the construction of the Communist Soviet régime but for the forging of the Russian Communist Party, and the founding of the Comintern, has recently been developed in masterly detail by Lazitch and Drachkovitch in Vol. 1 of their *Lenin and the Comintern* (Stanford: Hoover Institution Press, 1972).

historical Marxist piety—and it seems unlimited—can produce anything more than the evidence that it was possible, and a remote possibility at that. As a Marxist, however, Althusser claims that it was *historically necessary.* The nearest he comes to this is the assumption, implied but never explicitly stated, that any historical result is determined by the state of the world which precedes it, a postulate compatible with the non-occurrence as well as the occurrence of the October Revolution. For all his talk about the necessity of "rigor" and "a rigorous conception of Marxist concepts, their implications and their development," this collection of essays is singularly free of it. It suffers from tergiversation, and terminological distinctions that are more ingenious than relevant to an objective understanding and evaluation of Marx's thought.

Space does not permit more than a brief mention of Althusser's exposition and defense of dialectical materialism which he regards as the general theory of scientific practice.

This philosophy, which is not a science, and which "represents the class struggle in the realm of theory," is declared to be "indispensable" to the development of all the sciences including the natural sciences. Althusser does not describe the impact of dialectical materialism on the development of the natural sciences in the Soviet Union, and the continuous purge of science and scientists undertaken in its name. But since he explicitly denies that there is any dictatorship in the USSR (p. 222) since "antagonistic classes have disappeared," and assures us that "the State is no longer a class state but the State of the whole people (of everyone): in the USSR men are indeed now treated without any class distinction, that is, as *persons,*" he probably would deny that dialectical materialism has served as a premise to justify purges of science and scientists. The excesses of the terror can always be blamed on "the cult of personality," *on Stalin,* but never on Lenin: the normal or endemic terror is "socialist humanism."

4. A NEW (POST-1932) MARX?

With the publication of the early *Economic-Philosophical Manuscripts* a new Karl Marx has burst upon the world. The most fantastic interpretations have been placed on these groping efforts of Marx toward intellectual maturity. An extensive literature has already developed which on the strength of these writings subordinates in importance all of Marx's published work to Marx's *Ur-philosophie* of alienation. It is widely asserted both that the meaning of Marx's philosophy has remained unchanged from the early to the later years, and that the real key to its meaning can be found only in the early manuscripts.

Thus Father Calvez in his massive volume on the thought of Marx presents the Marxist philosophy as "a complete *system* of man, nature and history." [13] This is already questionable. He then goes on to devote by far the major part of his exposition to the doctrine of alienation in its various forms. Erich Fromm boldly claims that "it is impossible to understand Marx's concept of socialism and his criticism of capitalism as developed except on the basis of his concept of man which he developed in his early writings." [14] This might suggest to some unwary readers that no one understood Marx until his early manuscripts were published in 1932.

To the unsectarian mind, to the student of the intellectual history of ideas without *parti pris,* the difference in interest and emphasis between the old and the new Marx is tremendous. The old Marx was interested in the mechanics or organics of capitalism as an economic system; in politics, as the theater of clashing economic interests; and in the theory and practice of revolution. He is so impatient of the rhetoric of piety and morality that he gives the impression of a thinker who had no moral theory whatsoever, and whose doctrines logically do not allow for considered moral judgment. The new Marx, barely out of his intel-

---

13. Jean Yves Calvez, *La Pensée de Karl Marx* (Paris, 1956), p. 39.
14. Erich Fromm, *Marx's Concept of Man* (New York, 1961), p. 79.

lectual swaddling clothes, sounds like nothing but a moralist, with a religious dedication to the conception of man in a co-operative society which could easily be re-phrased in the ethical idioms of Christ, Spinoza, Kant, and Hegel. The traditional view that Marx, the "scientific" socialist, did not have, and was not entitled to have, a moral position is untenable. But this certainly does not justify the view that all Marx really had was a morality.

Nor does the fact that the new interpretation of Marx as a moralist provides a wonderful weapon against Bolshevik-Leninism and all its varieties of terror, and at the same time makes it possible to preserve an intransigent opposition to the evils of capitalism, have any relevant bearing upon its validity. What is "useful" in a political or personal context has nothing to do with the criteria of practice or experimental consequences in a knowledge-getting context. Myths and lies may sometimes be useful, too. And there is sufficient humanist fire (including the rhetoric of freedom, democracy, and independence) in the *published* writings of the mature Marx to achieve the same effect. No minority party dictatorship which tries to conceal its dictatorship by sleazy words about its leadership of the masses can find the slightest support for this kind of double talk in the published writings of Marx.

How shall we go about determining without question-begging the truth in this matter? This is not the place to lay down the objective methodological criteria for deciding how to establish the basic meaning of a corpus of writings. Suffice it to say that—in the face of Marx's explicit repudiation in the *Communist Manifesto* of the verbose lamentations about "the alienation of man" as "philosophical nonsense," his mordant, indeed needlessly cruel and somewhat unjust, criticism of the *Liebesduselei* of the "true socialists" in his other writings as sentimental vaporings, and his subsequent concentration on historical and economic analysis—it requires some impressive evidence to reverse the traditional interpretations of his thought. For all their variations, these interpretations exclude the notion of Marx as an anguished precursor of existentialism. Certainly it is not sufficient to claim that "Marxism is anything which can be found in Marx's own writings" because these writings contain incompatible things.

Even the exegetes of the new Marx must admit that there are some things which those writings contain which are not Marxist.[15]

To be sure, any change in doctrine is an event in a thinker's biography. Even a sudden and violent conversion from one position to another in any field may disclose elements of psychological continuity. But psychological continuity is not logical continuity. We may recognize Saul in Paul but it would be absurd to argue that Saul was a believer in Pauline Christianity. This confusion is illustrated in the position of Adam Schaff, once *Vertrauensmann* between the Political Committee of the Polish Communist Party and the Polish intellectuals eager to make the best of both worlds. He asserts that even when a philosopher abandons idealism for materialism, there must be continuity between the two phases of the process. To deny this, he contends,

is impossible if only for psychological reasons; we still have to do with one man working on his system, and the transitions from one stage to another are determined by something and must in some way be interrelated within a certain whole.[16]

This is a ponderous truism reinforced by a dogmatic apriorism—both irrelevant to what must be concretely established in

15. I have developed this point in the new Introduction to the second edition of my *From Hegel to Marx* (University of Michigan Press, 1962): "To seek what was distinctive and characteristic about Marx in a period when he was still in Hegelian swaddling-clothes, or when he was still more or less of a Feuerbachian, before he had fought his way clear of every variety of seductive idealism and reductive materialism, is to violate accepted and tested canons of historical scholarship. A period of intellectual maturation, surveyed and evaluated from the perspective at which a thinker has subsequently arrived, is significant more for the doctrines and attitudes which have been abandoned than for those which have been retained. Otherwise there is no explanation of development and we should have to conclude that Marx was born a Marxist. . . ."

16. Adam Schaff, *History and Theory* (Vol. II, No. 3, 1963), p. 316.

any specific case. Obviously a convert from Christian Science to Catholicism or vice versa is the same man but this is utterly irrelevant when we seek to ascertain whether, and when, he believes one set of dogmas rather than another. And although anything a man believes is determined, the specific causes of his belief may not be psychological determinants which explain *how* he holds his beliefs but rather the grounds or reasons on which the belief rests.

5. THE MEANINGS OF ALIENATION

Let us look a little more closely at the doctrine of alienation which is central to the new conception of Marx.

It is perhaps unfair to examine critically a youthful manuscript which together with other early writings Marx left to "the gnawing criticism of mice." But for its resuscitation by latter-day Marxists, its chief interest would be biographical. It breathes a brave and generous spirit and is marked by the same kind of passionate moral indignation against the conditions and nature of labor under early capitalism manifested by Engels in his account of the life of the English working classes after the introduction of the factory system. It is full of interesting insights and striking phrases, shows that Marx had been reading widely in political economy, and that under the influence of Moses Hess he looked to communism as an ideal society in which man would be liberated from all his oppressive restrictions. But in the light of Marx's own development, candor requires one to point out that philosophically his whole treatment is incoherent, incompatible with the principles of his own subsequently formulated historical materialism, that the truths it expresses were unoriginal and wildly exaggerated, and that it teems with ambiguities, puns, tautologies, and *non sequiturs.* Parts of it read as if a poet were reacting against the abstractions of political economy. William Blake and William Morris are far more interesting.

Historically the doctrine of alienation is derived from religious and idealistic traditions, and in most of its expressions, presupposes an abstract, unhistorical notion of natural man. Its very language indicates its origins. In the strictly religious tradition all separation is evil, a consequence of man's disobedience to God. In the idealistic tradition from the time of Plotinus on, otherness and multiplicity result from a mysterious but necessary diremption in the bowels of the One. The alienation of man or the soul lies in its descent into the realm of matter, work, and pain. The life of man or the soul is the career of a fallen spirit whose alienation from its initial bliss is overcome by a pilgrimage in which it returns to God or the One. In Hegel, the theological doctrine is deepened and at the same time transformed. Alienation loses its previous connotations of strangeness, lack or deficiency. It is integral to the process of growth, of necessary development in nature, society, self, and even the advance of knowledge. The Absolute (God or the One) realizes its potentiality in a continuously enriched differentiation. The world and man, human society and history appear progressively more reasonable despite, or rather because of, the manifestations of conflict and evil. If anything, it is the unalienated man in the Hegelian view who lacks true virtue and being, for he is someone who has remained petrified in a particular state, without conflict and therefore without the prospects of growth and development. Virtue must overcome vice or temptation to escape from the innocence of arrested development.

In Feuerbach, the Hegelian "alienation of the Idea" is demythologized. It becomes the alienation of man, alienated because man has not properly understood his own nature, its needs, wants, disguises, and illusions. In religion man worships as transcendental the projections of his own needs. Philosophical anthropology, therefore, is the secret of theology in all its variations. Inspired by Feuerbach, the Young Hegelians declared the disregard of man's true nature to be the secret of all human institutions. They embarked upon a program to liberate men from the fetishism of their own abstractions in morals, politics, and economics. Alienation became not a metaphysical or theological phenomenon but an intellectual, psychological, and ultimately social one. Liberation can be won from the abstractions that obsess the human mind, that divert attention from the workings of institutions that seem to have a life of their own and in consequence exact human sacrifice, by exposing the way in which these abstractions arise and actually function in social life.

The influence of the Hegelian, Feuerbachian, and Young-Hegelian concepts of alienation is apparent on almost every page of the *Economic-Philosophical Manuscripts.*[17] It professes to be a continuation of the Feuerbachian and Young-Hegelian mode of analysis applied to political economy whose precursors have been Weitling, Hess, and Engels. Political economy is viewed as the study of the forms of human alienation which underlie all economic categories. Special emphasis is given to labor and the human laborer as expressions of alienation. But in discussing these latter Marx confuses different kinds of "alienation." He uses the same term to cover the relatively innocent and inescapable fact that men must work in situations of scarcity with the deplorable exploitation which occurs in factory labor unprotected by welfare laws. The emotive overtones associated with exploitation are carried over to activities in which there is no human exploitation whatsoever. The consequence is that what is distinctive about the alienation of labor under capitalism, or a phase of capitalism, gets lost in a *mélange* of widely different conceptions.

The main thing Marx is trying to say in these manuscripts, it seems to me, may be made clear by asking: whom, and under what conditions, would he regard as the unalienated man, the man truly himself? The closest we can come to an answer is: the man who finds personal fulfillment in uncoerced, creative work. He is the person who under an inner not outer compulsion is doing some significant work. He is the creative artist or the dedicated professional man who in pursuit of some vision or task has found a center around which to organize his experiences, a center which gives a rationally approved and satisfying meaning to his life and yet does not obsessively exclude other interests. As an ideal by which to criticize and modify our social institutions in order to make it possible generally for human beings to find

17. *Marx-Engels Gesamtausgabe* (Berlin: Marx-Engels Verlag, 1932, Erste Abteilung, Bd. 3), pp. 33-172.

significance in their practical life, a great deal can be said for this notion. As an expectation that the labor of an entire society can acquire this character, even if science succeeds in banishing *material* scarcities, it is as Utopian as any of the ideals of the great Utopian forerunners of Marx and Engels.

That this is what Marx intended may be gathered from what he says about the "alienation of labor" which suggests labor under the factory system.

> Work is *external* to the worker, that is to say it is not part of his nature, that he therefore does not fulfil *(bejaht)* himself in his work. His work is not voluntary but coerced, *forced labor (Zwangsarbeit)*. (p. 86)

This is the alienation which produces the familiar dualism between earning one's living and living one's life. But there are other kinds of alienation distinguished by Marx. Alienation is found in the fact that the objects produced by the worker are not his, he has nothing to say about how they are used, distributed, or consumed. They have a life of their own, independent and opposed to his own, a hostile and alien force. Here we begin to tread on dubious ground. Whether anyone except an independent producer can control the use or disposition of his product in *any* society is questionable. And even in capitalist society a man who builds bridges, schools, roads, and tunnels, even if he does it merely to earn a living, cannot reasonably regard them as independent powers which threaten him.

But there is a third sense of alienation, even more questionable. This is expressed in the phenomenon of "objectification" *(Vergegenständlichung)*. By becoming dependent upon physical nature and upon the gratification of his own physical wants in production, man reduces himself to the level of an object or natural thing, and his activity to mere animal activity. But "what distinguishes human life-activity from that of animal life-activity is its awareness." Man is indeed a part of nature, but a distinctive part. When he labors to gratify his hunger, without respect for the elements of beauty, truth, social significance, he is betraying what is human within him. He is converting what should be an expression of his *human* life-activity into a means of satisfying his merely biological existence. This seems very farfetched, indeed. Man is human but he cannot always live at the top of his ideal form. Apparently for Marx any production under "the compulsion of physical need" is degrading; so that if a man builds a shelter to protect himself and his own from the elements, he is caught in the toils of self-alienation. Man's ascent to humanity can be traced from cave to cottage to mansion but it is still man who dwells in the cave.

Marx distinguishes a fourth type of alienation—the alienation of man from other men. This takes place in two ways: as a consequence of betraying one's own humanity in working to gratify physical need, one acts like an animal toward other men; and further, because of the relationship which man acquires in the process of production, he regards other men not as brothers, but as competitors or exploiters. What the worker produces does not belong to him but to someone else—to another man. And this man in the nature of the case must find "pleasure and enjoyment in the activity which the worker experiences as torture." This is a purely gratuitous generalization. The laborer who is worthy of his hire is not always degraded by his work.

Alienation now is piled upon alienation. The existence of private property is not the cause of alienated labor but the necessary consequence of it, so that private property far from being the means by which man humanizes himself is the primal crime of man against man. The existence of a wage system is another infallible sign of alienation. So long as human beings work for wages they are not fulfilling their true human nature or essence. Even if the workers are better paid this would be nothing but a "better remuneration of slaves." Even if *everyone* received the same reward, this would mean that what is true for workers in relation to their specific work would also be true for everyone in society no matter what their task. "Society would then have to be conceived as an abstract capitalist." Everyone would be equally enslaved.

The inventory of alienations is not complete but it is time to

bring it to a halt. Suffice it to say that from the primary alienation of labor, which creates private property, is derived the
alienation imposed by the division of labor, which fragments
man; the alienation embodied in the use of money, especially
gold, as a medium of exchange; the alienation of man from the
community by the rise of the political state; the alienation of man
from a truly human culture and human society by man's greed. It
is not difficult to find in this mixture of insight, fantasy, and
balderdash, intimations of the latest varieties of alienation celebrated among the literary sophisticates of Paris and New York.

It can hardly be disputed that in these early manuscripts and
particularly in his view that alienation is the fundamental cause of
the existence of private property, and not vice versa, Marx is not
even a thoroughgoing naturalist or materialist. For what makes
man human, according to Marx, is his *spiritual* nature, his traits of
mind and consciousness which differentiate him from the animal
and plant world. Indeed, to the extent that man is determined by
material conditions and needs, by his body, he is not truly human.
To be truly human, his life, like his mind, must be expressed in
vital choices which are autonomous. He functions, so to speak, in
angelic fashion, free from the compulsions of matter and natural
necessity. The de-humanization of man, which in his mature
writings Marx attributes to specific historical and social conditions, he characterizes as "alienation," as something foreign to his
true nature, as imposed from without. In the mature Marx, however, what is objectionable about alienation is the consequence of
the way in which certain forms of private property operate in a
determinate historical society.

In asserting that alienation is the *cause* of the existence of
private property, the young Marx is unconsciously expressing the
fables of Genesis. Man is sentenced to hard labor by God for his
disobedience and therewith his very nature as man, and Eve's as
woman, is transformed. Marx surrendered his belief in God but
not in the Fall, in the curse of alienation. But whereas the
religious believer has an "explanation" of alienation, Marx actually has none. The very terms "alienation" and "estrangement"
are completely foreign to a robust materialism for which man is *at*

home in nature, not a stranger, as much at home as any other creature. The image of man which rises from the poetic texts of these early manuscripts of Marx is of a fallen angel struggling to liberate himself from the mire of matter, not of man as a tool-making, symbol-using animal. Actually, Augustine and Calvin could make more effective use of a theory of alienation which explains private property as a manifestation of greed or human selfishness than Marxists who have, following the published Marx, explained the prevalence of selfishness and greed by reference to the state of private property.

It is an open question whether the various types of alienation enumerated by Marx are always and in every respect morally objectionable. This is obviously true for the division of labor which is held heavily responsible for human alienation under capitalism. And it often is. But historically, and also today, many kinds of specialization have served to liberate and enrich both personality and community. Not all forms of specialization are narrowing because they sometimes presuppose mastery of a whole range of activities. Division of labor like other forms of specialization arises from the fact that not all men can do all things equally well. This does not doom man to the assembly line except where production for the sake of production or for the sake only of profit is the rule. Even where social or personal goals control production, division of labor may be a means of self-integration, not self-alienation. The religious roots of Marx's early thought appear clearly in his interpretation of the division of labor as *necessarily* a form of self-alienation. Although not omnipotent, man is conceived as a creature capable of doing all the things that God can do to a preeminent degree. If not self-created he is self-creating. As soon as he becomes specialized, he is limited, subject to external restraints, alienated from his true nature or self. Marx believed that sexual reproduction is the most primal form of division of labor, which can be interpreted fancifully as self-alienation only if the ideal of a true unalienated being is a self-copulating creature as some ancient divinities are.

Even the most sympathetic approach to Marx's *Economic-Philosophical Manuscripts* cannot overlook a fundamental difficulty, to which we have already alluded, in the doctrine of alienation and self-alienation. This is a difficulty which appears all the more glaring from the standpoint of the historical approach developed by Marx in his maturer writings.

What is man estranged or alienated *from?* A natural self or an ideal self? It cannot be the former because according to Marx's social psychology there is no such thing as a natural or real self, counterpoised to the world of nature and society, to be estranged *from.* Already in these manuscripts, following Hegel, Marx rejects the notion that society is an abstraction which confronts the ready-made individual. "The individual is the *social creature.*" By acting on nature and society, man continually modifies his own human nature. Man cannot betray or distort or alienate his true nature because he has no true nature. Whatever his nature is at any definite time, it can be explained in terms of the interacting antecedents out of which it developed. Marx admits that at one time human life needed private property for its development, that alienation therefore was both natural and necessary. If human life now requires that private property and the products and processes of alienation be abolished, it can only be in virtue of what Marx conceives man *ought* to be, not because of what man *really* or *naturally* or truly is. Precisely because man is a creature who makes his own history, and therefore ultimately his own nature, whenever we deplore the facts of human alienation, it can only be in the light of our *ideal* of man, of what he *should* be. That Marx's ideal of man was influenced by the Greek conception of the liberal-minded free man and by the Goethean ideal of the active and creative man does not militate in the least against its normative character.

Another way of making this point is to call attention to a kind of alienation which Marx does not discuss but which his own life superbly illustrates. Marx was preeminently alienated from his own society but he would have scorned the notion that he was *self*-alienated, that he had fallen short of his "true" nature. Marx was the kind of man he wanted to be even though not the kind of man others thought he should be. Alienation from society may be a good thing if one lives in a bad society. Internal emigration—the flight from an evil society—is not necessarily a state of self-diremption. In any society, short of Heaven—and judging by Lucifer possibly there, too—there will be at least two possible kinds of alienation: one in which the individual is rejected by society in such a way that he finds himself degraded in his own eyes, and one in which he rejects society, or the powers-that-be in it, in such a way as to affirm himself and live with courage and dignity. These are choices open to all men so long as they are not under the compulsions of physical torture or extreme hunger.

The historical materialist's objection to conceiving of alienation as if it meant a departure from an original or natural norm does not hold against the role played by the doctrine of alienation in a system of historical idealism such as Hegel's. For the empirical self in that system grows by virtue of its alienations until it is absorbed into the Great Self or Totality which functions as a substitute for God. An immanent teleology controls the process, and properly considered there is no place in it for chance, individual decisions, objective possibility and genuine evil. Marx had not freed himself completely from the Hegelian influences he was combating when he penned this youthful work. Subsequently, without abandoning the humanist ideal, he shifted the basis of his social criticism from the murky ethics of self-realization to an empirical account of the development of the capitalist economy in an effort to discover what policies and programs would facilitate social revolution and usher in a new social order and a more desirable kind of man.

To be sure the *linguistic* traces of the doctrine of alienation are found in the *Communist Manifesto* and in a few places in *Capital*, notably in the section on the fetishism of commodities. But their meaning is quite different—empirical and practical. In the mature Marx, the sensible way of combating human alienation is by reducing the length of the working-day and by making power, economic and political, responsible to those whom its exercise affects.

What I am asserting is, first, that the contemporary revival of Marxism in the main has been spurred by the view that the conception of human self-alienation is the key to Marx's philosophy; and, second, that this conception is itself alien to Marx's mature thought.

That the theme of self-alienation is Marx's central concern has been affirmed not only by Marxists who regard it as valid but by some scholars who repudiate it as a myth. Far from agreeing that the doctrine of self-alienation is metaphysical tripe or the intellectual rubbish Marx himself declared it to be in the *Communist Manifesto*, Professor Robert Tucker in his *Philosophy and Myth in Karl Marx* defends the thesis that "human self-alienation and the overcoming of it remained always the supreme concern of Marx and the central theme of his thought." [18] Tucker grants that the doctrine as developed by Marx reveals insight but in contradistinction to latter-day Marxists asserts that it is nonetheless a great myth. Its aberration results from the fact that Marx mistook the true locus or source of human alienation. The alien power which distorts man's nature and against which he must struggle to achieve liberation is man's own inner self of greed, pride, and selfishness. Marx therefore mistakenly substitutes a program of social revolution for the revolution within. According to Tucker, it is human selfishness not capitalism which is the real evil from which men must be liberated.

We can leave to Marx's own dual critique of Christianity on the one hand, and of Stirner and Bentham on the other, the appropriate rejoinder to Professor Tucker's own conception of alienation. What concerns us here, however, is Tucker's contention that there is an obvious answer in Marxist terms to the question I have posed above: "From what true or natural self is man alienated?"

Defending his book against criticism, Tucker asserts that Marx views human nature as "both an historical variable and a constant." Man's variable nature changes with variations in the mode of production: the constant element is "the producing animal, a being whose nature it is to find self-fulfilment in freely performed productive activities of various kinds." (*Slavic Review*, March 1963, p. 188)

18. Robert Tucker, *Philosophy and Myth in Karl Marx* (Cambridge University Press, 1961), p. 238.

The only thing obvious about this distinction between man's variable and man's constant nature is that from the Marxist point of view it is obviously wrong. First, this is not a *description* of anything observable in all human behavior; it expresses a normative goal—something man *should* be. Secondly, how can man's constant nature first come into existence at the *end* of the human history of class societies, as Marx contends, for in no society of the past has man found fulfilment in freely performed productive activities? What is constant must be present from the first. Third, and most important, what Tucker distinguishes as constant and variable in human nature are for Marx in continuous interaction with each other—so much so that Marx even denies that a clear distinction can be made between man's biological nature and his social-historical nature. Human psychology is not only dissolved in social psychology but even human physiology is radically affected. In the very manuscripts which Tucker cites to justify his discovery of a radical dualism between man's constant and variable nature, Marx declares that

> the senses of social man are *different* from those of non-social man; it is only through the objectively developed wealth of the human creature that the wealth of subjective human sensibility is in part first created and in part first cultivated, *e.g.*, a musical ear, an eye for beauty of form, in short *senses* capable of human satisfaction, senses which validate themselves as essential human capacities. For it is not only the five senses but also the so-called spiritual senses, the practical senses (will, love, etc.), in a word *human* sensibility, the human character of the senses, which arises only by virtue of the existence of its object, through *humanized* nature. The education *(Bildung)* of the five senses is the work of all previous history. (*Gesamtausgabe*, loc. cit., p. 135)

Presumably, Marx would be prepared to believe that if there were any toothaches under communism they wouldn't hurt as much, or not in the same way, as in other societies. He carries themes suggested by Hegel and Feuerbach to absurd and

Utopian lengths. But nevertheless the citation above shows as conclusively as any text can that the distinction between a constant and variable human nature is untenable. For Marx, human nature or the human self is not something antecedently given which finds natural fulfilment in the way in which, loosely speaking, an acorn fulfils itself as an oak. Whether man has one self or many selves, he redetermines them to some extent in the light of some reflective ideal. Marx's ideal of the good life in the good society is, as we have already indicated, of great nobility—a community of creative individuals living cooperatively in pursuit of beauty and truth. If *this* is Marxism, Marx need not have published a line, since its secular and religious expressions antecede him not only by decades but by centuries.

This is pretty much the judgment of Tucker. *"Capital,"* he writes,

> the product of twenty years of hard labor to which, as Marx said, he sacrificed his health, his happiness in life and his family, is an intellectual museum piece for us now, whereas the sixteen-page manuscript of 1844 on the future of aesthetics [economics?], which he probably wrote in a day and never even saw fit to publish, contains much that is still significant. (p. 235)

Instead of seeing irony in this observation, I regard it as very weighty evidence of the untenability of Tucker's interpretation. If it is the unknown writings of Marx in which his true significance is to be found, from what source, then, did the great mass movement which centered around Marx's name and doctrines catch fire?

6. WHITHER "IDEOLOGY"?

It is not only Marx's concept of "alienation" which has been blown up beyond reason and evidence in order to provide a basis for revolutionary criticism of the *status quo* as well as criticism of the revolution betrayed. There are signs that the same thing is happening to the Marxist concept of "ideology." I predict we shall hear more about this in the future but it warrants some attention in this sketch.

Here the intellectual phenomenon is not the resuscitation of an abandoned notion but the inversion of a position taken by the mature Marx so startling that the exegesis reveals seams of incoherence. For Marx, an "ideology" is a set of beliefs or doctrines which rationalize the interests of a class engaged in struggle with other classes for social and political power. It conceals the interests at stake in a given period as much from those who hold the ideology as from those who oppose it. The function of Marxist historical and sociological analysis, among other things, is to criticize and unmask ideologies in order to lay bare the stark clash of economic class interests beneath the rhetoric and abstractions about God, country, national honor, universal love, peace, and freedom. Marxism itself on this view is *not* an ideology but a true or valid doctrine which honestly expresses the interests of the working class, and ultimately, of all humanity, on the basis of scientifically valid assertions about the nature, functioning, and collapse of the economic system. From the Marxist point of view, if an "ideology" has a genuinely cognitive meaning, it is false. But cognitive or not, an ideology always has the meaning of a diagnostic sign. It reveals the way in which the true state of affairs about the power struggle is being concealed either by overt deceptions or, more likely, by self-deceptions. And it has an effect on the behavior of those who believe it. That is why it must be combated.

If contemporary Marxism is the belief that human beings can be liberated from the burden of all social evils (which are regarded as the root cause of most personal problems) merely by the socialization of the means of economic production, achieved by a social revolution based on the working class, it is a triple myth.[19]

First, the socialization of the means of production is not a *sufficient* condition of such liberation. In the absence of deeply

19. See my *Reason, Social Myths and Democracy* (New York, 1940); also *The Ambiguous Legacy, Marx and the Marxists* (New York, 1955).

rooted and effectively operating democratic institutions, it may become the engine of a more terrible despotism than Marx ever conceived, and certainly worse than any experienced under capitalism. Total socialization may not even be a *necessary* condition for the realization of the humanistic ideals of socialism. A mixed economy under plural forms of ownership all ultimately responsible to regulatory bodies, within a democratic political order that upholds the civil and personal freedoms of all citizens,, and guarantees a living wage for all who are able and willing to work or an adequate minimum family income, may achieve the best results with the fewest dangers.

Secondly, even when *the* economic problem is solved, if this is defined as the abolition of poverty and gross physical want and the achievement of decent minimum standards of existence for all, other grave social problems will remain, aside from new ones which may develop, not to speak of certain classes of personal problems which cannot be settled merely by social re-arrangements.

Thirdly, the social revolution, if and when it comes, whether peacefully or not, is not likely to be based primarily on the working class, and in some countries it may be begun even in the absence of a developed working class in the Marxist sense.

In the light of the historic experience of the Soviet Union, Mao's China, and every Communist régime in the world, this triple myth can be held only in the same way as the more traditional eschatological beliefs. Marxism in this sense is an ideology not only of *some* working-class groups but of *intellectuals,* especially in under-developed countries, who see in rapid social change not only a promise of plenty for all but of additional opportunities for their skills and talents. An ideology differs from a false social theory in that it cannot be refuted by any tests of experience. Just as some protagonists of a free market system explain all its malfunctions to government intervention so those for whom Marxism is an ideology rather than a set of scientific hypotheses about how to reorder society to get certain desirable results, explain the failure of socialization in terms of vestiges of the past, accidents of leadership, sabotage, etc. always *ex post facto,* without ever abandoning their faith in Marxist dogmas.

In recent years Marxist ideology of this variety has increasingly come under attack because of its claims to offer *total* solutions of the problems of poverty, war, peace, and meaningful vocations. This *type* of criticism of total solutions had been effectively and justly made by some Marxists and by non-Marxist social reformers of the ideology of "free enterprise." In rejecting total solutions, those who have called attention to "the end of ideology" (an unfortunate because ambiguous phrase) have left open how large the piecemeal approach to problems should be. Some problems *are* interrelated and require bold and fundamental reconstruction of the areas in which they are found. For example, if a government finds it necessary to take over an industry in the interest of social welfare, it may have to make a profound change in its fiscal and tariff policies. Or if large-scale educational reconstruction is planned to improve opportunities for minority or disadvantaged groups, this may require far-reaching changes in housing and in employment policy. Other problems can be met only by radical political action (e.g., complete independence for Algeria). Those who have contributed to the literature devoted to the "end of ideology" (Raymond Aron, Arthur Koestler, Seymour Lipset, Daniel Bell, and others) have been notable for their liberal and socialist sympathies. Far from urging resignation toward the acute social problems of the day, they have sought to make social criticism more intelligent and responsible.

It has remained for an American professor of philosophy [20] to take up the cudgels to halt the intellectual revolt against ideology. The strategy of his defense is very curious. He begins (1) by accepting Marx's critique of ideology as a great insight; he continues (2) by attacking current analyses which herald and approve the end of ideological thinking as constituting merely a defense of the *status quo;* and he concludes (3) with an interpretation and spirited defense of "ideological" thinking as an expression of concern to improve the lot of man! This would make Marx's

20. Henry Aiken, "The Revolution Against Ideology," *Commentary* (April 1964).

rejection of all ideological thinking evidence of hostility to attempts to improve the lot of man. Professor Aiken's zeal, however, is not so much to defend Marx as to denigrate the contemporary critics of orthodox Marxist ideology. Despite their professions, all who declare themselves for "an end of ideology" are really committed, he asserts, to the position of "that most determined and most consistent of anti-ideologists, Michael Oakeshott," the staunch conservative critic of rationalism in all its varieties.

Aiken's reasoning will not bear close examination for a moment. It reduces itself to the charge that because one denies that there is a cure-all for disease one thereby denies that there is a cure for anything. Because the critics of ideology deny there is one, single, over-all technique for solving social problems, because they contest the viability of a total plan for the final amelioration of the lot of man, they are rebuked by Aiken as if they were *philosophes fainéants.*

> I cannot, as a pragmatist [he writes] see how one can be said actively to seek a less cruel lot for humanity if one can trust no technique, and no plan for its amelioration.

What he cannot see was seen very clearly by John Dewey, one of the founders of pragmatism, who long before the current discussions about the end of ideology vigorously criticized orthodox Marxism for its quest of total solutions, its disregard of the continuity between means and ends, and of the distinction between ends-in-view and ultimate ends, and its consequent hypostasis of a social ideal into a fixed metaphysical goal.[21] There are many plans and techniques for the amelioration of human suffering in society but there is no one plan, no one technique that will work in the way some ideologists of revolution claim that socializaton of all the instruments of production, destruction and exchange will work.

---

21. John Dewey, *Liberalism and Social Action* (New York, 1935), and *Freedom and Culture* (New York, 1939).

Like so many others, Aiken wants to have his cake and eat it—explicitly to reject Marxism and even socialism and yet to refurbish it with doctrines that would make all liberals, progressives, men of good will, indeed anyone who sincerely and actively commits himself in the struggle to improve the lot of mankind, "Marxist ideologists," too. As if it were necessary to have an "ideology" in order to have a moral passion for freedom or peace or social equality or the prevention of cruelty to children and animals. This is a kind of popular-front conception of crypto-Marxism according to which there are no enemies to the "left." This illusion of perspective reinforces the illusion of those conservatives from Herbert Hoover to Whittaker Chambers who regarded the New Deal and the welfare state, for all their piecemeal solutions, as "the piecemeal triumph of Communism."

Where those who proclaimed the "end of ideology" proved to be mistaken was not in their criticism of the validity of the faith in total solutions but in their predictions of the erosion of this faith among the intellectuals. For in recent years this faith has reasserted itself more strongly than ever. This is true not only among those who have espoused revolutionary collectivism but also among some exponents of extreme *laissez-faire*.

7. THE TEMPLE OF THE TEN THOUSAND MARXES

To the extent that Marx has made contributions to the study of history, sociology, social psychology, economics, and politics, they are integral to the scholarly traditions in those fields. But whatever these contributions, they do not explain at all the perennial appeal which Marx and Marxism have exerted on the proletariat of some countries of the West and on certain circles among the intellectuals of the West. For those *constituents* of Marx's thinking which represent abiding contributions—like his historical approach to all social tendencies and "laws," his insights into the development of capitalism, his hypothesis that economic and class influences always limit the alternatives of effective social choice and also influence the choice of different groups among these alternatives—*all* can be accepted without subscribing to any Marxist revolutionary program. Even non-socialists like Pareto, Max Weber and Schumpeter could regard Marx as an intellectual pioneer, albeit one not free from some of the illusions of those Marx criticized.

To what then can we attribute the recurrent allegiance to Marx, the battle cries which invoke his name even when his doctrines are rejected or transformed beyond recognition? I shall conclude by listing a few of the motives which seem to me to account for the phenomenon.

1. The dominant intellectual mood in the Western world is critical. The cultural role of the intellectual is primarily to be "against." Dissent from, and nonconformity with, existing traditions and institutions are regarded as virtues, even when they do not rise above the level of gut reactions, because they seem continuous with the dissenting attitudes of the great figures of the past. Since the enemy is usually assumed to be on the right, no association with the dissenting movements and ideologies from *this* quarter is conceivable. The spectrum of professedly liberal views is unexciting and unheroic. Their sane attitudes appear merely safe, and their reasonable programs timid. In consequence, allegiance to a vague and free-floating Marxism, no longer handicapped by seemingly organic ties to the murderous regimes of Communist police states, provides the break with the imperfect present, continuity with the revolutionary past, and absolution for the "excesses" or "mistakes" of the Stalinist cult of personality. From this arises the complex of views which are *de rigueur* for the doctrinally well-equipped intellectual of our times.

2. Non-Marxist or anti-Marxist reformisms do not by far exercise the same attraction for intellectuals because their programs of piecemeal change strike the impatient as halfhearted. And most intellectuals (not the scholars so much as the opinion-makers) are impatient. Although the specific doctrines and principles of Marxism are rarely defended, nonetheless as a system of total opposition Marxism still has a strong appeal. It is against religion, against the state, against the existing family, against the profit motive and against the vulgarities of mass culture which the profit motive breeds. In short, Marxism "explains" everything even if a

little vaguely and hazily. Like Thomism, although not so well-knit, the system gives a resiliency to the attitude of the believer. He is buoyed up by its inflated claims and airy hopes enough to float securely despite rents and tears in the fabric of the argument.

3. Another source of attraction in Marxism is its strong sense of social justice, its passionate protest against social inequalities rooted not in reason but in tradition and arbitrary power. And this despite some of its hardboiled pronouncements. It opens the vista of a world in which the exploited, the enslaved, and the oppressed—and there are many such!—come into their own. The balance-wheel of history is set right not by a mythical *deus ex machina* but by processes which modern man can accept as natural, even if not merely physical, and to which he can contribute.

4. Marxism is a philosophy which promises fulfilment of age-old dreams of material betterment, and justifies hope in man. After all, there is no point in crying stinking fish in the world if that has always been the fare of mankind and always will be. The Paretos, Moscas, and Michels, with their "iron laws" of the circulation of the *élite,* of the political supremacy of minorities, and organizational oligarchy, are unable to account for the phenomena of *degree,* which may spell the difference between the Weimar Republic and Hitler, sometimes between the very life of the free mind and its death. Marxism, no matter how reinterpreted, always appears the optimistic variant in the reading of the future. To the literary mind, indifferent to recent history, it suggests a dimension of depth because it expects the felicity of the future to be accompanied by a little blood and tears (of others). In a world where there has already been so much evil, and in which so many have scared themselves witless by fears of accidental nuclear holocaust, a view which sustains hope in a triumphant future, and helps cheerfulness to break out, is not without attraction.

5. As a system Marxism is now invalid. Its theory of historical materialism was exploded by those most "orthodox" of Marxists, the Bolshevik-Leninists, who demonstrated that politics determines economics in our age, not vice versa. Nonetheless there is no rival system freer of difficulties, especially for those who

hunger for the emotional security of feeling that they are thinking and living with the true drift of things. In addition, with a little ingenuity, its doctrines can be qualified to make them not obviously wrong. Let him who is without any *a priori* assumptions throw the first methodological stone! Further, for some periods of history, and in some regions of the world, some of its general propositions about the state or imperialism or the overriding character of economic class struggles appear to be valid. What is easier than to assume that what is true at some time may turn out upon further exploration to be true at any time? Despite the niggling objection that upon further exploration what seemed true at some time may turn out false at another time, there is just enough semblance of truth in the reconstruction of Marxism to give it an aura of intellectual plausibility to those predisposed to revolt against the present in fervent hope for a better future.

6. Another reason for the strength of Marxist ideology is the apparent use of the theory of historical materialism in undergirding the view that the conflict between Communist and non-Communist/worlds is gradually disappearing, that there is a growing "convergence" in their economies, and that their cultures are rapidly becoming mirror-images of each other. The view is held by those who deplore it, and who take pride in their lonely feeling of revolutionary integrity against both the democratic philistines and the equally philistine Communist Commissars of People's Culture. That the democratic philistines cheerfully accept their critics, when they do not comfortably support them in their role of dissenters, while the Communist philistines purge and punish dissenters severely, sometimes by imprisonment, torture, and confinement to insane asylums, is dismissed as an irrelevant observation. The degree of "economic" convergence is hard to establish because of the variety of notions the term "economic" connotes. But in the main, the structural similarities are found in common technological and bureaucratic phenomena which reflect the place of science and the size of the industrial enterprise in the modern world.

Does it follow that the more similar the basic technology of different societies is, or even their modes of economic production with which technology is vulgarly confused, the more similar will be their cultures? This is an empirical question for which the evidence, although not conclusive, strongly suggests a negative answer. Cultural and political phenomena of vastly differing significance are compatible with similar economic structures. Consider, for example, the difference which free trade unions can make, and have made, to the way in which the economic system itself functions. Consider the variations in religion which can flourish in the same economy. The predictions of Hayek and others that only a free enterprise economy can support a free culture and that the more socialized the economy of a culture, the less cultural freedom and political democracy it can enjoy, have been refuted by events. (Others besides orthodox Marxists are crypto-historical materialists!) The predictions that the Communist and non-Communist worlds will converge and develop a common cultural and political pattern in the foreseeable future is today a gratuitous piece of dogmatism, not warranted by the facts.

7. Finally, there is the factor which I previously mentioned. The centripetal influence of established power, Communist power, forged in the name of Karl Marx, exercises a fascination on leftist circles in the West (and not only on leftist circles) almost in inverse relation to their own strength. Even the revolutionary pure become weary of being eternally right and politically impotent, and long for a sense of effectiveness in the world they live in. This they first get vicariously from the triumphs and achievements of Communist powers. They then rationalize their acceptance of the ideology of their Communist Big Brothers with the consoling myth that they can more easily change Communist thought and behavior by joining the movement than by cultivating perfection on the sidelines or in ivory towers. Similarly, in the middle and late 1930s, the apparent strength of the Italian and German régimes exercised a fascination on conservative (and not only conservative) circles in Western Europe. The phenomena, of course, are not identical and remain very complex but the simple upshot, now as then, of this attempt to influence totalitarians by joining or even cooperating with them is that the pure become more like the strong than the strong become like the pure, with

the consequent increase of coarseness and brutality in the world. In the end, the romantic souls become stern realists. Albert Camus has phrased this with his usual felicity:

> The will to power came to take the place of the will to justice, pretending at first to be identified with it and then relegating it to a place somewhere at the end of history, waiting until such time as nothing remains on earth to dominate.[22]

These motives for the revival of allegiance to vague Marxist traditions are not all consistent with each other. They appeal in different measure to different types of personality. Nor are they exhaustive. They are the main influences I have found among the Marxists and neo-Marxists of the postwar world. From such groups much may be expected in the way of a new literature of Marxist rediscovery—new expressions of dissent—new, much-needed (and despite exaggerations) praiseworthy exposures and disclosures of the evils and imperfect functioning of our mixed economies and our mixed-up cultures. But one thing in addition may be confidently predicted of them. They are not likely to serve as a basis for an international *revolutionary* movement or organization. This is true not only because of the influence of nationalism which, despite Marx, is as strong today as in the past century, but because current reinterpretations of Marx have stressed the individual, the deviant, the Utopian, and the anarchistic aspects of his beliefs. There is no central core of doctrine. There is no agglutinative element to tie or hold the new Marxists together in a Sartrian "group." Interpretations of Marx will proliferate.

In Japan there is a temple of the Tendai sect of Buddhism, Sanjusangendo, which contains ten thousand Buddhas, all shiningly indistinguishable from each other. If and when Marxism becomes a world ideology, without becoming the theology of

22. *The Rebel, An Essay on Man in Revolt* (London: Penguin, 1962; New York: Knopf, 1954), p. 195.

a universal church (an unlikely event but made possible by Communist polycentrism), history is likely to become the temple of the ten thousand Marxes, at which each culture or group will make its selective obeisance in accordance with its own particular needs, wishes, and hopes. Feuerbach will have revenged himself against Marx. The secret of Marxist ideology will be human anthropology.

ADDENDUM: MARX'S GRUNDRISSE

The claim has been made that most interpretations of Marx have been rendered invalid by failure to consider the contents of the mass of unpublished manuscripts that are now referred to as the *Grundrisse*. This is a manuscript which Marx composed in 1857 and 1858. Discovered in the early 1920s, published first in Russian in 1939, and in German in 1953, an English translation has recently appeared with a highly misleading and tendentious foreword by the translator, Martin Nicolaus.[23] All sorts of exaggerated claims have been made for it. It has been declared by David McClellan, Marx's most recent biographer, as "the most fundamental work that Marx ever wrote." [24] Nicholaus is even more extravagant in his characterizations. For him the *Grundrisse* makes visible the great mystery, to bourgeois scholars, of "the materialist dialectic method." It is the workshop not only of *Capital* but of every distinctive Marxist idea. The *Grundrisse* which McClellan believes to be a continuation of the *Economic-Philosophical Manuscripts* of 1844 threatens to play an even greater role in the future in sustaining a view of Marx as a thinker whose profundity and prophetic insight cannot be affected by prosaic empirical details that have falsified his major predictions. The argument of this chapter therefore requires some assessment of its content and of the claim made for it.

The simple truth of the matter is that the *Grundrisse* was earmarked by Marx as rough notes to *himself*—to be used, modified,

---

23. Pelican Marx Library (London, 1973).
24. "Marx and the Missing Link," *Encounter* (November 1970), p. 39.

or developed for subsequent publication. They should be taken as evidence of what Marx was trying to say, of his wrestling with ideas in order to achieve clarification. What he was trying to say emerged clearly in the *Introduction to the Critique of Political Economy* and in Volume I of *Capital.* These are the books that Marx himself wanted to be judged by. To second guess what Marx really meant is a gratuitous piece of presumption. To be sure the *Grundrisse* contains more than is contained in the text of *Capital* but it was Marx himself who rejected the pages that did not appear. He must have regarded them as unnecessary and perhaps in places incompatible with what he finally wanted to say. The English translator and editor of the *Grundrisse* who almost swoons with ecstasy about the significance of the work is hardly aware of the implications of his own words when he writes:

> The fact that one can read the *Grundrisse* at all today, and understand it, is due solely to Marx's labors in working its basic concepts *out*, in *presenting* the content in a form accessible to a public in a position to act on it. In 1858, not a single person in the world understood the *Grundrisse* except Marx, and even he had his troubles with it (p. 61).

What clearer acknowledgment do we need that to judge Marx's meaning by his own intent we must go to the published works for which Marx took public responsibility? Mr. McClellan seems to go further than Mr. Nicolaus in stating that "Marx never rejected any of his own writings." And speaking of Marx's intellectual development as "a process"—as if a development can be anything but a "process,"—he contends that "the central point of the process is neither the Paris Manuscripts [1844] nor *Capital* [1867] but the *Grundrisse* of 1857–8."

To assert that "Marx never rejected any of his writings," taken literally, is absurdly false. Not only would it fail to explain what Marx rejected for publication, it implies that he never wrote anything as a first effort or draft that he was not satisfied with as being true or adequate to his purpose. Even Marx's most vehement detractors never regarded him as a creature of such insufferable vanity. It makes a mystery of why he rewrote his manuscripts so often. The absurdity of McClellan's statement is no less striking if we take him to refer only to Marx's published writings. He admits that Marx spoke of rereading *The Holy Family* with embarrassment, but discounts this on the ground that in 1851 Marx was willing to reprint essays that went back to the *Rheinische Zeitung* of 1842. But there is an obvious difference between publishing or even republishing materials from one's past for purposes of historical interest or to illustrate the way in which one has reached his mature position and accepting or endorsing the position they express. After all Marx was not yet a Marxist when he wrote these essays and *The Holy Family*. The latter work contains some of the seminal ideas that he later developed but it cannot be considered a "Marxist" work. Marx was a socialist or Communist before he articulated the *distinctive* ideas of his social and economic philosophy. Broadly speaking Marx became a Marxist with the enunciation of the principles of historical materialism in some detail in *The German Ideology*. It simply makes no sense to regard the Paris Manuscripts written *before* Marx developed the theory of historical materialism as central to Marx's thought, and hardly more sensible to downgrade *Capital* because it does not treat all the themes referred to in Marx's notebooks in the course of the long gestation of the work that both he and Engels regarded as his masterpiece.

Let us grant that the *Grundrisse* contains more topics, and some treated more intensively, than those developed in *Capital* or in other published works. It is fair, however, to ask: what important ideas does the *Grundrisse* present that are not found elsewhere in Marx's publications? What important problem does it analyze more clearly than elsewhere? What does it illumine about the difficulties and apparent contradictions in the corpus of Marx's works?

Several claims have been made for the epochal significance of the *Grundrisse*. It has been asserted that the references in it to "alienation" are continuous with the uses of the term in the Paris Manuscripts. But the main points are whether or not these uses have the same meaning; and which one of several meanings of "alienation" is reflected in Marx's doctrine of "the fetishism of commodities" in *Capital.* The *Grundrisse* is primarily a critique of the economic categories. In it Marx works out his theory of surplus-value which is not found in the Paris Manuscripts. The most important sense of alienation in the *Grundrisse* is the appropriation of the alien labor of the worker by the capitalist in the course of a "free and equal" exchange of the labor power or capacity of the former for the wages paid by the latter. It transforms the nature of property: "The right of property originally appeared to be based on one's own labor. Property now appears as the right to alien labor and as the impossibility of labor appropriating its own product [Since out of this product comes profit, interest and rent]" (p. 458). The theory of alienation in the Paris Manuscripts presupposes an original and a fixed human nature which was abandoned soon afterwards in *The Poverty of Philosophy (Anti-Proudhon)* and is subjected to renewed, running criticism in the *Grundrisse.*

Another presumably novel feature of the *Grundrisse* is the attribution to Capital of "a very positive mission." McClellan makes much of this *(loc. cit.,* p. 42): "Within a short space of time it [Capital] had developed the productive forces enormously, had replaced natural needs by those historically created, and had given birth to a world market." But surely all this was already proclaimed by Marx, and much more eloquently, in the *Communist Manifesto.* The *Grundrisse* adds nothing here—and the historical sections of *Capital* are much more detailed and complete than anything found in these jumbled outlines. That "the ideas produced by capitalism were as transitory as capitalism itself," as McClellan puts it, was already stated in almost those words in Marx's published writings as a corollary of the theory of historical materialism. The difficulties of this theory which one would have expected Marx to explore at length in a work as comprehensive as this remain unmentioned except for a section already familiar to readers in material made available by Kautsky and reprinted in the English translation of *Introduction to the Critique of Political Economy.* For example, if "the arts are bound up with certain forms of social development"—ultimately with the relations of production—how account for their continued charm and validity when these relations have been transformed? Not only in art but in other areas of experience, validity may be independent of origin. The lame and inadequate explanation that Greek art owes its perennial charm, and its role as norm and model in subsequent societies, to the fact that it reflects the naïveté of historic normal childhood could hardly account for the moral validity of the Golden Rule or the logical validity of arithmetic and geometry.

Finally it is asserted that Marx's language is just as much and perhaps more Hegelian in the *Grundrisse* than in the Paris Manuscripts. The question is not one of language but of thought. No man completely emancipates himself from the language of his youth even after he outgrows his early thoughtways. In *Capital* Marx makes three claims that are hard to square with the contention that the Hegelian elements in his thought—except for the influence of the notion of organic totality—are profoundly important. The first is that he was "coquetting" with Hegelian expressions and that they were not essential to his distinctive contributions. The second is his emphasis on the fact that his approach was to be "scientific." The third and related point is his express opposition to Hegelian idealistic mysticism and his acceptance of materialism.

To take the last point first. For Hegel the culture of any society is an organic totality, in which everything in some sense is interconnected with, influences, and is influenced by, everything else. To the extent that we seek to grasp or explain the culture we must invoke some idea or ideal which pervades the totality of the culture, and whose logical ramifications account for the necessity of the historical development of the culture—why it blossomed where and how it did—and its subsequent disappearance. Marx rejects the idealistic approach as mystical because one cannot derive any concrete, existent facts from any ideal notion, and because what is actually experienced empirically seems arbitrary from its own standpoint. But the organic structure of a culture requires explanation. It is not self-generated. Nor is its historical development self-caused. The material factor which Marx some times calls, metaphorically, the "anatomy" and at other times "the foundation" of society and culture—viz., the social relations of production" is causally determining in a way in which Hegel would never accept. Ideas, however they be construed, are just as decisive for Hegel as relations of production.

Marx was proud of his scientific approach to history and social affairs. To be sure his conception of "science" reflects nineteenth-century conceptions as well as certain German connotations of the term *"Wissenschaft"* that suggest a rational discipline. But the fact that both he and Engels assimilate the Marxist approach to that of Darwin and of other great scientific figures, making allowance for the difference of subject matters, indicates the main drift of the meaning of the term "scientific" for them. In the nature of the case, however, every scientific explanation must assume that the phenomenon to be explained is *not* related to everything else in the world, that it can be relatively isolated in order to discover what changes are produced in other phenomena concomitant with or successive to changes within itself. The Hegelian view that truth lies in the totality of things—which is itself of questionable validity since we do not possess the truth about everything—makes any specific scientific inquiry or experiment impossible since we could never isolate any relevant independent variable.

Finally, there is no reason to dispute Marx's plain assertion that he was flirting with Hegelian terminology. And as for the dialectic method, either it is synonymous with or integral to scientific method or it is not. If it is, there is nothing expressed in Hegelian terms that cannot be rendered in ordinary scientific language. If it is not, then to claim that it can lead to valid results that scientific method cannot reach opens the door to two concepts or doctrines of truth which would subordinate scientific empirical findings to the deliverances of a higher philosophical truth. Something like this view is held by some expositors of Marx who dismiss scientific criticisms of Marx's economic predictions as the upshot of a vulgar empiricism that has not mastered the profound logic of the dialectic method. The claim of the editor and translator of the *Grundrisse* that Hegel's logic "served Marx in overthrowing the

Ricardian doctrine of profit" (p. 41) is not in the least established by a close perusal of the text. Marx's analysis ultimately depends upon his definitions of surplus value, constant and variable capital, rate of profit, and especially the concept of labor power or capacity whose output allegedly has more value than the value of the goods and services necessary to reproduce it.

The extravagant lengths to which those who cry up the virtues of the *Grundrisse* are prepared to go is evidenced in the claim that it is "the first known attempt self-consciously to change, and to apply the [dialectic] method, at the same time to major problems of theory." Mr. Nicolaus then goes on to add: "The materialist dialectic is not exempt from its own laws" (p. 43), which makes about as much sense as the assertion that the laws of thermodynamics are themselves not exempt from the principle of entropy or that the laws of gravitation gravitate.

The political bias and antidemocratic animus of the English translator of the *Grundrisse,* whose long introduction seeks to bend the reader's mind away from a plain reading of some of its pages, is apparent in his effort to Bolshevize Marx. He refers to the absence from *Capital* of the outspoken "revolutionary" passages in the *Grundrisse* and explains it in terms of the absence of a concrete illustration. Had the 1917 revolution already taken place, he concludes, "*Capital* would have had a far greater latitude of form" (p. 61). In other words Marx hesitated to announce his revolutionary intentions because there was no revolution to which he could point. For the kind of revolution he had in mind was the Bolshevik October Revolution of 1917!

This is bizarre to the point of incredulity. First of all, Marx, from the time of the *Communist Manifesto* on, makes many explicit references to revolutionary overthrow of existing society by the working class without any concrete historical revolution to serve as an illustration. Secondly, if the *Grundrisse*—out of which the famous introduction to the *Introduction to the Critique of Political Economy* grew—establishes anything, it is that Russia was the last place in the European world that Marx either expected, or would have approved of, a socialist revolution. All of the presuppositions of a socialist revolution were absent. Thirdly,

Nicolaus reads the text of the *Grundrisse* in such a way that when Marx speaks of the explosions, crises, cataclysms, and violence resulting from the *economic* contradictions of capitalism, he gives the term "violence" a political, revolutionary significance which it does not have except possibly in one sentence of the work. He even suggests that the reference in *Capital* to the "integument [that] must burst asunder" is a Pickwickian expression for violent political revolution, rather than the ultimate economic *Zusammenbruch*, that the expression is employed by Marx out of prudence. As if prudence was ever a consideration with Marx! Finally, the simple explanation of the absence of a call to violent revolution in *Capital* escapes Nicolaus's Bolshevik *parti pris,* viz., that by the time Marx published *Capital,* democratic institutions had sufficiently developed in advanced capitalist countries like England and the United States as to make a peaceful nonviolent transition to socialism at least possible.

One final observation. Sixteen years elapsed between the publication of the first volume of *Capital* and Marx's death. His failure to issue the second and third volumes of *Capital* which were practically complete by the time the first volume was published has been explained by the hypothesis that he could not make economic ends in his theory meet. Whether this is true or not would have no bearing upon the presumably non-economic aspects of his thought. What possible reason then would Marx have had for neglecting his brain children of whom he was inordinately fond?

The simplest hypothesis is that Marx left the *Grundrisse* to moulder away because he was not prepared to accept intellectual responsibility for all of the hastily written output during this period except where they could be reworked for *Capital,* which still remains his chief work. It must be judged by the same critical, scientific standards by which we judge other economic analyses and predictions of capitalist society.

CHAPTER TWO

The Enlightenment and Marxism

The relationship between Marxism and the Enlightenment is so tangled and complex that any general statement about it must be carefully qualified. The Enlightenment is many things. In this analysis I shall discuss only two of the things associated with it, its faith in reason or science and its belief in human rights or the natural rights of man. Marxism, too, is many things. But it is many more things. It is not only Marx but Marxist movements that span a century. There are Marxist movements which regard socialism as a means of furthering democracy as a way of life, and Marxist movements which regard democracy merely as a means of furthering socialism as an economic collectivist order.

If we turn our backs on the different varieties of Marxism and center our attention on Marx himself we still have many things. For there are many Marxs. There is Marx the revolutionary fighter against the European Restoration or the system of Metternich, and Marx the historical sociologist and political economist, deriving from a metaphysical theory of value the scientific equations of doom of the capitalist system. There is Marx the social and moral prophet denouncing the exploitation of man by man, and Marx the radical historicist for whom all moral ideals—freedom, equality, fraternity, integrity, independence —are deceptive abstractions concealing the economic class interests at their roots. And, to make the matter even more complicated, we must distinguish all of these Marxs, embodied in what was published over a period of forty years, from the Ur-Marx, of the so-called *Economic-Philosophic Manuscripts,* who quietly entered the world only in 1932, and was discovered almost a quarter century later to be the most effective ally of the Communist opposition to Stalinism.

In order to reduce my subject to manageable proportions I have selected two themes of the Enlightenment which seem to me to have the most comprehensive bearing in their continuity and difference on all varieties of Marxist movements, and on some central ambiguities of the thought of Marx himself.

Whatever else the Enlightenment is associated with, its very name, as well as its typical emphasis in most of the figures of the Enlightenment, suggests confidence in the use of Reason as the test of the morally acceptable, as the method of scientific discovery, and as the ultimate judge in resolving conflicting opinions about what is not scientifically discoverable, or in tolerating or learning to live with such conflicts where they could not be resolved. Even the Enlightenment critics of Reason like Hume and Kant do not denigrate the practical uses of Reason. They were concerned with its limits, to be sure, but in the spheres of human experience in which intelligence operated they recognized its authority, provided it did not immodestly claim to know what is beyond experience or with certainty about what is within it. Hume's thought was subversive of any conception of science that regarded it as a form of logical necessity or as completely empirical. Nonetheless despite his theoretical skepticism, like most of the Enlightenment figures he believed in the possibility of a science of human nature as well as a science of human society fashioned on a Newtonian model. To be reasonable, as distinct from being merely strictly logical, meant to be scientific.

For Marxism, too, Reason meant being not logical but scientific and therefore antiobscurantist, hostile to both religious and metaphysical superstition. The proudest boast of Marxist Socialists was that they were *scientific* socialists. To the extent that they were critical of the Enlightenment thinking about society it was on the ground that it sought to explain social and political phenomena in terms of psychological or ideal forces, i.e., by principles of individual psychology, instead of explaining individual psychological phenomena, including ideas, as the outcome of social, political, and ultimately economic institutions. Although they were not always aware of it, insofar as their conception of science was concerned, the Marxist notion was quite different from what might loosely be called the Enlightenment view of science. The nature and cause of the difference are to be found in the influence of Hegel. What the Marxists criticized as the method of vulgar empiricism was the method of the understanding which Hegel had denounced before them. This method of the understanding, whose abstractions were suggested, shaped, and criticized by experience, Hegel had rejected as inadequate to the organic unity of the systems encountered in nature as well as society. According to him, the phenomena of quality, of life, of experience itself were destroyed, not properly grasped by analytic methods. Hegel was critical of the Newtonian philosophy and approach which had been canonized by Voltaire and other Enlightenment thinkers. And it was this Hegelian conception of science which led Engels to refer to Newton with a quaint kind of arrogance as an *Induktionsesel.*

What was the difference between the Enlightenment conception of scientific method and the Hegelian-Marxist one? Briefly, the world of the Enlightenment, as of Newton, was conceived as a gigantic machine with invariant mechanical laws which determined the interaction of things down to the slightest detail. Knowledge of the laws governing the cosmic machine of which society and men are parts could enable men with insight and courage in principle to solve all problems, to discover or invent the social institutions required to provide human nature with the proper theater for its fulfillment. Just as men on the basis of their knowledge of laws and the ways of things could rebuild the houses in which they lived to let in the light and air and pleasing prospect required for a healthy and happy life, so they could shatter and rebuild the institutions of a society to make them fit or worthy for men. Only ignorance, religious superstition, and selfishness stood in the way of the needed resolution and reconstruction.

For Hegel and the Marxists, on the other hand, the world was not a machine but an interconnected set of processes. To this belief they added two fateful assumptions. The laws by which these processes were grasped must reflect the development they sought to explain, so that science itself becomes historical. Second, these processes, especially the historical process, had an immanent *progressive* direction or *telos,* so that when we truly understand human history we see not only that it is necessary but also reasonable. In consequence human beings can rely upon the immanent processes of history despite all setbacks and defeats to bring them to a world of universal freedom. These conceptions led Hegel and many Marxists to charge that the thought of the Enlightenment was characterized by an unhistorical approach to culture and civilization, indeed, by an indifference to history—a charge that seems unjust. The thinkers of the Enlightenment were profoundly interested in history; after all the chief actors of the French Revolution, nurtured on the literature of the Enlightenment, thought of themselves as reincarnated Romans on the stage of history. To be sure they moralized about the historical roles men played in past and present, but they also believed in a science of history whose dominant factors were geography, great personalities and ideas, and human nature with all its powers and vagaries.

The important difference between the Enlightenment and Marxist thinkers lay not in their concern for history but in their conception of what it meant to have a *science* of history. For the Marxists history could only be scientifically understood in terms of laws immanent in a developing social process more inclusive and complex in scope and subject matter than laws of physical nature, and therefore not derivative from them. Nature can only condition history, not determine it, and history can modify *both* nature and human nature. Just as the behavior of an organism in contradistinction to a machine cannot be explained merely by environmental stimulus and an invented design, but by the immanent processes of growth in relation to an environment which, within limits, is modified by them—so the development of society is conceived as being governed by immanent laws of economic production that determine the birth, development, and death of all societies until man as a truly free agent comes into his own.

What is most significant here are the consequences of these two different conceptions of science for the *making* of history, when they are combined with different specific hypotheses about society. If one thinks of society as a machine, as the Enlightenment did, there is a tendency to believe one can build it closer to one's heart's desire at *any* time, if only one is intelligent and resolute enough. One needs valid moral ideals, social ingenuity or inventive capacity, and the audacity to storm the centers of resistance manned by selfish lords of the manor or captains of industry and their superstitious or corrupt retainers. The men of the Enlightenment certainly had high moral ideals in profusion—the security of life, liberty, happiness, equality, fraternity; they had confidence in the power of human intelligence; and they and their descendants had courage and audacity. They therefore believed they could make revolutions any time and anywhere their ideals found a popular resonance. For them the willingness was all, the courage, the idealism, the sacrificial dedication to the public good, because aside from geography,there were no other determining tendencies in history outside of man himself. (This Enlightenment view still persists today among certain liberal thinkers who claim that anything can happen in history at any time.)

The Marxist approach was quite different even when it accepted the ideals of the Enlightenment. If there are laws that determine the development of society, then men are not completely free to make and remake history at will. The viable alternatives of action are determined by something outside their will, by the institutions and habits of the past. A revolution cannot be made by fiat, whether by enlightened despots, or by an intellectual élite. It must be prepared for. It is like a new birth. The violence and wrench with which new life is expelled from the womb of the mother is the final phase of the period of gestation. What the Marxists stressed was not the *willingness*, but the *ripeness*. The readiness was all.

The theory of historical materialism was developed by Marx to explain, among other things, not only when and where social revolutions do occur, but where they do *not* occur, and indeed where they should not be attempted. The French Revolution was prepared for by the growth of economic productive forces whose laws of development were hampered by restrictive feudal relations of distribution. The French Revolution to the Marxists was a complex phenomenon but *au fond* it was the act which cleared the way, as the English revolutions of the seventeenth century had done previously, for the development of capitalism.

Why didn't the French Revolution acquire a socialist character despite the existence of Babeuf and other socialist thinkers of the time? How did the Marxists explain this? Quite simply with the statement that the time was not propitious for it, i.e., the capitalist mode of production wasn't sufficiently developed to make possible the realization of the socialist ideals of organization and distribution. And according to Marx, "No social order ever perishes before all the productive forces for which there is room in it have developed." That is why not only Marx but Engels and all the Founding Fathers of Social Democracy down to 1917 expected socialism to come first in England or the United States.

There was one great insight and one great oversight in this Marxist approach. The insight was the recognition of the importance of the principle of social continuity or social maturity, which recognizes the constraints of rhythm, timing, and objective possibility, in proposals to reform or remake the human estate. Without it we would be hard put to draw the line between responsible and irresponsible social action, or distinguish between social sanity and insanity. The great oversight was a failure to realize that the principle of continuity was not sufficient as a guide to action, that without a moral point of view, or a set of explicit moral values, relatively autonomous in relation to economics and politics, which barred at least some alternatives of advance, certain actions could be easily rationalized as appropriate to the times, actions whose consequences could call into question the validity of historical materialism.

This is in effect what the latter day Marxists, who called themselves Bolshevik-Leninists, did. Despite their acceptance of the theory of historical materialism, these disciples of Marx seized political power in the most backward industrial region of Europe and then proceeded to build the economic foundations of a new order under it. The Marxists had refuted Marx. They had shown that with respect to the greatest social revolution of all time, naked will and force without stint or limit, and not the disparity between productive forces and property relations, provided the fuel to power the locomotive of history.

The apparent indifference to moral values that characterized traditional Marxism, which asserted that the real content of demands for justice reflected only the level of economic need of society, avenged itself on the entire humanistic and libertarian tradition of Marxism. Historical materialism taught that where social conditions are unripe, a new economic order cannot be introduced. Why not? Because among other things it would require that human beings be treated like things—like so much steel, iron, coal, and cement—and certainly not as fellow human beings, as ends in themselves. But to treat human beings in this way, or to change the metaphor, as so much fertilizer for the soil of history was beyond anything Marx dreamed would be undertaken on a systematic scale or be successful if anyone was mad enough to undertake it.

Lenin and Stalin and Mao did precisely what Marx never expected socialists would do or need do. The costs and horrors of capital accumulation under socialism have transcended the costs and horrors of primitive capitalist accumulation, and made them appear all the more onerous because on the classical Marxist scheme they were historically gratuitous. If we take seriously

Marx's and Engels's repudiation of "barracks communism," it would not be unfair to say that they would have had the last indignant words: the socialization of all instruments of production under primitive conditions by measures that respect no human rights can only develop another form of Asiatic despotism. The outraged moral sensibilities of those faithful to the ambiguous legacy of Marx is reflected in the emergence of a new form of Marxist revisionism according to which the real secret of Marx is not to be found in the *Manifesto* or *Capital* but in the early unpublished writings aptly characterized by Professor Lewis Feuer as the Dead Sea Scrolls of Marxism.

Nonetheless, even if we regard, as I do, the Bolshevization of Marx as a betrayal of the Marxian ethos, there was something in Marx's attitude towards the philosophy of the Enlightenment which prepared the way for it. This was Marx's interpretation of the doctrine of natural or human rights as pure ideology, his attempted reduction of them to mere expressions of personal and class egoism in civil society, despite his implicit and sometimes explicit invocation of them in the struggle for a society in which "the free development of each is the condition for the free development of all." This opens the complicated and largely unexplored relationship between the conceptions of human rights in the Enlightenment and in Marx.

For the thinkers of the Enlightenment the existence of the rights of man was a common article of belief however they differed in their definitions, enumerations, and justifications of the belief. To be human meant that one was morally entitled to a certain mode of treatment, formally positive, concretely negative, at the hands of one's fellows. Whether human rights were ultimately grounded in God, nature, or human nature, whether they were justified by reason or utility, were matters of dispute; but there was no dispute that all individuals possessed these rights, that they were not created or granted by any society or state or government, whose moral right to existence could and should be judged by whether it furthered them or not. Where enumerated these rights expressed the moral conscience of the time revolted by injustices and cruelties.

In Marx and Marxism, the practical strategy of natural rights is at war with the theory of natural rights. By this I mean that Marxism as a movement of social protest, reform, or revolution talked a language which made no sense in the light of the doctrines of historical materialism. In the Enlightenment tradition, the language of natural rights is the natural language invoked to curb the excesses of power. It was this language that Marxists eloquently and often persuasively employed when they voiced the demands of the suffering and oppressed for relief as well as for justice. But according to the theory of historical materialism all talk of the rights of man was simply an ideology, a rationalization of the needs of a burgeoning capitalist society. It denied the existence of any component of independent moral validity or autonomy in the appeal to human rights. If the issue was merely one of power or interest there is no more reason for one class or party in the social conflict to prevail than another, "right" should be a synonym of "might" and "wrong" of "weakness," a view which no Marxist can consistently hold when he speaks of exploitation of labor or protests against the suppression of human freedom. To say that the principle of freedom for which so many human beings willingly died during the French Revolutionary Wars was merely a slogan whose real content was the demand for freedom to buy cheap and sell dear, for freedom of contract, mobility, accumulation of capital, despite and against feudal restrictions, sounds utterly cynical. And it actually does a profound injustice to those Marxists whose ethical sensibilities are revolted by some proposed methods of achieving relief from social injustice. I know of few Marxists who escape incoherence and inconsistency when they speak of natural or human rights from the standpoint of historical materialism.

Here is a typical passage from the writings of an English Marxist, H. M. Hyndman; speaking of the ideas of the French Revolution, he says:

> Never in human history were great ideals prostituted to baser ends. "Liberty, Equality, Fraternity" is the glorious motto still inscribed on the buildings and banners of the

French Republic. But what did those noble abstractions mean to the class triumphant in the French Revolution, the class whose members were its leaders throughout? Liberty to exploit by wage slavery and usury. Equality before laws enacted in the interest of profiteers, and justice administered in accordance with their profiteering notion of fair play. Fraternity as a genial brotherhood of pecuniary exploitation. The "Rights of Man" was deliberately perverted to the right to plunder under forms of equity.[1]

But it makes no sense to charge that moral ideals have been betrayed or perverted unless we believe that they have a meaning and validity independent of the historical activities with which they have been identified. It is amusing to note that when Hyndman justified the support by the British workers in 1914 of the war against Germany, which "in spite of her tyrannous militarism and Junkerdom took more care of the physical and educational condition of her people than the governing classes of England did of their wage workers and dependents," he falls back upon implicitly ethical principles.

Nonetheless there was a supplementary reason which led at least the more revolutionary wing of Marxism to treat the concept of "the rights of man" gingerly. The exigencies of the struggle for power reinforced the reluctance to face up to the ambiguities of "the economic reduction" of the rights of man. For the latter profess to state in universal form certain bounds or limits of what man or state can do to man. Those, however, who set out to overthrow a social order by revolution must in the nature of the case violate, overturn, or recast laws whose customary character is invariably sensed to be fitting or natural or just by those who have benefited from their operation. From this point of view the Revolution may be imperiled by too faithful a respect for the rights of man of those opposed to it. The frank acknowledgment by Marx in the *Communist Manifesto* that the Revolution cannot proceed except by "despotic inroads against property" indicates

1. *The Evolution of Revolution* (London, 1921), p. 236.

that even if property were considered—and it was so considered by Locke and the philosophers of the Enlightenment—a human right, it would not be held sacred. But what if it is necessary to make "despotic inroads" against freedom of speech and press, against privacy and security, against life itself, if this is necessary for revolutionary victory? The problem of course is not unique to Marxism. It confronted Robespierre, the priest of reason and freedom, and even Jefferson, whose softer and more compassionate version of Deism was free from any trace of the stern fanaticism of virtue. Whoever proclaims that "the health or welfare or safety of the republic or the people" is above all law, positive or natural, or that it is the supreme natural law, must be prepared to sacrifice any or all of these sacred and inalienable rights of man whose exercise threatens the triumph of the Revolution. Once we make absolutes of any human right and under no circumstances justify its modification, then we cannot escape the Kantian, otherworldly position: "Let the right prevail, though the heavens fall." Morality would then become something too good or exalted for man!

As we shall see, Marx's recognition that one could not reasonably accept the absolutist conception of human rights contributed to the readiness with which he embraced an historical-economic monism that reduced human rights to rhetorical masks of economic class interests. But before showing this, one must explain the puzzling fact that many who accepted the doctrine of natural and human rights on moral grounds not only welcomed the Marxists as allies in the common political struggle against despotism, but even accepted their criticisms as illuminating. How was this possible? For two allied reasons. First, the Marxists claimed that human rights were abstract and formal unless certain institutional economic changes were introduced to make the expression of that right possible. If I have the right to life it means little if I have no right to the means of subsistence on which that life depends. Marx was keenly aware that property as a social relation is not merely a form of power over things but especially over men. Therefore ownership of the means of production by whose use men must live—an ownership which legally means the right to exclude others from the use of things owned—ultimately by the arms of the state, carries with it real power over the life of anyone who must work in order to live. As Marx put it, the worker is "the slave of other men who have made themselves the owners of the material conditions of labor. He can only labor by their permission and hence only live by their permission." [2] This would make the workers the slave of any group, independently of the forms of ownership, that has the power to exclude them from the productive process on which their lives depend. Socialism without democracy for its workers, on Marx's own analysis, would therefore be a new form of enslavement. If workers can only have access to the instruments of production by permission of others, whether they be capitalists or state or party bureaucrats, they "only live by their permission," and are to that extent enslaved.

Secondly, the Marxists pointed out that although equality of rights is a necessary condition for social justice, by itself equality is not sufficient, for it was compatible with many different modes of treating human beings, some of which are experienced as intolerable. The prophets of the Enlightenment declared that all men are or should be equal before the law. Article V of the French Constitution of 1795 reads: "Equality means that the law is the same for all, whether it protects or punishes." The nub of the Marxist position is that where economic disparities are substantial the law cannot and does not protect or punish equally. The burden of a fine which represents one man's income for a week and another's income for a day, even assuming the absolute incorruptibility of the judge, is not the same burden for the same offense. The case is no different even if equality is defined in terms of equality of opportunity, for inequality of economic status and economic power spells inequality of opportunity.

All this is good sense even where exaggerated claims are made. These exaggerations can be trimmed away. The position is at least intelligible. Every right, according to the Marxists, is affected by the conditions of its operation, whether it is the right to a fair trial, or to an adequate education, or to freedom of speech and press.

2. *Critique of the Gotha Program* (New York, 1933), p. 22.

Therefore commitment to equality of rights in a stratified economically privileged class society carries with it a mandate for continuous social reconstruction. The upshot of this critique is that political democracy—conceived as respect for the cluster of human rights—is *incomplete* without some form of economic democracy. Economic democracy would abolish the vast gulfs in living conditions or wealth between man and man which ultimately reflects itself in a different status between citizen and citizen. When Marx claims that "every right is in general a right of inequality in its *contents*" he is not denying the validity of the principle of equal rights. He is merely saying that given different individuals with different or varying needs, the application of an equal standard will result in treatments that are not identical but which for all their differences are equally just. A physician who treats all his patients with equality of consideration and concern does not prescribe identically for all of them. Once we understand this, we can also interpret Marx's contention that "right can never be higher than the economic structure and cultural development of society conditioned by it" as a common sense restriction on the scope and number of the human rights we can at any moment reasonably demand, e.g., there is no right to leisure if there is no surplus available, etc.

If only Marx, and especially the Marxists, had stopped at this point! But often when political rights were criticized as bourgeois rights, as formal and abstract, they were regarded not as partial and incomplete, but as unreal and mythical. In the struggle for an economically classless society, which presumably would provide social and economic democracy, compliance with the forms of political democracy was deemed unnecessary. Rights were formal, therefore inconsequential, unimportant, and hence if they interfered with concrete social progress, they could be ignored or violated. The Marxists of the Bolshevik-Leninist persuasion turned their backs on the democratic political means to achieve socialist goals and attempted to impose them by the dictatorship of a minority political party. When Fascism in its different varieties appeared on the political horizon, the significance of political rights in terms of natural or human rights was reasserted, but by that time the Marxists had thoroughly demoralized themselves with their semantic double-bookkeeping about human rights, and aroused the deep suspicion of their possible allies. How could one consistently appeal to human rights in the struggle against Fascism and at the same time dismiss them as outworn bourgeois notions or prejudices, irrelevant to the practices of the Communist minority one-party dictatorship?

It was not only Marx's disciples who were at fault, but Marx himself for the ambiguous legacy he left behind concerning the nature and meaning of human rights, human freedom, and political democracy conceived as resting on freely given consent. For he shifted between two different conceptions—one which regarded human rights as precious and which sought to preserve and strengthen them by extending their sway to economic and social relationships; the other which regarded talk about human rights as an expendable because anachronistic ideology. Had he taken the first view seriously and consistently, he would have recognized that the difference between ancient and modern conceptions of democracy had less to do with conflicts of economic classes than with the preservation of the rights of minorities as a restriction on the power of majority rule. If democracy is defined only as rule by the majority without any curb on the power of the majority, then society is always in a state of potential civil war. If a democracy recognizes the limitations on majority power set by firm observance of a Bill of Rights, minorities can by peaceful means become majorities and modify the operation of the economic system itself. Here Marx seems to have fallen behind Hegel who stressed the category of *Wechselwirkung* or reciprocity among the various factors that constituted the life of objective mind or culture. Although here and there, Marx acknowledged the existence of this reciprocity, and admitted in his later years that political democracy could make a difference to the mechanics of the road to power, he did not realize *why* and *how* it could make the difference, or how powerfully political democracy could affect the operation of the capitalist system of production. In short, Marx's political economy was not politically sophisticated enough because of his underestimation of the democratic process undergirded by respect for human or natural rights. Political democracy, conceived as the institutionalization of the rights of man without which there can be no freely given consent on the part of a majority, led the state to intervene in the economy, not only on behalf of the dominant class, but in some Western countries on behalf of the working class acting in concert with other groups and classes. It made collective bargaining a powerful countervailing force, sanctioned by law, which protected the worker against arbitrariness. It diverted into the public sector large amounts of goods and services. Through taxation it has already affected to some extent a redistribution of wealth —and it could do more, much more. It gave birth to the welfare state whose horizons can be progressively expanded. And it explains why so many of Marx's economic prophecies proved to be false.

Where did Marx go wrong? If I am right, quite early in the development of his thought—in some of the earliest of his publications. In his *Zur Judenfrage,* published in Herwegh's *Einundzwanzig Bogen aus der Schweitz* (1843), and also in *Die Heilige Familie* (1845) Marx delivers himself of a well justified and soundly argued criticism of the views of his erstwhile teacher, Bruno Bauer, on the question of Jewish emancipation. In the course of his argument, he also criticizes the French *Declaration of the Rights of Man and of the Citizen* of 1791. On the European continent this document has always been taken as the classical expression of the Enlightenment philosophy. Marx launches a strong attack on the assumption that the rights of man are the rights of citizens. It is the rights of man which draws Marx's fire in contradistinction to the rights of citizens. Why? Because Marx identifies the "man" of the Declaration with "the member of bourgeois society." On what ground? On the ground that these rights are individually and egoistically conceived, that they are rights *against* others rather than with others.

Who is this *homme* who is distinguished from *citoyen?* None other than the member of bourgeois society. Why does the member of bourgeois society become "man," simply man, why are his rights called human rights? How do we explain this fact? By the relation between the political state and bourgeois society, by the nature of political emancipation.

Above all let us note the fact that the so-called rights of man, the *droits de l'homme,* as distinguished from other *droits de citoyen,* are none other than the rights of a member of bourgeois society, i.e., of egoistic man, of man separated from man and the community of men.[3]

Marx cites the various natural and imprescriptible rights of man and shows that their very definition presupposes that the person who enjoys these rights exists as an atom or monad separated from others. For example, liberty is defined as "the power of each man to do anything that does not infringe on the rights of others"; property is defined as "the right belonging to each citizen to enjoy and dispose as he pleases of his goods and income, the fruits of his labor and industry." What is wrong with these conceptions? What is wrong with "liberty" defined this way? Marx tells us:

The human right of liberty is based not on union between man and man but on their separation. It is a right to separation, a right of a limited individual to his limitation.[4]

And what is wrong with "property" thus defined?

The human right of private property is the right arbitrarily *(à son gré)* to enjoy and dispose of one's wealth without relation to other human beings, independently of society; it is the right of private use *(Eigennutz).* Individual freedom, like this

3. *Marx-Engels Gesamtausgabe I,* Vol. 1, p. 593.
4. Ibid., 594.

particular application of it, is the foundation of bourgeois society. It permits every man to find in other men not the *realization* of his freedom but its *limit.*[5]

Down the line Marx goes on to show that "human rights" are precisely the powers and privileges which separate man from the community since they reflect only private interest, individual need, selfish desire. We must look to the rights of the *citizen* to establish a political community. We must avoid the error of considering membership in the political community as "a mere means" to preserve the so-called "human rights" whose exercise destroys genuine political community. This is the theoretical error the French Revolutionists made which their practice, according to Marx, happily nullifies.

It is interesting to observe that Marx does not list the "rights of the citizen," and it would indeed be difficult to list rights of citizens without finding at least some rights of man among them. Further, however a right of a citizen is defined, it cannot avoid implicit reference to the limits of actions of others. If I am politically free to vote this means that others are legally not free to prevent me from voting. Bentham saw more clearly than Marx that every law which bestows a political right is a restriction of the freedom of some possible actions by others. And despite Marx's attempted reduction of human rights to masks of interest, individual need, and selfish desire—surely this goes too far—even in civil or bourgeois society there are some *shared* interests, *common* needs, and *compassionate* or disinterested desires that can support a schedule of human rights. Further there is nothing morally wrong in a right to *some* separation, call it a right to privacy or a right to be left alone, which every community should respect that does not conceive of itself as a bee-hive or military barracks. A limited individual may enjoy some of his limitations. He may not want to walk with, talk with, be friends with, or make love with everybody.

There are at least two misconceptions of the nature of human rights by Marx that were to have fateful consequences on Marxist

5. Ibid.

theory and practice. The first was the view that because under some circumstances the specific rights of man could be reasonably abridged, they therefore need not be taken seriously, and had no more moral authority than any other legislative enactment, and sometimes less. Marx quotes from the Declaration of 1791, Article 2, "The end of all political association is the preservation of the natural and imprescriptible rights of man." But he complains that the French Revolutionists could not have meant this since some of these rights were on occasions abandoned. If secrecy is a human right, how could the right of the secrecy of correspondence be violated? If Article 122 of the Constitution guarantees "unabridged freedom of the press," how could Robespierre proclaim that "freedom of the press cannot be permitted when it compromises public liberty." If property is a human right, with what justification are hoarded stores seized to feed a famished town? In each case the justification of the violation of some human right was offered in terms of other human rights. This does not prove that there are no human rights but that they often conflict, and that when they do, the decision, although not arbitrary, cannot be deduced from a fixed second order rule but expresses a judgment about the relative weights and priorities among human rights—all relevant things considered here and now. What is true for human rights would be just as true for political rights or the rights of citizens. If they are conceived as absolutes, we cannot live in safety with them if there is more than one absolute right.

Secondly, Marx seems dissatisfied with "human rights" because they do not go far enough. For example, the right to be religious, to worship God according to one's conscience, the right to property, to speak freely, etc., are human rights and he urges that they should be extended to all citizens. But Marx also warns that these human rights are not enough. Men receive religious freedom properly but they are not freed from the sway of religion: they have a right to speak freely, but they speak nonsense. Man has freedom to trade but he is not free from the egoism or selfishness of commerce.[6]

6. Ibid., 598.

Those who deplore these possibilities, instead of accepting them as part of the necessary risk of freedom, are tempted to curb or abolish human rights once they have reason to believe that they can prevent what they deplore by other and more vigorous means. Whatever the dangers deplored are, they can be better met as a rule by strengthening and extending human rights rather than by abolishing them. Freedom of religion is more precious than either salvation by indoctrination or irreligion by prescription. The right to *seek* the truth is more basic than the right to speak the truth. Error has no rights, but the right to freedom of inquiry carries with it freedom to err, and to test the consequences of erroneous hypotheses on which progress in science depends.

There are certain obscurities and difficulties in Marx's conception of the "rights of a citizen" which neither he nor any of his followers adequately clarified. I should like to conclude with a few exploratory suggestions.

If one denies that the "rights of man" are literally natural rights, rights men have outside of society, *a fortiori* there are no rights of a citizen except in a community. But one can live in a community in various ways—as a citizen or as a subject, or as a free citizen or as a slave or serf. And one can live as a citizen with his nose to the grindstone, narrowly limited in possibilities of development, or as a free citizen able to live a life rich in possibilities of variation. Marx writes: "Only in association with others has each individual the means of cultivating his talents in all directions. Only in a community therefore is personal freedom possible." [7] Yes, but whence comes the right to be free and not to be enslaved, the right to cultivate one's talents in all directions rather than in some, to be more free rather than less free? If these are not natural or human rights, what are they and how can they be justified? Marx does not tell us.

What is impressive about Marx's critique of the thought of the Enlightenment is his refusal to counterpose the individual and social as if they were fixed, separable, polar concepts applicable to different entities. Using a modern idiom, Marx could have said

7. *Die deutsche Ideologie,* MEGA. 1/5/p. 634.

with John Dewey that "individual" and "social" are adjectival not substantive distinctions. The social relations into which a man enters as child, sibling, and parent, wife or husband, friend or lover, student or teacher, townsman or countryman, worker or employer enter constitutively into his personality. They are not additions to a hard kernel of natural individuality, any more than the thoughts and notions that language alone makes possible are additions to an original stock of ideas in the pristine mind of the individual. Only the biological *capacity* for language and organic activity is given—minds, personality, and everything else are consequents of the processes of acculturation.

All this may be granted as a necessary condition for a community in which "the rights of citizens" are not the "rights of man" but represent organized and harmoniously functioning social powers in "daily life and work"—the classless society of the future. But it is not a sufficient condition. Even if we attribute to Marx the view that human emancipation can be achieved only when society is organized on the model of a family, we cannot derive the "rights of citizens" from it. There are families and families. The "rights of citizens" are based not on universal love but on universal respect, self-respect and respect for others, courage, and the sense of independence.

When Marx makes explicit the values he regards as central to the life of the free citizen, what is suggested is not Christianity or the fraternity of the Enlightenment but rather the life of the free man in the Greek *polis*—Aristotle rather than Christ or Rousseau. Marx sounds this note at the very outset of his career, and its overtones can be heard in all his subsequent writings. In his correspondence with Ruge, which opens the campaign for revolution in Germany, in 1843, he writes:

> The self-respect *(Selbstgefühl)* of man, his freedom, must still be awakened in the breasts of these men. Only this feeling of self-respect, which disappeared with the Greeks from the world and into the blue haze of the heavens with the Christians, can make out of society once more a community

of men in pursuit of their highest end, the democratic state.
(MEGA, 1/1/561)

A year later in his *Critique of the Hegelian Philosophy of Law,*
Marx writes:

> The criticism of religion ends with the doctrine that man is
> the highest being for man, therefore with the categorical
> imperative to overthrow all conditions in which man is a
> debased, an enslaved, a forsaken, a contemptible creature. . . .
> (loc. cit., 615)

A few years later in a passionate criticism of the social philosophy of Christianity, Marx writes that "the proletariat will not
permit itself to be treated like canaille; it regards its courage, its
self-respect, its pride, its sense of independence as more necessary
to it than its bread" (MEGA, 1/6/278).

Of course, Marx is here speaking for himself, and only of his
hopes for the proletariat. Nonetheless, his writings and his life are
eloquent evidence of the fact that for all his dedication to social
reform and revolution, he was not a utilitarian. He speaks of
Bentham's philosophy as a shopkeeper's morality in the same
unjust way as does Nietzsche. It is not the happiness or welfare of
mankind which inspires Marx to hail and support the socialist
revolution. Otherwise he would have had to reckon the costs of
revolution more carefully and consider the claims of religion
more sympathetically. His conception of "the rights of citizens" is
a conception of a society of morally autonomous men. In the end,
he is committed to the same moral postulate as the men of the
Enlightenment. As distinct from them, he tries to support his
choice by an obviously circular appeal to history. In the end, I
believe, we must trace his ideals to his own personality rather than
to his philosophy of history. This is not surprising considering the
options in the theories of human rights which were closed to Marx
because of his other views. The rights of man cannot be derived
from the nature of man *qua* man because human nature is an
historical variable in "progressive transformation." Nor can they

be derived from the nature of society, since societies are even more obviously historical and diverse than human nature. What society is to serve as the matrix of human, universal rights? It is no objection to a schema of human rights that they are projections of personal values, if reasonable grounds can be offered for universalizing them. But Marx himself does not offer any grounds, and few among those whom he has influenced, unfortunately, have concerned themselves with the problem.

CHAPTER   THREE

Myth and Fact in the Marxist Theory of Revolution

Many expositions of the Marxist theory of revolution and violence have been politically motivated. By selective exegesis of texts they aim to invoke the authority of Marxist tradition either to prepare and launch violent revolution or seizure of power when social and economic conditions are ripe or to allay fears that socialist groups whose increasing strength has brought them to the threshold of power by the use of political democratic processes will abandon them for direct action. The first interpretation looks to armed insurrection, prepared by illegal as well as legal means, ultimately to smash the existing state machine and consolidate revolutionary power. The second interpretation stresses the processes of democratic legality to transform the basic economic-social-legal relations of society.

As far as Marx and Engels are concerned, once certain distinctions are introduced, their views on violence and revolution are relatively clear. Obfuscation has resulted primarily from the fact that the Leninist revision of Marx has been read back and into the Marxist position.

According to Marx and Engels, revolution can be violent or peaceful depending upon the presence of democratic political possibilities, but whether peaceful or not the socialist revolution must be democratic. At the time of the *Communist Manifesto* there were no realistic possiblilities, in view of the severe restrictions on suffrage, that profound social change could be introduced through parliamentary means. Indeed the *Manifesto* indicates that among the first things that would be done after the revolution would be to introduce democratic institutions. Nonetheless both Marx and Engels assumed that revolutionary action even under oppressive or narrowly restrictive political institutions would have the support of the majority of the population behind it, and that it could justifiably be considered democratic. (The empirical evidence, however, that the working class constituted a majority of the population was lacking. It was based on an extrapolation of certain economic tendencies of capitalist development.) Subsequently, Marx and Engels, as is well known, anticipated the possibility that socialism could be introduced peacefully by parliamentary means in countries like England, the United States, and Holland. Toward the end of his life Engels explicitly declared that "the dictatorship of the proletariat" would express itself under the political form of the bourgeois parliamentary republic.

Marx and Engels, and their followers, disassociated themselves strongly from men like Blanqui and Bakunin on two grounds. The first was the latter's failure to recognize the controlling importance of the objective economic-social situation as providing a necessary condition for a successful political revolution. The second was their undisguised élitism. For Marx "the emancipation of the working class can be achieved only by the working class." This is of central significance in distinguishing between Marx's conception of revolution and the Leninist-Stalinist (Bolshevik) view. There is not a line in Marx's writings which states or implies that "the dictatorship of the proletariat"—a phrase employed a few times to characterize the economic and social content of the democratic socialist revolution—must be exercised through "the dictatorship of the Communist Party."

For Marx the concept of dictatorship is primarily social and economic. The "dictatorship of the bourgeoisie" refers to the fact that the rule of the bourgeoisie is to its economic advantage and the economic disadvantage of the working class. But the dictatorship of the bourgeoisie could be exercised through nondemocratic political forms or through democratic political forms. For Lenin "dictatorship" is primarily a political concept. "Dictatorship," he tells us, "is rule based directly upon force and unrestricted by any laws." It is really unmitigated *Faustrecht*. Whereas for Marx and Engels "the dictatorship of the proletariat" could be established through peaceful parliamentary victory, for Lenin "the revolutionary dictatorship of the proletariat is rule won and maintained by the use of violence by the proletariat against the bourgeoisie, rule that is unrestricted by any laws." [1]

In contradistinction to Marx and Engels, Lenin proceeds to interpret the "dictatorship of the proletariat" as viable only through the dictatorship of the Communist Party, which constitutes a small minority of the population, many of whose members are not even proletarians. Although Marx and Engels's interpretation of the Paris Commune of 1871 as a socialist revolution is extremely dubious, nonetheless they both refer to it as an exemplification of "the dictatorship of the proletariat" in which there was no dictatorship of any political party whatsoever. The followers of Blanqui seemed to be in the majority; after them in numerical strength came the followers of Proudhon, while the partisans of Marx and Engels, whose chief spokesman was Leo Frankel, were minuscular. Actually there was no socialist content whatsoever to the reforms of the Paris Commune. No industries were socialized. The abolition of night work for bakers was no more socialist than the abolition of child labor and other "bourgeois" reforms. The real achievements of the Paris Commune, whose launching Marx disapproved, was the extension of democratic processes and principles, most of which could be

---

1. Lenin, *Selected Works* (Moscow, 1951), Vol. 2, Part II, p. 41 ff.

implemented in a non-socialist economy. The Leninist view that the Russian socialist revolution of October 1917 is a continuation or fulfillment of the heritage of the Paris Commune is a sheer myth.

Lenin makes no bones about the fact that "the dictatorship of the proletariat" is exercised through "the dictatorship of the Communist Party." In his pamphlet on *The Infantile Sickness of Left-Communism,* he states: "Not a single important political or organizational question is decided by any state institution in our republic without the guiding instructions of the Central Committee of the Party." And Stalin, here as elsewhere when he touches on doctrinal matters, echoes his teacher.

> Here in the Soviet Union, in the land of the dictatorship of the proletariat, the fact that not a single important political or organizational question is decided by our Soviet and other mass organizations without directions from the Party must be regarded as the highest expression of the leading role of the Party. *In this sense* it could be said that the dictatorship of the proletariat is *in essence* the "dictatorship of its vanguard," "the dictatorship" of its Party, as the main guiding force of the proletariat. *(Foundations of Leninism* [Moscow, 1934], Ch. VIII)

If as Lenin declares "dictatorship is rule based directly upon force and unrestricted by any laws," the dictatorship of the Party entails that it may very well be a dictatorship not *of* the proletariat but *over* the proletariat as well as over others.

Aware of the enormity of this transformation of the concept of the "dictatorship of the proletariat" into the "the dictatorship of the Communist Party," Lenin and other Bolshevik leaders adopt several semantic devices to conceal their abandonment of the democratic component of the Marxist theory. But in the early years the exigencies of the struggle for power lead them to a forthrightness of utterance that becomes qualified in subsequent apologetic rationalizations when faced by critics invoking Marx's democratic principles.

Nothing signifies the non-Marxist undemocratic stance of Bolshevik Leninism more clearly than Lenin's writings on the Constituent Assembly. Referring to his theses on the Constituent Assembly, Lenin observes: "My thesis says clearly and repeatedly that the interests of the revolution are higher than the formal rights of the Constituent Assembly. The formal democratic point of view is precisely the point of view of the bourgeois democrat who refuses to admit that the interests of the proletariat and of the proletarian class struggle are supreme." [2]

The plain meaning of this declaration exposes as a hypocritical rationalization the pretexts Lenin offers for bayoneting the Constituent Assembly out of existence after the Bolshevik's miserable showing in the elections (19%) and after the Social Revolutionary and Menshevik majority refused to accept Lenin's ultimatum to yield power to the Bolsheviks. Justifying his refusal to accept the legitimacy of the Constituent Assembly, Lenin claims that although elections to the Constituent Assembly had been held *after* the Bolsheviks seized power in October, the mood or sentiment of the masses had changed by early January and that in reality they favored the Bolsheviks.[3] Rosa Luxemburg in sharply criticizing Lenin's view retorted that if this were so the Bolsheviks could have called for new elections without disputing the legitimacy of the Constituent Assembly, particularly since in their propaganda against Kerensky they had agitated so fiercely for the convocation of the Constituent Assembly.

In the light, however, of Lenin's thesis on the Constituent Assembly cited above, his ex post facto talk about improper lists and unrepresentative elections is revealed as a feeble and irrelevant cover-up. For assume that the election on the basis of new lists had been as democratic as Lenin had desired. If, as he unwaveringly claims, "the interests of the proletariat and the proletarian class struggle are supreme," what difference would it have made to Lenin if the new electoral results showed that the Russian masses had even more completely repudiated the Bolsheviks than they did on the basis of the old lists? Would Lenin

2. Lenin, op. cit., p. 78.
3. Ibid., p. 81.

have recognized the sovereignty of the Constituent Assembly? Certainly not! For if as he insists "the interests of the proletariat," as interpreted by the Bolsheviks, of course, are "supreme," Lenin would have felt justified by his political philosophy to take power against the Constituent Assembly even if it had an overwhelming mandate from the masses—provided he could get away with it.

If there is any doubt about this an analysis of Lenin's article *On Slogans* will confirm it.[4] When Lenin seeks excuses to ban the Constituent Assembly, he bases himself on the authority of the Soviets. But in July 1917 when his article "On Slogans" was published, he repudiates the slogan of "All Power to the Soviets" because the Soviets "are dominated by the Social Revolutionary and Menshevik parties" (p. 95). In January, having seized power and already begun the terror and acquired a majority in the Soviets of Petrograd and Moscow, the slogan: "All Power to the Soviets" is restored and used as a foil and excuse to prorogue the Constituent Assembly. In every case what is decisive for Lenin is the question of *power*, not the question of democracy, formal or concrete, or representation, authentic or not, viz., whether the Bolshevik Party has a likely prospect of seizing and retaining power.

Lenin and Stalin explicitly disavow Marx's belief that socialism could be legally and peacefully achieved through the democratic political process in countries like England and the United States. Further, the conditions of affiliation to the Third International drawn up by Lenin imposed on every Communist Party of the world the organization of illegal cadres and the resort to armed insurrection in the conquest of political power in all countries including "the most free in the world." Even ambiguity on this point was not tolerated except as a linguistic maneuver to disarm the political enemy, and to win sufferance to organize the seizure of power. The Russian road to power became the paradigm for all Communist parties of the world under the discipline of the Third International. This may be illustrated in the programmatic declaration of William Z. Foster, head of the Communist Party of

4. Ibid., p. 87 ff.

the United States, at a time when it enjoyed complete legality and freedom of propaganda:

> Even before the seizure of power, the workers will organize the Red Guard. Later on this loosely constructed body becomes developed into a firmly-knit, well-disciplined Red Army. The leader of the revolution in all its stages is the Communist Party. . . . Under the dictatorship all the capitalist parties—Republican, Democratic, Progressive, Socialist, etc.,—will be liquidated, the Communist Party functioning alone as the party of the toiling masses. Likewise will be dissolved all other organizations that are political props of bourgeois rule, including Chambers of Commerce, employers' associations, rotary clubs, American Legion, Y.M.C.A. and such fraternal orders as the Masons, Odd Fellows, Elks, Knights of Columbus, etc. *(Towards Soviet America* [New York, 1932], 275)

Under Khrushchev's rule the Leninist dogma of the inevitability of war between the Communist world and the Western world was abandoned although the inevitability of world Communist victory was still proclaimed. But the insistence upon the view that the triumph and rule of the revolution could be achieved only through "the dictatorship of the party" was retained. It was asserted that the Communist Party in a "coalition" with other parties might come to power peacefully but only if the Communist Party exercised leadership which meant at least control of the Ministry of the Interior (police).

An analysis of the concept of "the dictatorship of the party" in official Communist literature (as well as the historical evidence) will show that even where Communist parties, either alone or in formal coalition, come to power peacefully, their rule is based upon continuous exercise of force and violence. For the very meaning of "dictatorship," in the words of Lenin, "is rule based directly upon force and unrestricted by any laws." This dictatorship is directed not only against overt hostile elements seeking to restore the overthrown economic and social order but against any dissenting thought in art, literature, science, and philosophy of which the Central Committee disapproves.

With some variations, depending upon a number of historical and national factors, all Communist states that profess to be inspired by Leninist doctrine follow the Russian Soviet pattern, which is demonstrably incompatible with Marx's and Engels's commitment to socialist democracy and their criticism of élite rule. These Communist views have remained unaffected by the Sino-Soviet split and by the emergence of "polycentrism."

Naturally, in democratic Western countries, where there are large Communist parties (and/or dissident Communist groups critical of the Leninist tradition) engaged in the parliamentary political process, attempts have been made to soften and tone down the harsh features of Leninist principles according to which "the dictatorship of the proletariat" results in the terror of a Communist Party dictatorship of varying degrees of intensity over the proletariat and all other groups of the population until the advent of the classless society. In these countries some theoretical spokesmen of Communism tend to blur the difference between the Marxist views on revolution and the possibility of a peaceful transition to socialism through a multiparty democratic political process, and the Communist Leninist position.

The lineaments of that position have been authoritatively restated most recently by the Institute of Marxism–Leninism of the Central Committee of the Communist Party of the Soviet Union, and reprinted in the Soviet official theoretical journal *Kommunist* (No. 3, 1972) under the title "Falsifiers of the Theory of Scientific Communism and their Bankruptcy." It is directed against Communist dissidents, characterized as "modern revisionists" who envisage the transition from capitalism to socialism as a process of "evolution" or "reform" or "renovation," and who believe that "the dictatorship of the proletariat" is possible without the dictatorship or leadership (a euphemism for dictatorship) of the Communist Party. The article declares:

We know the numerous statements in which V.I. Lenin developed the basic Marxist thesis that the dictatorship of the proletariat is inconceivable without the leadership of the Communist Party. Practical experience has shown that even the existence of a multiparty system does not refute the necessity of such leadership. The Communist Party is the vanguard of the working class, its most conscious, organized and unified part. Only under the leadership of the Party can the working class implement its dictatorship over the defeated exploiting classes.

As if to leave no doubt that the Leninist line applies not only to the seizure of political power but to its exercise after the Communist Party has come to power, the article concludes:

> The grave consequences of any attempt to depart from the Marxist-Leninist teaching on the leading role of the Party and to renounce Leninist organizational principles are well illustrated by the events of 1968 in Czechoslovakia.

Although Marx's views on revolution, violence, and democracy are quite different from those identified as Bolshevik-Leninist, they suffer from certain basic difficulties. These flow from the failure clearly to recognize the primacy of political freedom in relation to all other desirable social and cultural freedoms, and the consequent underestimation of the possibility of modifying the economic structure of society by politically democratic means. Historically the influence of political democratic processes on the economy has resulted in a mixed economy and welfare society which is neither purely capitalist nor socialist. The choice then becomes not so much one of *either-or* but of *more-or-less*. In this sense it is not the mode of economic *production* that in many crucial situations becomes the key determining factor, if any, but the mode of political *decision*.[5]

Whatever the inadequacies of Marx's theory of revolution are, his commitment to a *scientific* or rational method of achieving a

---

5. Cf. Chaps. 25-28 in my *Political Power and Personal Freedom*, (New York, 1959).

nonexploitative society permits—actually it should encourage—a modification of his specific views on political strategy in the light of historical evidence. Marx was not born a socialist and certainly not a Marxist. What was distinctive about his theories concerning how socialism—which *au fond* was an extension of democracy to a way of life—was to be achieved was largely disconfirmed by historical events. He underestimated the capacity of capitalist societies to raise the standard of living of its population, including even the longevity of the working class; he underestimated the growth and intensity of nationalism; he was mistaken in interpreting all forms of coercion and exploitation as flowing from private ownership of the social means of production; he ignored the prospect of bureaucratic forms of collectivism; and the very possibility of war between collectivist economies, illustrated in the nuclear threat of Communist Russia against Communist China, was inconceivable to him by definition. He shared the naïveté of anarchist thinkers in believing that the state would disappear with universal collectivism, and that "the administration of things" could ever completely replace administration by men and the possibility of its abuse. He underestimated the role of personality in history, and although he contributed profoundly to our understanding of the determining influence, direct and indirect, of the mode of economic production on many aspects of culture, he exaggerated the degree of determination and its "inevitability" and "necessity." That is why those who have learned most from Marx, if faithful to his own commitment to scientific, rational method, should no more consider themselves "Marxists" than modern biologists should consider themselves "Darwinians" or modern physicists "Newtonians." "Marxism" today signifies an ideology in Marx's original sense of that term, suggestive more of a religious than of a strictly scientific or rational outlook on society.

In speaking of Marx's failure to do justice to personality in history, one may cite the life and work of Lenin, the greatest revisionist of Marx, as decisive evidence. The Russian Revolution of October 1917 has been regarded as among the most influential events, and some have even characterized it as *the* most influential

event because of its consequences, in world history. Yet it is in-
ontestable that if Lenin had not lived there would in all likelihood have been no Russian October Revolution.[6] Among the
fateful consequences of the October Revolution under Lenin's
guidance was the creation of the Communist International which
organized Communist Parties in most of the countries of Europe,
Asia, and America. The Communist International, as Zinoviev,
his close collaborator, once put it was "Lenin's creation." And it
was Lenin who above all not only insisted on the organization of
the Communist International but that "Bolshevism *can serve as a
model of tactics for all.*"[7] Since the Bolshevik model prescribed
armed insurrection and the dictatorship of a minority party as the
indispensable means of achieving political power, it provoked a
backlash and reaction in most countries in which Communist
parties were active.

It has been argued by some that the October Revolution was
responsible for reforms introduced in non-Communist countries
and that the development of the welfare state was primarily
motivated out of fear of domestic Communist revolution abetted
by the armed intervention of the Red Army. It would be very hard
to establish this. The history of political and social reform in
Western Europe and America was impressive long before the
Russian Revolution and was primarily the result of indigenous
class struggles that strove to extend the democratic ethos to
economic and social life. The New Deal in the United States, for
example, as well as the emergence of the Welfare State in Great
Britain, were in no way undertaken to meet any danger of a
Communist revolution.

It is far closer to the truth to assert that rather than inspiring
democratic social reforms in the Western World, the Bolshevik
Revolution and the operation of the Communist International
were largely responsible for the rise of Fascism in Italy and

6. Sidney Hook, *The Hero in History: A Study in Limitation and
Possibility* (New York, 1943).

7. *Collected Works,* Vol. 28, emphasis in the text, quoted with other
supporting documents in *Lenin and the Comintern* by Lazich and
Drachkovitch (Stanford, 1972), Vol. I., p. 46 ff.

Nazism in German, not only by weakening the democratic structure of pre-Mussolini Italy and Weimar Germany but by its activities, including abortive attempts at insurrection, which provided a mass base and support for the demagogic propaganda for the forces of social reaction. It is overwhelmingly likely that if there had been no October Revolution and attempts by the Communist International, serving as the instrument of the Kremlin, to organize revolutions in Western Europe, there would have been no victory of Fascism in Italy and of Hitlerism in Germany. It may be difficult to predict in detail what the history of Western Europe would have been if Lenin had not succeeded in overthrowing Kerensky's regime and destroying the democratic Constituent Assembly. In the light of what actually occurred as a consequence of the rule of Bolshevism, Fascism, and Nazism, it is hard to see what could have been worse.

It remains to ask what light this analysis casts on identifying contemporary expressions of Marxism with respect to revolutionary thought and action. A position, of course, may be morally sound or justifiable regardless of whether it is Marxist or not. The question I pose here is: what are the criteria for determining the truth of the claim of any party program or activity, independently of its own labels, to be Marxist? On the above analysis, any movement based on the ideas of Herbert Marcuse is clearly non-Marxist. This follows not only from his repudiation of the working class as unfit for the role and honor of carrier of the socialist idea but because of his undisguised élitism and unabashed justification of forcible repression of ideas, persons, or institutions that are not "progressive" according to his lights. Here Marcuse is a faithful Leninist.

Where socialist parties, alone or in alliance with others, come to power through the democratic political process, the crucial question is whether or not they permit freedom of political propaganda to parties that reject their program, and in the event of an electoral defeat, relinquish the reins of government to those who have won the support of the majority. Any political party, regardless of what it calls itself, which holds on to power by refusing to conduct free elections or to abide by their consequences is not Marxist.

The theory of Marxism makes no claim that the working masses are always right or even aware of what is to their best interests. At any definite time a Marxist party may know better than the masses what their best interests are. But this knowledge does not give it any right to impose upon the masses a program in opposition to their wishes and will. Indeed, this is integral to the very meaning of "democracy" in any political context.

In envisaging the democratic role to political power, Marx and Engels were realistic in considering the possibility of an antidemocratic revolt to defeat the will of the majority. This possibility has led some Leninists to justify the seizure of power without the support of the majority of the population, and when in power, to repress parties and individuals who dissent from the socialist program, and even from the Leninist version of that program, on the pretext that they *may* revolt. But such rationalizations are transparent evidence that they have no faith in the democratic process.

In dealing with children or mental incompetents, it is sometimes necessary, and therefore justifiable, to act in behalf of their genuine interests even when it runs against their wishes and will. What Marx would have thought of such procedure with respect to the proletariat or working class may be inferred from his declaration that this class "regards its courage, self-confidence, independence, and sense of personal dignity as more necessary than its daily bread." [8] Marx may have been wrong in believing this but it is not wrong that he believed it.

8. *Gesamtausgabe*, Abt. I, Bd. 6, p. 278.

CHAPTER FOUR

The Rationale of Revolution

I

There are more people in the world, including the world of higher education, prepared to make a revolution than to understand the nature of revolution. Some of them are convinced that this is the only way that revolutions can be understood. Although they would be quite dubious about the statement that the only way we can understand experiences—say, loving, fighting, dying —is by undergoing them, they seem to make an exception for the experience of revolution. Yet reflection will show that experience at most can supply data for understanding. The whole history of medicine is convincing evidence that having an experience is not the same as understanding it. Millions have suffered from diseases they have never understood. The same history has shown that it is possible to understand many things without having personally experienced them. The same is true of the historical experience of revolution.

The very word "revolution" like all large words in human experience, stands for a broad cluster or family of ideas that share some vague qualitative overtones rather than a clear and precise meaning. And these overtones have a wide emotional range. Say "revolution" in Spain and to most adults it will bring memories of the Civil War launched by Franco against the Loyalist regime. Say "revolution" in Hungary or Cuba or France, it will unloose a flood of other memories. The associations of the term are much more various than its meanings; and of these meanings one must flatly say that only the specific context of *use* can determine what kind of "revolution" one is talking about. Who would surmise when he picks up a book entitled *The Revolution in Philosophy* or reads an announcement or lecture on "The Sexual Revolution," that the term "revolution" is derived from astronomy?

Despite the enormous variation in the use and usage of the term "revolution," attempts have been made to find some meaning common to all or most of them. I regard them as semantic traps productive of greater confusion than enlightenment. I shall say a few words about them before dismissing them.

The late Professor Paul Schrecker in his *Work and History: An Essay on the Structure of Civilization* (Princeton, 1948) offers us a definition, extrapolated from the field of law and politics, which he defends as valid for developments called revolutionary in any discipline. "A revolution," he asserts, *"is an illegal change of the conditions of legality."* The only virtue this definition has is its brevity. The phrase "conditions of legality" has a clear meaning in law but it becomes a metaphor when transferred to the arts, sciences, and practical disciplines. In such fields the phrase "conditions of legality" can only mean the dominant style or norm. An "illegal change" in "the conditions of legality" can only mean a marked change in these dominant styles or norms. To call it "illegal" is confusing because the old conditions are upheld by no sanctions, and there is no way of distinguishing between legal revolutions that culminate in something new in art and thought, and sudden changes that replace customary modes of style or thought. In the first case we do not recognize a revolution until it is over. If we admit that revolutions, so to speak, can take place behind the backs of people, like the industrial revolution, there is no question of legality or illegality no matter how loosely these categories are interpreted. And as for the sudden changes that replace customary modes of style or thought, this would give us too many "revolutions" by far. And oddly enough it would not permit us to refer to Hitler's or Mussolini's "revolutions" because these were not brought about by illegal changes in "the conditions of legality" but by fundamental legal changes.

Even if we restrict ourselves to political and social contexts, there is a danger in using the term "revolution" in a too encompassing sense. A revolution is a social change but not all social changes are revolutionary. How does a revolutionary change differ from other kinds of social change? Shall we say with Sorokin that it is "a profound disturbance of the sociocultural framework"? If we speak this way we shall end up as Sorokin does in classifying revolutions with the phenomena of criminality also classified as disturbances. Here is Sorokin's wisdom on the subject:

> The phenomena of social disturbances are fundamentally like the phenomena of criminality. The main difference is in scale. When a few individuals kill, steal, or rob others, the isolated cases are called "crimes." When the same actions are perpetrated on a large scale and by the masses, the phenomena are called "riots," "disturbances," "revolutions," and so on. Accordingly most of the disturbances spring from, and develop in, exactly the same sort of situation as does criminal demoralization among individuals. The determining factor in each case is the condition of the sociocultural network of values and relationships.[1]

1. Pitirim Sorokin, *Cultural and Social Dynamics* (New York and Boston, 1937), Vol. 3, p. 401.

This comparison between "crime" and "revolution" seems to me absurd for many reasons. Suffice it to say, however, that the term "crime" always carries with it a deprecatory moral connotation whereas the term "revolution" is problematic; independently of context and justifying reason, good or bad, its moral connotation is indeterminate or neutral.

The revolutions I shall be talking about are fundamental changes in the *power* relation of classes within society, or between societies where both are part of one nation or empire and in which the changes result in the establishment of a new nation or new society. They are the kind of changes preeminently illustrated in the English, American, French, Russian, and Algerian revolutions. When large-scale attempts at such fundamental changes fail, we call them "rebellions." We classify what is sometimes called a "counterrevolution," when it succeeds, as a revolution, too, e.g., the Nazi Revolution, whenever it is not a restoration of the *status quo ante*. Hitler obviously did not restore the Wilhelmine Empire nor the power of the Rhenish industrialists and Junker landowners. On the other hand, I shall not regard as revolutionary sudden changes, whether violent or not, in the regimes of countries that leave the basic power relations among classes unaffected, like military takeovers in a South American or African republic. These are properly called a *coup d'état* or *putsch*.

The conventional Marxist wisdom about the proper use of the term "revolution" is that only a transformation in the economic structure of society—its mode of production—can be legitimately regarded as a revolution. All other social changes are dismissed as superficial if they do not result in basic changes in property relations. The American Revolution of 1776 is regarded as merely a political change, not a genuine social revolution like those in France in 1789, Russia in 1917, and mainland China in 1949. This usage, sometimes uncritically adopted by those who are not Marxists, is predicated upon the prior acceptance of the theory of historical materialism according to which all important cultural and social changes depend upon changes in the mode of economic production. But until this theory is empirically established, the Marxist conception of what constitutes a revolution is completely question-begging. Other changes in society besides economic ones may have pervasive cultural influences.

A pluralistic theory of social causation might recognize on empirical grounds the great role of economic change on social and cultural changes at one time, and deny priority of weight or importance to economic factors at another time. The American War of Independence of 1776 as well as the American Civil War of 1861-1865 and even the American New Deal of the mid-1930s had such profound consequences for the cultural and social life of the American people that despite the fact that no formal change occurred in the mode of economic production we can very well refer to them as "revolutions." Sometimes without initial formal changes in the mode of economic production the power relationships of different classes may be so transformed that it is more illuminating to refer to that transformation as a revolution than as a reform. Mexico and Turkey in the twentieth century, Japan in the latter half of the nineteenth century are cases in point.

There is also the element of practical purpose or interest that enters into judgments of causal determination. Those who desire to transform society to achieve certain changes of transcendant purpose to them are likely to judge the weight of the overriding social factor in relation to that purpose—whether it be religious or secular, national or racial.

II

When I speak of "The Revolution" as a *symbol* I refer to it in its capacity to evoke a deep emotional response whether of hope or fear among the classes it affects. The hope is found among those who stand to gain by changes that will liberate them from an invidious social or national status, or from a system of oppression. The fear is felt by the beneficiaries of the existing class relationships and their servitors whose interests are interrelated in a material or empathetic way. No easy symmetry can be drawn, however, between *hope* in revolution and the absence of power and *fear* of revolution and possession of power. For as Marx knew, although his theory of class cannot account for it, there are always some elements of the ruling classes who in a spirit of vicarious atonement or out of a sense of justice throw in their lot and their hopes for revolution with the subordinate class and make common cause with it. And there are always members of the powerless or less powerful classes who, despite their present lacks and hardships, fear revolution as a harbinger of evils much worse than those they now endure. Nonetheless the rough correlation holds, influenced by the political climate, i.e., by whether revolutions are in the ascendant or in decline in consequence of defeat or Thermidorian betrayal.

"Revolution" as a symbol is a concretion of historical memory and piety. Since a revolution as distinct from a revolt has the aura of victory about it, its words and legends and monuments acquire a patina of patriotism. Almost every nation can boast of at least one revolution which it celebrates as a triumph of liberation or a new birth of freedom. Looking back to it, the very word "revolution" is like the sound of a trumpet and like the bright color of blood. But when the word is heard in a context of contemporary disorder, it is like the sound of a machine gun and like the color of death. Ernst Renan signalized the difference when he observed: "Happy a people who inherits a revolution: woe to those who make it." This expresses a truth already grasped by those geniuses of common sense, the philosopher-statesmen of the American Republic, who pointed out in their seminal Declaration that even when men have right on their side, they are not easily moved to revolution, that men are "more disposed to suffer, while evils are sufferable, than to right themselves by abolishing the forms to which they are accustomed."

The intensity with which people react, positively or negatively, to revolution as a symbol in political experience determines the character of the myths about revolution that prevail among its protagonists and antagonists.

The number of myths about revolution is legion. I shall mention only a few. The first is that revolutions are not made. They happen. They happen with the elemental force of natural necessity when the mounting pressure of need, privation, and suffering, pent up by cruel and confining institutions and laws, bursts through the police barriers of the régime, and engulf the society. On this view, the worse conditions are, the better, for the nearer at hand becomes the salvationary, revolutionary outbreak. Despair serves as the fuel of action. When the tension has reached its height, any ordinary outrage or casual piece of official repression is sufficient to trigger the inevitable explosion. So the myth goes.

This myth has many uses. For one thing, it absolves everyone of responsibility for the inescapable revolution. It absolves those whose egoism and cruelty blinded them to the consequences of their acts of omission and commission in creating the intolerable conditions of oppression. It also absolves those whose folly and bankrupt leadership often lead revolutions to disaster.

Nonetheless this is a myth. Revolutions do not merely happen. Revolutions are made. For if and when they are successful, they must be led, usually by those who are not altogether unknown before they occur. A riot or demonstration may happen, may be truly spontaneous, but a revolution never. For its direction requires a program and goal, and these are not hatched in a fit of revolutionary passion but by preliminary thought.

Further it is not true that abject misery and acute suffering are the necessary preconditions of revolutionary disturbance. If this were true most of mankind would be in a state of perpetual revolt. Or, at least, the history of revolutionary attempts would run parallel to the history of human misery. This is notoriously not the case. The song of the revolutionary working class, *L'Internationale,* begins: "Arise, ye prisoners of starvation!" But prisoners of starvation do *not* arise or revolt. If they have any energy left, they are out foraging. St. Just, to the contrary, *les malheureux* are *not* the most powerful force on earth. In order to be that they would have to be organized. And although social *disorganization* may be compared to a disease, social organization may not. It does not spread by contagion. It must be built.

That incomparable observer de Tocqueville is justified in remarking:

Revolutions do not always come when things are going from bad to worse. It occurs most often when a nation has accepted and indeed has given no sign of even having noticed, the most crushing laws, rejects them at the moment when their weight is being lightened. The regime that is destroyed by a revolution is almost always better than the one preceding it, and experience teaches us that usually the most dangerous time for a bad government is when it attempts to reform itself.[2]

But just as the opposite of an absurdity can be just as absurd, so a misleading myth can generate a misleading opposite or counter-myth. This is the view that because it is false that revolutions just happen, it is true that they can happen at any time, that revolutions are conspiracies engineered by a comparative handful of professional agitators or revolutionists. This is the view that Burke seems to have had of the French Revolution and with which reactionaries explain all the revolutions that occur in their lifetime. It is a view also held by some revolutionists, too, notably by August Blanqui who spent more years in jail than out plotting *coup d'états* that never came off. It was a view held by Bakunin, Nechayev, and some of Marx's early colleagues, Willich and Schapper, whom Marx and Engels severely criticized. It is a view which has been encouraged by a too simple reading of Lenin's *What's to be Done?*

Lenin, of whom it can be said more than of any one man in history that he made a revolution, argued that the theory of spontaneous revolution was a myth. Left to itself the workers' response to oppression and brutalizing conditions would peter out in sporadic outbursts of opposition or violence, without direction, without cumulative force. They would therefore be politically futile. Only where a political party or group of professional revolutionists is at hand to lead and control, to encourage and restrain these outbreaks, can a revolution succeed. For Lenin the Communist Party,

2. Quoted by M. Richter, "Tocqueville's Contribution to the Theory of Revolution," *Nomos* (New York, 1966), Vol. 8, p. 119.

under any name, is a revolution-making party. But it does not or should not attempt to make a revolution without the necessary ingredients or independently of the objective features of the revolutionary situation whose existence does not depend on the will of the revolutionists.

Later on, Lenin and his followers by postulating a state of objective *world* readiness for revolution became more and more voluntaristic. They gave the Communist Party such a dominant role in making a revolution that they ended up denying even the facts of spontaneous outbreak, and claimed credit for them. Thus in answer to the question: "Who led the February 1917 Russian Revolution?"—an event that took the Bolsheviks inside and outside Russia by complete surprise, Trotsky replies in his *History of the Russian Revolution,* "Conscious and tempered workers educated for the most part by the party of Lenin," [3] for which he offers not a particle of evidence.

The Communists came to power with the thesis they adopted from Trotsky that world capitalism had broken down and that therefore the world revolution could begin at the weakest link in the world chain of nations. By definition the weakest link was wherever political power could be seized. Instructions were issued to Communist countries everywhere to organize illegal cadres and engage in underground work "in all countries, even the freest, 'legal' and 'peaceful' in the sense that the class struggle is least acute in them" and to organize cells especially "in the army, navy, and police." [4] This was tantamount to converting Communist parties into conspiratorial organizations in those countries of the world where an objective revolutionary situation could not reasonably be assumed to exist—i.e., in most countries. But what may be true for a Party is no longer true for a movement when the party succeeds in organizing it.

A third myth which seems to attend most revolutions in the making is that no matter where begun, the revolution must end in

3. Leon Trotsky, *History of the Russian Revolution,* Vol. I, p. 132.
4. V. I. Lenin, *Selected Works* (English trans.), Vol. 10, p. 172-3.

total redemption of man or society. The initial goal, the introduction of specific and limited ends, is soon abandoned for the ideal of a new world out of which a new order of society, a new order of man, will arise, free from taint of present vice and past depravity. Even when a new calendar of time is not adopted, the general sentiment is that with the revolution a new era of change must begin everywhere. A total reordering is required uninhibited by the restraints of the past. Even when a revolution begins with limited objectives, once the reins of leadership fall into the hands of the ideologists, whether they are Robespierrian fanatics of Virtue and Reason, or Marxist prophets of historical necessity, the achievement of these objectives is made to appear bound up with the larger justifying goals of the new man in the new society.

The natural consequence of this totalistic conception of revolution is that difference of opinion or criticism at any point is sensed as latent or concealed opposition at every point, since everything tends to be interrelated in the minds of those who view society as a totality rather than pluralistically. Opposition becomes suspect as treason. Failures to achieve victory in any field appear as confirming evidence of the truth of the suspicion. In a few short steps opponents become enemies of the party, and before long "enemies of mankind."

Historical reality, however, makes a shambles of any ideal of total transformation for society or man or culture. Even when progress is made in some respects old evils reappear in a new guise, not to mention new evils unanticipated by anyone. Those who revolt were never nought—and they discover that they have *not* become all. The very rights which the revolutionists invoked as a protective shield in the old order behind which they carried on their revolutionary activity is brutally denied to those—even to erstwhile comrades—who cannot accept the new dispensation. There is room only for the new truth not for the renewed quest for truth. The new values in art, in freedom of personal relations which were prevalent on the eve of a revolution are frowned upon once the revolution is consolidated. The censor comes back—not merely with a blue pencil but with a sword.

A fourth myth about revolution is that it is necessarily opposed to reform. But unless the revolution becomes an end in itself, it ultimately must be judged by its costs and consequences. It may be that proposed reforms are insufficient to remove the evils and achieve the goals the revolutionists aim at but this has to be demonstrated in fact, *after* the effort at reform has been made, not assumed by fiat. Some of the measures that Marx listed in the *Communist Manifesto* on the agenda of action to be taken *after* the revolution have already been adopted by some Western countries as part of the program of social reform. It is possible to score a touchdown and win the game by a succession of small gains as well as by one long end-run.

Finally, a myth related to the one that counterposes reform to revolution is that a revolution is inescapably violent, and that it can only insure its victory by bloodshed and terror. This in part stems from a kindred confusion between a democratic revolution and a violent one.

At the time Marx wrote the *Communist Manifesto,* there was little possibility of introducing fundamental social and economic changes through peaceful legislative processes because of the absence of broad forms of political democracy. In France at the time, property and other qualifications restricted the suffrage to about 300,000 voters. In Germany and other European countries conditions were worse. In the nature of the case, under such conditions, unless one fell victim to Utopian illusions, even for mild reformers a revolution was not the order of the day. Within a generation, because of the growth of democratic institutions, Marx and Engels freely admitted that in England, the United States, and Holland, a social revolution that transferred economic power to the producers could be achieved without a violent political revolution. This presupposed of course that the economic structure of the new society had already been built up within the shell of the old, that the work of capital accumulation had been completed, the workers educated by their industrial and political struggles, and organized in a political party. Marx predicted already in *Die Deutsche Ideologie* that if a revolution was made in an economy of scarcity it would lead merely to the socialization of poverty and, to use his inelegant idiom, "all the old crap" would come back again—class rules and exploitation. Lenin revised Marx in denying that a peaceful transition to socialism was possible *anywhere*. He insisted that in every country of the world, independently of the maturity of the productive forces and relations, or the presence or absence of democratic processes, it was necessary to seize power, smash the state, and create a new one in order to build socialism. Lenin and his heirs succeeded, despite their professions of Marxist orthodoxy, in refuting the theory of historical determinism. But at what a price! Not only was the magnitude of human suffering greater than what has been experienced in any fifty-year period in the industrial development of any other great nation, every humanist and socialist ideal was sacrificed in the process. Even the programs and promises with which Lenin rationalized his destruction of the Kerensky regime—a regime that he had declared to be the freest in the world, turned out to be fraudulent. In short order, the slogan "All Power to the Soviets" turned out in practice to mean "All Power to the Communist Party," then all power to its Political Committee—and finally all power to its General-Secretary.

The pattern has been the same everywhere—at least in Europe. Despite the use of democratic slogans and rhetoric, wherever revolutionists have come to power by force and violence they have instituted dictatorships, sometimes as bad, sometimes even worse, than the régimes they replaced.

III

This brings me to the rationale of revolution by which I understand the question: what valid justifications can be offered, if any, for revolutions in the world today? This question cannot, of course, be answered except from the standpoint of basic moral and political principles. Nor can these principles by themselves decide particular cases, independently of historical application.

My standpoint is one of commitment to the politics and ethics of democracy, by which I understand a government that rests on the freely given consent of the governed and whose politics reflect an equality of concern for all persons within the community to develop themselves to the full reach of their powers. This, as I understand it, is the ideal expressed in the Declaration of Independence—which I still regard as valid and am prepared to defend against criticism. It is an ideal which challenges every conception of government based on political rule by an élite of blood, religion, social status, money, education or ideology. It is an ideal quite different from the ancient conceptions of democracy as the rule of the many, because integral to it is the recognition of natural or human rights, however theoretically grounded, as limits upon the power of government. It presupposes that political *consent* can be free only where there exists freedom of speech, press and assembly, an objective judiciary, and the institutional provisions that make it possible for a minority peacefully to become a majority, and through its representatives to control the government.

I contend that this philosophy of government, with modifications and extensions implicit in its principles, is still a viable guide to action, and that except in cultures that are primitive and uncivilized, it provides a more adequate model for progressive social change, even revolutionary change, than the Bolshevik-Leninist model, illegitimately derived from Marx's revolutionary project. The Bolshevik-Leninist model of revolution fits badly the needs of any society that takes seriously the notion of human rights. It presupposes that the leadership of a minority political party knows better what are the true objective interests of the people than the people do themselves. In addition, it postulates the existence of a proletariat, which in many countries simply does not exist—a myth that makes it easier for a group of intellectuals and bureaucrats to seize power in its name. It must adopt draconian methods to achieve economic growth or even to preserve economic stability. It drives out its entrepreneurial talent precisely at a time when the key to economic development is rationalization, and application of sophisticated technologies to the production of wealth.

Although Marx was highly critical of the "rights of man" in contradistinction to "the rights of citizens"—which, where the phrase had meaning, took the presence of the rights of man for granted—his central insight was perfectly compatible with the principles of the Declaration. This great insight was that property is not a thing but a social relation of power over man by means of things. Private property in the instruments of production meant power over the lives of people who must live by the use of them. Unless that power can be made responsible and shared, it violated the democratic ethos of equality, freedom and human dignity. Where democracy does not exist, according to Marx, *it is the first thing that must be established,*[5] not only to improve the workers' living conditions but to remove the obstacles that prevent all human beings from becoming free persons in a society in which "the free development of each will lead to the free development of all."

As we have seen from our previous studies, Marx does not counterpose bread to human dignity.[6] He held that want and hunger and the servitude they generate are incompatible with human dignity, that their existence is irrational in a society of potential plenty, whose just distribution of social goods and services should be used to make possible a life of dignity for all.[7]

Where Marx went astray, and his orthodox followers with him, was in underestimating the rejuvenating powers of the capitalist system in expanding the forces of production and tapping new sources of wealth. Far more important, he underestimated the growth and the impact of the democratic process upon the redistribution of wealth and power. One may cite as paradigm cases of the effects of political democracy on the economic order, the adoption of the Wagner Labor Relations Act and the complex of New Deal legislation that ushered in, however imperfectly, the welfare state in the United States, or the postwar transformation England in which standards of living, modest enough from our point of view, and a degree of political control over industry and agriculture were reached, that have produced vast social

5. cf. *Communist Manifesto.*
6. *MEGA*, I, 1, 615.
7. Ibid., I, 6, 278.

changes. In no country of the world, where democratic political processes prevailed did the workers become poorer and poorer, despite the pressure of the population explosion, but together with their allies they were able to effect in those countries a series of changes whose consequences on the culture and economy make it difficult to apply the traditional economic categories to them.

Now if the socialist movement depends merely upon the presence of poverty, then the advent of prosperity, even with pockets of poverty, must lead to the evanescence of the socialist movement. All the more so, if we recall Marx's reminder that poverty is a relative term. (Not many of those whom we call poor in this country are considered so by Europeans.) There are no economic grounds for doubting that the elimination of poverty, considered as an absolute state of deprivation, is possible today in the era of cybernetics and automation. But to a humanist and socialist it is not only a question of poverty. As fundamental are questions of human dignity, freedom, and justice. These still remain on the agenda of history.

It is in this sense that the political and human rights, originally expressed and implied in the Declaration of Independence, remain fundamental to all other social rights. For they give direction and justification to the continuous, even if incomplete, revolutions required to realize their promise, to convert them from frozen abstractions into living realities by broadening the scope of participation and responsibility of citizens for the institutional arrangements of their society, and hence deepening the meaning of their consent.

To deny this is to misconceive and blunt the ethical drive behind the whole of Marx's thought. The very concept of "exploitation" in most contexts, is more than an economic category. Together with the critique of "the fetishism of commodities," the heart of Marx's sociological economics, it expresses his passion for justice as well as for the autonomy of the human spirit against the worship of objects and things. After all, human beings can be exploited even when they are not suffering from dire want. The parasite sometimes has a lively interest in the welfare of his host—for the fatter the host, the fatter the parasite. But he is no less a parasite for all that!

It is a sad mistake to contrast political democracy, as some Marxists have done, with economic democracy or ethnic democracy and to imply that the latter can exist without the former, at least temporarily, until they are fused. If economic democracy has any meaning at all, it entails the right of the worker to help determine the conditions, organization, and the rewards of work—at the very least, free trade unions and the right to strike, in the absence of which we have forced labor. And if ethnic democracy has any meaning it entails the right of ethnic groups to develop freely their culture, art and religion. But neither economic nor ethnic democracy can be exercised without the presence of the complex of basic freedoms and rights—of speech, press, assembly, the protection of law—which defines political democracy. Consequently we may say that political democracy without economic or ethnic or social democracy is *incomplete;* but we *must* say that economic or ethnic or social democracy *without* political democracy is *impossible.*

That is why in the strategy of the struggle for the extension of the democratic way of life, the principles and practices of political democracy, in their varied forms, and on every level from the village to the nation, are of primary importance. They are the levers by which sooner or later, with sufficient courage and intelligence, obstacles can be removed and programs of social welfare introduced. The poverty program is not working properly? It can be improved. After all, that the elimination of poverty is now a national objective is a remarkable advance. It encourages us to push on for a guaranteed family income minimum which can rise higher with GNP. Note that this is a conception of a political democracy with a built-in commitment to human rights that may not be overridden at the first cry that the republic or state is in danger, or sacrificed to some conception of social or public welfare arbitrarily defined by whoever holds power in a moment of crisis or danger.

It is or should be an old story by now but it still remains true—the sacrifice of political liberty, even when it exists in primitive forms, for security or equality or what not, usually ends with the loss of one and the diminution of the other. This is the cruel logic of Jacobinism which has always proved fatal to the very ideals that are invoked to sanctify the sacrifice. When Robespierre with his own hand drew up the instructions for his law of Terror issued on the 22nd Prairial (June 10, 1794), he sacrificed "the rights of man and of the citizen" in the name of the public welfare, and therewith signed the death warrant of the revolutionary government. Within six weeks the Thermidorian reaction took over.

"The enemies of the Revolution," said Robespierre's instructions, and the language is echoed in decrees of some recent revolutions, "are those who *by any means whatsoever* and under no matter what pretext have tried to hamper the progress of the Revolution and prevent the establishment of the Republic. The due penalty for this crime is death: the proofs requisite for condemnation *on all information,* of no matter what kind, which may convince a reasonable man and a friend of liberty. The guide for passing sentence lies *in the conscience* of the judge, enlightened by love of justice and his country, their aim being the public welfare and the destruction of the enemies of the fatherland." [8]

To be sure, we sometimes hear that democracy and respect for human rights is a luxury that only industrially developed countries can afford or that it is a unique disposition of the Anglo-Saxon and Norse genius. I have never been convinced of it. These countries enjoyed considerable political freedom *before* they developed their industry, not as a result of it. Nor do I believe that there is a racially determined freedom-reflex or a gene for love of freedom. It is an acquired value, and like other human values can be acquired by all peoples and races.

I also tend to be skeptical of the argument of those who justify

8. My emphasis, quoted by Kropotkin in *The French Revolution* (New York, 1927), Vol. 2, p. 557, Eng. trans.

the overthrow of civilian governments by military or personal dictatorships in countries painfully groping their way to democratic political forms, on the ground that their peoples are not sufficiently developed; or that they need the harsh rule of the drill sergeant to march them forward, to accumulate capital, to build factories and achieve the prosperity and affluence without which, they say, the assertion of human rights is a rhetorical irrelevance.

I would be more impressed by such pleas if there was any evidence that the military or personal dictatorships do in fact improve the economy, do raise the level of education, do encourage the growth of the local, self-governing institutions alleged to be the pre-prerequisite for a free society, and then ultimately restore the rights of self-determination negated by their *coup d'état*, I have not seen this happen. But if the goal of these revolutions is *merely* to raise the standard of living or introduce modernization, it becomes puzzling why some of these countries threw off the bonds of colonial rule, which even when it exploited them, transformed their economy in the process and brought them further along industrially than they could go by their own efforts. In some of the Asian countries I have visited, I have been told by members of all classes (except the Harijans in India) that economic conditions on the whole were better before their colonial liberation than after. I do not know whether India and Burma were more prosperous under British rule than they are now, but even if they were the unanswerable rejoinder to that was made by an Indian judge to an English colleague who was enlarging on the advantages to Indians of British rule, "Yes, you gave us roads, hospitals, machines, the British law and the British peace: but you took away what we now value more: our self-respect."

The only apparent exceptions to my contention that military and personal dictatorships, despite their promises, do not achieve ordered progress under just laws are the rule of Mustapha Kemal in Turkey and of Salazar in Portugal. In the case of the first the progress was indisputable, but what his rule replaced was not a democratic régime, even of embryonic character, but a corrupt

and archaic dictatorship. There was no viable democratic alternative on the scene. In the case of Portugal, there was a functioning, although disorderly, democratic political life in operation. That has still not been restored. Neither the state of the
economy nor of cultural and intellectual freedom in Portugal
today is such that one can confidently say that either one is better
or more secure than what would have developed without
Salazar's accession and dictatorship.

IV

I turn now to a problem which arises when the Declaration of
Independence, which proclaims the right to revolution, is invoked
to justify revolutionary violence to further its own implicit ideals.
This is a problem attended by old and stubborn confusions. In
1860 when South Carolina seceded from the Union it justified its
action in terms of the right to revolution with specific reference to
the Declaration. And today some of their descendants, and some
of those at dagger's point with them, use similar language.
"Freedom was born," they say, "when we took the law into our
own hands—and it may be necessary to do it again." But this is
absurd! There is no such thing as a right to revolution in the
abstract. If there were, one couldn't distinguish it from a right to
counterrevolution. This in an invitation to perpetual war—and to
the worst of all wars, civil war.

The natural right to revolutionary overthrow recognized by the
Declaration is not a legal right to revolution. A legal right to
revolution is a contradiction in terms because it would require
governments to carry out revolutions against themselves. The
natural right to revolution is a *moral* right. What makes it moral is
not that it is a mere demand or claim—anyone can demand or
claim anything!—but that it is a justifiable, a reasonable claim.
The reason and justifications are spelled out in the Declaration "a
long train of abuses and usurpations, pursuing invariably the
same object, evinces a design to reduce them under absolute
despotism." This is condemned in the light of the underlying
principle that those persons who submit to the authority of

government and are affected by its decisions must have a voice in determining that authority.

To a principled democrat once a responsible government is set up along democratic lines, the situation becomes fundamentally different from one in which responsible democratic government is absent. Now in the new situation, if a law is lacking or a law is evil, if an institution is functioning improperly or badly, so long as the processes by which freely given consent is determined still obtain, it is open to the democrat to agitate, to educate, to demonstrate, to alter, to amend, or to repeal them. What is not open to him as a democrat is the use of revolutionary violence against the democratic system itself. For when he advocates or resorts to violence, he has abandoned his faith in self-government, and espoused either anarchy, or what is more likely, the despotism, allegedly benevolent, of a party or church or charismatic leader. For despotism and anarchy are the only alternatives to democracy. And as for benevolent despotism, earthly or even divine, the overwhelming historical evidence warrants a greater confidence in its despotism than in its benevolence. If all forms of government rest on faith, the faith of the democrat is that the evils of a democracy—and it has many evils—can be remedied by the patient efforts to achieve a better democracy.

There may be situations in which on moral grounds one may abandon his belief in democracy—one may conclude as some philosophers have from Plato to Santayana—that most human beings are too stupid and/or too vicious to be entrusted with the power of self-government, not to speak of power over others. When such views are defended the usual assumption has been that democracies are really majoritarian despotisms.

It would be much more difficult, although theoretically conceivable, to fault on moral grounds a democracy whose powers are circumscribed and limited by a respect for human rights, if the consequences of its operation resulted in widespread suffering and injustice. It was situations of this kind that Lincoln had in mind when he said in his First Inaugural, "If by the mere force of numbers a majority should deprive a minority of any clearly written constitutional right, it might in a moral point of view justify revolution—certainly would if such a right were a vital one."

Even in such a situation where the moral case is unexceptionable, it does not necessarily follow that resort to revolutionary violence is justified. For the human cost must be counted. Wisdom and prudence may show that the consequences in blood and agony and hatred may be worse, much worse, than the hardships that inspired the revolutionary action. It may or it may *not*. We cannot legislate about these matters in advance. Force cannot be banished from the world because under some conditions it may be necessary to use force to prevent the unjust use of force. If we had followed the absolute pacifist's noble policy toward Hitler, most of us would have been dead by now. But the great lesson of human experience confirms the wisdom of Edmund Burke when he warned, at the height of his powers, that force is often temporary and uncertain, and should be used only as a last resort. "If you do not succeed [in the use of force] you are without resource; for conciliation, failing, force remains; but force failing, no further hope of reconciliation is left."

The heavier responsibility rests on those who defend democracy than on those who would breach it to achieve relief from social evils. The democrat must be committed to the arduous and never finished task of defending and expanding the area of human freedom. "To leave social criticism to those who are freedom's enemies is to abandon freedom." Sometimes overwhelmed by the magnitude of the task and unhappy about the rate of progress, it appears as if no progress has or can be made. But anyone who has any memory of the state of the United States fifty, thirty, and twelve short years ago, or of England in the 1930s, can be heartened by the substantial gains won. Compared to the tasks that must still be achieved the gains have been modest, too modest, but there have been gains all along the line—economic, social, cultural, political, and especially with respect to the right and scope of dissent. The illusion that no progress has been made results from the fact that we have raised our sights as we have advanced, as we should.

The despair that alienates some extremists from political life and leads them to regard the democratic process itself as an obstacle to a just society is shortsighted and self-defeating. It reflects their failure to convince or persuade those in whose interests they presumably speak. Their rage which should be directed against their own easy and unexamined assumptions expresses itself almost as often in contempt of the "dumb masses" as in hatred for those who keep them in intellectual servitude. But failure to win over the masses is not necessarily a sign that they are dumb or enslaved. There is no remedy for this failure in a democratic society except harder, more patient, more intelligent work. The impatient, no matter what their political complexion, have a short political life. They may make headlines but without a political organization and political program, especially when they refuse coalitions with labor and other groups whom they regard as unenlightened, their chief political effect is to alienate some sections of the electorate that could be won to progressive causes, and to drive others into the arms of political reactionaries.

There is need for much new legislation on local, state, and federal levels of government. But just as important in the democratization of American life is the enforcement of legislation already enacted.

If the Civil Rights Acts of 1964 and the voting acts of 1965 were effectively enforced it would transform large sections of the South in which Negroes since the Civil War have lived in virtual peonage. Here is where the mass pressure should be brought. Psychologically and politically it makes a vast difference when a just cause has the highest law of the land on its side. A just cause that finds itself outside the highest law of the land and believes that it must go beyond peaceful civil disobedience and violently break the laws, harms those it would like to help and ultimately helps those who are responsible for the greater, continuing harm.

The American Civil War was the most violent in the annals of mankind up to that moment in time. It is still an open question whether the Civil War was inescapable or whether slavery could have been abolished by purchasing the freedom of the slaves at an infinitely lesser cost than the price paid in blood and treasure.

One thing, however, remains clear. It was not John Brown who liberated the slaves but Abraham Lincoln.

V

I return, very briefly, to the question of revolution in a political democracy. It is bound up with the question often asked: why did not the American Revolution lead to the terror and excesses of the French and Russian revolutions? This is sometimes answered by the statement that the American Revolution was merely a political but not a social and economic revolution. I do not find this answer convincing. For many political revolutions have been far more bloody than some social revolutions. Further, by the time of the French Revolution the social revolution in France had practically been completed. The terror played a political role not a social one. As many scholars have observed, the Revolution "removed *the last vestiges* of serfdom, the *remaining* privileges of nobility." [7] And the Bolshevik terror began from the very moment the power was seized, with the outlawing of entire political groups and *before* the socialization of industry and forced collectivization of agriculture was begun. If there have been other political revolutions which have been followed by a succession of purges, *coup d'états,* and bloodbaths, the political character of the American Revolution cannot explain the absence of sustained terror.

Nor do I find in the least plausible Toynbee's discovery of a "general and enduring historical 'law' which decrees that the material goals of a revolutionary advance must always be paid for by losses of corresponding magnitude in the currency of liberty." [8] In other words the more bread, the less freedom. This law was discovered by Toynbee at the very time when postwar social and economic changes in England were illustrating, as the American New Deal had done before, that im-

7. Plamenatz, *Man and Society* (New York, 1963), Vol. 2, p. 306.
8. Toynbee, *A Study of History,* Vol. 8, p. 343.

mense material gains, far from limiting freedom, could expand it. Like all of Toynbee's laws it is tailored to fit a special case. The irony is that even for this special case, the October Russian Revolution, the law is a singularly poor fit. The curtailment of human rights and liberties did not produce more bread. If anything it produced less bread, and prevented exposure of, and outcry against, the greatest man-made famine in human history. Indeed, many long years of debasement of the currency of liberty have hardly increased the size of the loaf of bread available for consumption in 1914. In justice it should be admitted that there have been large and impressive gains in certain industrial respects but by no means substantially larger than gains for a commensurate period of time in some nontotalitarian countries.

The explanation of the American experience is not simple but a large part of it was given by Lincoln when he asked whether a democratic government must be too strong for the liberties of its own people, or too weak to maintain its own existence against subversion. He answered that question by expounding the theory of sovereignty expressed both in the Declaration of Independence and the Constitution, from which he later derived the rationale of the Proclamation of Emancipation. "A majority," he declared, "held in restraint by constitutional checks, and limitations, and always changing easily with deliberate changes of popular opinions and sentiments, is the only true sovereign of a free people." [9] It is the way the majority decision is reached which is crucial here. If any group is denied a hearing, if there is a monopoly of education and propaganda, the majority loses its legitimacy. In other words, when issues are in dispute, if we refuse to sit down to reason with each other, we will end up fighting each other. In that fight everyone is likely to lose.

The Declaration of Independence and the Constitution are very imperfect documents. But their meaning and validity *transcend* whatever class interests inspired them. True, they declared the equality of man and his natural right to freedom but they did not abolish slavery. In this they reflected an estimate of the his-

9. Abraham Lincoln, Second Inaugural Address.

torical possibilities of the epoch, as well as the weaknesses found
even in the best of men. But what is much more significant, they
expressed the principles that can be used to abolish not only
chattel slavery but in time every other slavery of the body and
mind. And it is these very principles which have swept the world
to a point where even those who are opposed to them dare not say
so openly but seek by semantic outrage and the degradation of the
word to speak of "higher" democracy or "organic" democracy or
"directed" democracy or "people's" democracy.

If we lose the sense of history, nothing in the past becomes
usable. Although we must of necessity add to the past, there is a
need to preserve continuity with its best elements. The Magna
Carta was employed in England to justify the expansion of the
liberties of the people against tyrannical government. Under
Coke it helped build a thick hedge of law against arbitrary personal rule. But its actual text is largely concerned with restoring
baronial privileges. Some of its measures flagrantly discriminated
against Jews and women (e.g., "No one shall be arrested or
imprisoned upon this appeal of a woman, for the death of any
other than her husband"). Nonetheless if anyone were to scoff at
or dismiss the charter on these grounds, and disregard the respects
in which in 1215 it marked an *advance* over the past and a promise
for the future, he would be sadly deficient in historical perspective.

It is in this sense that the Declaration is not merely an historical
document but an expression of a still viable philosophy directed
to the enlargment of freedom. It conceives of the *pursuit* of happiness as an expression of liberty, and of happiness as its fruit. It
makes central to the ethos of government, freedom of choice, the
right to say "no" to entrenched power, the right to self-determination. The assumption is that such freedom of choice, extended to all institutions, including the economy, will produce
more happiness for mankind than the rule of any élite, if only
people remain free to learn from their experience. It is not happiness itself under any condition that is the goal. For happiness
may be secured by serenity pills, narcotics, and other forms of
intellectual and physical servitude. There are some forms of

happiness, according to the philosophy of democracy, which are unworthy of man. Happiness in a human society must have a proper foundation in justice. It seems to me that this is what John Adams meant when he wrote in a Jeffersonian vein: "As the happiness of the people is the sole end of government, so the consent of the people is the only foundation of it."

CHAPTER FIVE

The Cult of Revolution

The theme of this chapter concerns a disturbing phenomenon in the recent cultural and political life of the United States but not only of the United States. Although it is more muted elsewhere, signs of it are apparent in other industrial countries of the West. I refer to the emergence of a revolutionary political perspective encouraging deliberate episodic resorts to violence in hopes of precipitating consequences, including reprisals, that will increase the potential of revolutionary change and the ultimate likelihood of its success. These episodes sometimes evoke justifications for violence in the guise of explanations, penned by intellectual sympathizers, who maintain that those who initiate the violence are really the victims of society, not the aggressors. When the aggression is so bestial and unprovoked that it cannot be regarded as a defensive action, the bold claim is made that ethically crimes of the weak against the strong must be judged in a different light from other crimes.

To some extent this shift to a revolutionary stance has been facilitiated by the climate of opinion of our time, and by the very idioms in which we discourse about change. During the nineteenth century the term "evolution" was extended from biology, the field of its primary application, not only to all the arts and sciences but to the universe itself. Sometimes the historical approach itself was carelessly identified with the evolutionary approach. By the end of the century the term "evolution," independently of a specific context, was so vague that despite its vogue it had little cognitive significance.

In the twentieth century a similar fate has overtaken the term "revolution." Never has there been a century in which judging by its literature have so many revolutions occurred in so many societies and nations, and in so many diverse disciplines and fields of thought. In no previous century has so large a proportion of books been published which flaunt the term, "revolution" in their titles. The word "revolution" has become the shibboleth of our era, the attention-getter, the quickest way to capture the ear of an audience. It has become so fashionable that even theologians have sought by means of it to breathe fresh life into the dry bones of their dogma. One theologian apparently more convinced of God's omnipresence than of his omnipotence assures us that: "Not even God can escape radical thought today." According to him, God is not dead, despite Nietzsche. He has come alive. "He is the God of Revolution." Small wonder then that the verbal counters of other periods—"reform," "reason," "compromise," "gradual or evolutionary progress" are currently at a discount.

Sometimes this invocation of revolution seems comical in its juxtaposition of the serious and the trivial, and confusion of blood and ink. Here is a book on education, picked up almost at random, which tells us ". . . it took only a few men and women to start three of the greatest revolutions of our time, in America, in France, in Russia. Who among us doubts that we are witnessing the beginning of the Fourth Revolution? *And who among us will not play his part?*" One wonders what the revolution means to this writer, in whose part he is playing a self-conscious role, since he approvingly quotes Burke in condemnation of the French Revolution and also assures us that "revolutions have occurred which do not change institutions." Instead of proclaiming stirring and spine-tingling revolutionary educational changes, alas! he turns out to be a pedagogical paper tiger, high on rhetoric. "The liberal arts colleges, with the dawning of the Fourth Revolution, must find a new democratic purpose, and it is hard to see how that purpose will be all that different from that of the old normal schools although teaching styles, curriculum, and level of profundity will assuredly be different." [1]

It would be a mistaken linguistic purism to object to the proliferation of usages of the term "revolution" provided that we keep their contexts clear; and a futile intellectual exercise to attempt to discover some nuclear meaning common to all usages. I shall be talking about social and political revolution in the modified Marxist sense in which it designates *a fundamental change in the power relations of classes within society* effected through economic controls. I say in the "modified" Marxist sense because Marx's theory of classes and class conflicts is much too narrow and cannot do justice to what Pareto, Mosca, and Michels prophetically saw long before the victory of any Marxist-led revolution, viz., that even when the mode of production is socialized, classes and bitter class struggles are still possible. From this it would follow that a classless society is a Utopian myth. The difference between reform and revolution on this view becomes one of degree, between small scale and large scale changes designed to eliminate the evils and lacks of existing society. So long as the mode of political decision remains democratic, the *ideal* of social revolution can be regarded as a large-scale reform, and historically all genuinely Social-Democratic parties function as reform parties. Where Communist parties, whether oriented toward Moscow or Peking, despite their rhetoric, genuinely participate in the political life of a nation (and drop their role as Fifth Columnists) they, too, despite themselves will gradually become reform parties and accommodate their ideal of revolution to the democratic process. So far there is no evidence that any Communist party has truly committed itself to the preservation of

1. *The Liberal Arts and Teacher Education—A Confrontation* (University of Nebraska Press, 1970), pp. xxxiv, xiv.

all the political rights of those opposed to its program in the event that it comes to power. To guarantee that other political groups in a socialist society, including those who peacefully oppose socialism, will enjoy the freedoms of the Bill of Rights, invoked by Communist parties when they have not yet acquired power, is to repudiate the Leninist version of Marxism. So far as I am aware no Communist party has done so. Politically the heritage of Lenin has remained sacrosanct among all Communist parties.

Revolution as a "cult," as I shall use the term, as distinct from revolution as an ideal, is the position that rejects the processes of democratic social change, as hopelessly ineffective or deceptive or both, and makes a fetish of various forms of opposition ranging from passive uncivil disobedience to open violence. Those who have accepted this cult—or violent revolutionary faith—are often critical of the political position of official Communist parties, even when they declare themselves as still sympathetic with their ideology, and accuse them of betraying the authentic social revolution conceived as a total transformation of traditional, social, economic, political, and cultural institutions. The leaders of the cult are disaffected intellectuals of the Western world whose followers are other intellectuals, would-be intellectuals, militant students, and certain politically conscious elements of marginal or minority groups. Among them are Sartre in France and Marcuse in the U.S. and the late Ché Guevara, whose writings have an appeal to erstwhile social reformers disillusioned with the rate of social progress or outraged by some institutional practice of injustice toward some nationality or race that stubbornly refuses to yield to the corrective measures of legislation. Their influence has been mediated mainly through adult student leaders of the New Left.

There are several paradoxical features about the resurgence of the revolutionary myth among intellectuals of the Western world, whose influence the public media of the market economy they so scornfully condemn have helped spread out of all proportion to their numbers. The basic paradox is that as the welfare state moves to ever higher and more inclusive levels of social reform, even to the consideration of an annual guaranteed wage for every family, that would in effect wipe out traditional poverty, and to the progressive elimination of electoral discriminations, thus increasing the potential political power of the masses, the attacks on the system which makes this progress possible mount in frequency and ferocity. This paradox is accentuated by the fact that the commitment among student leaders of the New Left to a position of revolutionary opposition grows at a time when the likelihood of *successful* revolutionary uprisings in advanced industrial countries is extremely small, and when the costs of any attempts at such action would be catastrophically high.

Nonetheless the cult of revolution, even when the term "revolution" is not expressly invoked, flourishes above ground even more than underground. Its rhetoric has become chic and fashionable. Those who broke with the authoritarian régimes of the past used "to go to the people." Today those who denounce the welfare state or "the system," whose nature they cannot adequately analyze with the tired concepts of Marxist orthodoxy, proclaim they are "joining the resistance." To join the resistance is something quite different from going to the people—for "the people," whether the blue collar working class or the white collar lower middle class, seem to have little stomach and some revulsion both for violent revolution and revolutionists. Even the traditional parties of revolution—the Communist parties of the West, despite the existence of their underground apparatus, shun this extremist propaganda of the word and especially the terrorist propaganda of the deed with which the revolutionary rhetoric is occasionally punctuated. For in their experience such words and actions have been associated with the work of *agents-provocateurs* and irresponsible anarchists, long since read out of the organized workers movement by Marx and his followers.

The failure of classical Marxist theory to interpret and predict historical events may be attributed chiefly to two factors. First, the phenomenon of nationalism which in crucial situations overrode considerations of class interest; and second, the relative material prosperity of the major capitalist countries attributable in a considerable degree to the influence of the democratic political process in redistributing wealth. In consequence, the economy of welfare states obeys neither the equations of doom of Marx's *Capital* nor those of equilibrium that hold for a perfectly free market. Those for whom Marxism was a scientific theory and practice of achieving a classless society, and therefore refutable by events, abandoned its apocalyptic doctrines according to which the increasing misery of the masses would culminate in the act of revolutionary overthrow. In general this is the development followed by Social-Democratic movements and parties. If the objective presuppositions of revolution were lacking, the revolutionary attempt itself must be condemned as adventurous and suicidal. And there is, in a sense, a Marxist wisdom in this dying grasp of renunciation of Marxist eschatology—in this refusal to transform the scientific predictions, refuted by historical events, into an ideology which in principle is beyond empirical refutation. These Social-Democratic movements in good conscience and good logic have become people's parties for social reform. And it is safe to predict that to the extent that Communist parties in the West become organizationally independent of Moscow and Peking and sincerely practice what they currently profess, a willingness to submit to the arbitrament of the democratic political process, they, too, in effect will ultimately become parties of social reform.

As the Marxist ideal of revolution fades today, it is being replaced by the "cult of revolution" among the small but influential groups in the West that are identified as the New Left in whose eyes even the Communist parties are already hopelessly reformist. And by the "cult of revolution," to repeat, I mean the attitude which rejects the existing system no matter what its political form as inherently repressive. It repudiates principled reliance upon the democratic and judicial process even for the redress of specific grievances, especially of those regarded as acutely and overwhelmingly evil, whether it be war or minority repression. And although it *says* on occasion that it will employ all means to transform society, peaceful if possible and violent if necessary, it leaves little doubt that it believes peaceful means are not possible, that violence of one kind or another is inescapable, and that immediate resort to violence is imperative.

The cult of revolution has various roots. They not only feed the blossoms of its rhetoric but its violent fruit. The longest and strangest of its tap roots grew out of the writings of those who, having revised Marx's theory and ideal of revolution, still wish to be considered his dialectical successors and heirs. Marx had proclaimed that the emancipation of the working class can be the work only of the working class. Marcuse who typifies the current revolutionary revisionism is dismayed by the decision of the working classes, through their political parties and trade unions, to emancipate themselves gradually and peacefully, even if militantly, by integration into the welfare society. He is even fearful that the proletariat and its allies, if they dissociate themselves from those who today make a cult of revolution, "may well become, in part at least, the mass basis of a neo-Fascist regime." [2]

According to Marcuse, the organized working class, and even all but the poorest sections of the unorganized working class, have betrayed their historical mission. They have preferred to luxuriate in the shoddy goods and the vapid leisure time excitements that modern capitalism makes possible rather than risk their comforts by heroic revolutionary action. Nonetheless Marcuse still clings to the view that he is within the Marxist canon, a position made even more odd by his neo-Freudian notion that under Communism human beings will be free of all class-infected "civilizing" restraints upon natural sexual impulse. Theoretically, however, despite his reaffirmed allegiance to the Marxian dialectic method, Marcuse's is a dialectic of retreat to the standpoint of the early Marx, which we have already seen in an earlier chapter is a standpoint that Marx himself repudiated as an abstract, unhistorical moralism expressed as a fetishism of human nature, the Feuerbachian *Gattungswesen* which functions as an absolute norm, the true self from which the historical self has been alienated.

There are many devotees of the cult of violence whose intellectual origins are not Marxist. Disheartened by the gap which is

2. "Re-examination of the 'Concept of Revolution,' " *New Left Review*, July-August, 1969.

ever present between our social ideals and their imperfect fulfillment, they are prepared on high moral ground to support violent action against the system. They tell us that we must finally make an end to all human oppression and exploitation including that of women by men and of students by their teachers. When they realize that this has eschatological overtones, they sometimes moderate their language. The revolution is then justified as necessary to *reduce* "oppression, exploitation and alienation." But if that is our aim then there is no moral difference between the reformer and the revolutionist. Every reformer is in favor of this reduction but insists on translating these grandiose abstractions into concrete goals. We can then measure the extent and pace of progress toward them. If poverty diminishes as real wages increase together with more adequate social insurance, pensions, and opportunities to participate significantly in decisions affecting one's life, the natural response of the reformer is: why not more of the same, why not continue on the same course?

The cultists of revolution are impatient with this historical progressivist and reformist perspective. They come down hard on it, irritated all the more by its seeming air of reasonableness. There are two generic criticisms made of the reformers. The first is that the progress is spurious despite all the quantitative indices which show that real wages have increased and living conditions improved. Comparison is made not between the past and the present but between the relative incomes of the extremely wealthy in the present and the average working-class income. Even if the workers in the present are much better off than workers in the past, compared to the income of the extremely wealthy in the present they are worse off. Or alternately, attention is focused upon an extreme instance of utter deprivation and an inference is drawn about the entire system which permits such an unmitigated evil to occur. How valid are these critical responses to the reformist approach?

Semantically, the expressions "better off than before" or "worse off than before" are usually employed in comparisons made between the states of the *same* person or group in the present and the past, not in comparison with the states of different persons and groups. If with respect to one's health it is said, "He is better off this year than last year since he was ill only for ten days and not five months," it would be extremely odd to hear in response: "Not at all—he is worse off than he was last year since there have been others who have been ill for only five days." Or with respect to knowledge, if I say of John: "He is better off than he was last year—he knows so much more this year as measured by all the tests," it would be a plain abuse of language for someone to retort: "Not at all, he is worse off, he really knows less than last year because his friends know far more than he does." John's relative standing this year may be worse than last year's despite the improvement in his knowledge and understanding. But the precise point at issue is whether the relative standing has any bearing or effect on the positive improvement made. Except as a desperate move in an argument to save a theory, we do not make this relative judgment when discussing improvements in the standards of living of a specific person or group—granting the legitimacy of such inquiries for other purposes, e.g., tax and fiscal policies. Tell a man who was quite familiar with hunger pangs in the past but can now eat to repletion on nutritious fare that he is worse off than before because some others can eat and overeat more often and more expensively, and he will feel he is being made sport of. What is true of individuals is true of groups. Compared with the state of affairs less than a century ago the longevity of the American people has increased and infant mortality decreased, both in spectacular fashion. The fact that the current records in Scandinavia are better shows only that there is still room for improvement, not that the improvement is unreal.

In one sense, of course, poverty is a relative term but not in the sense in which the Gospels mistakenly assures us "For ye have the poor always with you" (Matthew, 26:11). In the Biblical sense, poverty could be wiped out in short order in the industrialized countries of the West. The sense in which poverty is "relative" involves questions of justice where that is defined simply in terms of equality. If my real wages double but the wages of others (whom I judge as no better qualified or worthy) quadruple, I may regard this as unjust but not as worsening my lot. Where there is no question of physical need and deprivation or suppression of basic human freedoms or punishment for criminal actions, the desire for justice, if defined in terms of equality, may express resentment or envy of the better fortunes of others, deserved or undeserved. It may show poverty of spirit, not physical poverty. "A hut is a hut," observes Marx, "but build a [mansion] beside it and it becomes a hovel." [3] This is a profound psychological observation, not an economic truth. And even as a psychological truth it is historically conditioned although the insight remains. A hut with all modern conveniences, heated in winter and air-conditioned in summer, overlooking a couple of acres and a pleasant view does not become a hovel no matter what is built beside it. Does a mansion, in turn, become a hovel when a palace is built beside it? The absurdity of conceiving of poverty only in relative terms is apparent in the fact that in a community of oil-sheiks, all of whom are millionaires, we would have to refer to those whose income was only one million as "poor."

When this first response to the case for reform is shattered by the avalanche of incontrovertible facts concerning improvements in the standard of living, the revolutionist shifts ground. He argues that the improvement is only temporary. His confidence that it is only temporary sometimes derives from an expectation of an economic earthquake or catastrophe that will level society. Even if we grant that possibility it would constitute no more of an argument against reforms than the possibility of a real earthquake against building houses. At this point a further shift occurs. The cultist of revolution contends that the reformist outlook makes for ethical and psychological complacency, for a self-congratulatory fixation upon the distance society has come from the darkest days of the past rather than upon the distance yet to go. Without denying the possibility that the very success of reform may undermine its spirit or *élan*, psychologically this seems unlikely. At any rate, what does the historical record of the last two centuries show?

Some writers have suggested that the history of health care for

3. I am aware that in the quotation from Marx, he used the term "palace" instead of "mansion" which I use to make my point clearer.

the masses be taken as a paradigm of the progress of social reform. They argue that once the social responsibility of the community for the health of its citizens is recognized, every achievement becomes the basis for an eager and more daring advance on the frontier of the yet to be accomplished. With some justification it may be objected that this is a special case bound up with the growth of scientific knowledge and not comparable to the history of social and political progress that involves fiercer conflicts than over the distribution of tax funds. Let us then examine the history of electoral reforms, of civil rights, labor unionism, welfare legislation, and public support of education in democratic countries. Do they show patterns of expansion or of the exhaustion we should find if the cultist of revolution were right? To be sure, the pattern of expansion shows some resting on plateaus and even some setbacks induced by the pace and success of the reforms and sometimes by resistance and backlash to violence that has accompanied demands for reform. But in every respect there has been a large net gain. This by no means guarantees continued gains but it places a heavy burden of proof upon those who would urge another course.

Psychologically, there is even less reason to believe that awareness of historical gain reinforces complacency. The natural momentum of a successful reform opens up possibilities whose existence may not have been suspected before the reform was introduced. Sometimes it generates a buoyant mood that the Zeitgeist, if not the cosmos, is on the side of the reformer. It is this mood that everything has become possible, that the gains won are natural and irreversible that makes so dangerous the frustration of the popular expectation for more progress. The paradox of rising expectations shows that hope does not wither but flares with success. Far from making reformers complacent, awareness how far one has come may even strengthen the resolution to continue in situations where grave injustices and needless suffering still exist.

The cult of revolution sometimes develops out of a consuming rage against a specific evil that looms so large that it blots out everything else. This is typified by the observation of one academic devotee of the cult: "Revolutionary violence in Sweden or Canada would be quite unjustified ... Rhodesia and the United States are something else again." Since Sweden, Canada, and the United States are capitalist welfare societies of approximately equal living standards for the working population, since no reference is made to the possibility of justified revolutionary violence in the Soviet Union or Mainland China, and since the political system of the United States is more like that of Canada and Sweden, while that of Rhodesia resembles the dictatorships of Russia and China, the coupling of the United States and Rhodesia obviously indicates that the author is referring to "racism" in the United States which he believes can be eliminated only by revolutionary violence. In passing, it should be noted that there are some cultists of revolution that do not draw the line at Canada. There are French revolutionary nationalists in Canada who are as *enragés* about their grievances as American Black Panthers. We shall discuss the problem posed by minority groups who conceive of themselves at war with a majority in another chapter. But from the point of view of a citizen opposed to any form of invidious racial discrimination what shall we say to this bland blanket justification of revolutionary violence?

First, it could only be made by someone insensitive to the tremendous progress in race relations that has been made in the last two decades *without* revolutionary violence, a progress much greater materially, socially, and educationally than was achieved by four years of the most violent civil war in human history up to that time and which resulted in a change in the legal status of the Negro but not his genuine political enfranchisement in former slave-holding states. Second, it overlooks the suicidal character of any attempt to tie the movement for *further* reduction of racial discrimination to a movement of revolutionary violence. This was understood by the NAACP, the largest and most representative of all Negro organizations, from its very founding, and reluctantly and belatedly grasped even by the Black Panthers. Third, anyone capable of a cool look at history should realize that neither racism nor nationalism would be destroyed even if a minority despite the odds against it succeeded in putting down a majority by force. At best the character and direction of the repressive nationalism and racism would be reversed.

The ways in which a social evil is attacked may in the long run breed consequences that are as bad or worse than the evil that spurred the original opposition. When minorities that suffer injustices at the hands of a majority in politically democratic societies reject existing legislative and judicial mechanisms instead of using them, and invoke the slogan "all power to the people," they are really invoking lynch law. When individuals join the so-called revolutionary resistance because of the presumed injustice of the draft or a war, they seem unaware that they may be committing themselves to the support of a wider draft or a more protracted war if by some historical fluke their revolutionary action was victorious.

Not all cultists of revolution exempt Sweden as a possible locus of revolutionary violence. Jan Myrdal, the Maoist son of a Social-Democratic father, protests that reforms are not adequate because "We have not solved the problem of the alienation of the individual." Whatever the problem of alienation is, there is not the slightest reason to believe that if it should be solved, about which there can be legitimate doubt, it will be solved by violent revolution rather than by reform unless the liquidation of multitudes is considered one form of solution. But, as we shall see, this talk about alienation reveals some significant facets of the cult of revolution and some of its moral pretensions.

The ideologists of the cult of revolution usually reply to their critics by trying to force upon them a position of either absolute pacifism or of absolute opposition to revolution under any conceivable circumstance. But it is not necessary to adopt the position of the absolute pacifist to oppose the cult of revolution any more than principled opposition to lying or deception entails that a person must always tell the truth regardless of consequences. Opposition to violence may sometimes necessitate a violent defense against those who resort to it. There is nothing inconsistent here. Morally to equate the two is like equating the violence of the thug with the violence of the victim who defends himself against the thug or with the force used by an arresting police officer. Of course one can easily *conceive* of historical situations in which a revolution would be justifiable as the lesser evil. But speculative possibilities are here irrelevant. Only a fanatic would justify revolutionary action in a specific situation on the basis of the merely *conceivable*. For the political issue is always of a specific time and place, here and now. Past revolutions may or may not have been justified: future revolutions may or may not be. They have no bearing on our responsibility in the present.

Another interesting aspect of the thought of present day cultists of revolution is that they also claim to be principled believers in democracy. And yet they consistently overlook the fundamental difference between the resort to revolutionary violence in order to *establish* the processes of political democracy, in whose absence the just and peaceful settlement of grievances is not feasible, and the resort to revolutionary violence in a democracy to transform it. To an ethical absolutist it may make little difference whether one is revolting against a tyrant who refuses to accept representative institutions or whether one is revolting against the alleged tyranny of the democratic majority. To the democrat, however, there is a fundamental difference. His decision whether or not to engage in revolution against the tyranny of the despot is largely prudential but, as a democrat living in a democracy, if he rejects the decisions of an *unenlightened* majority, he is in principle bound to appeal not to violence but to an *enlightened* majority. When he rejects that appeal to the enlightened majority on the Platonic ground that most human beings are either too stupid or vicious to be entrusted with self-government, he has rejected the democratic process. The cultist of revolution instead of admitting that *he* has abandoned his faith in democracy wants to eat his cake and have it, too. He denies that the existing democratic political system is truly democratic, denounces it as formal, pseudo, bourgeois, or with whatever deprecatory adjective comes to mind. He then defines democracy in vague and grandiose terms as a community in which individuals enjoy complete autonomy, self-determination, and freedom. When these terms are rendered meaningful, it turns out that no earthly community could possibly exemplify them. And so ignoring the necessity of determining whether any given society is more or less democratic in its basic institutions—which always defines our concrete choice—he can condemn *all* existing political democracies, praise—indeed cooperate with their totalitarian foes—and still proclaim himself as the only true and authentic democrat.

It is at this point that present-day cultists like Marcuse reveal that despite their insistence upon the authenticity of their democratic faith, they are really in direct line with the original totalitarian traditions of Bolshevik-Leninism from which they seek to differentiate themselves. The Leninists contrasted "the wishes and will of the masses" and the "real interests of the masses." They then claimed to know these real interests better than the masses themselves, and in their light oppose and correct the expressed wishes and will of the masses, and punish them for the form they took.

What was shamefaced in the Leninist revision of Marx is open in Marcuse who declares that "the Marxian concept of a revolution, carried by the majority of the exploited masses is overtaken by the historical development." [4] The working masses are to be replaced by the middle-class student intelligentsia, allied with the ghetto population and other discontented groups on the margin of society—all of whom together do not constitute a majority of the producers, still less, as Marx claimed for the workers, a majority of the population. Together with aid from Third World revolutionists, this is the composite group that replaces the working classes which history has found wanting.

And why have the working classes been found wanting by the cultists of revolution? Because they have been corrupted by the affluence of the welfare society. They have been infected with consumerism. They desire the housing, the schooling, the clothing, the leisure and entertainment, the automobiles, the swimming pools, and holiday jaunts abroad which until now have been the monopoly largely of the prosperous middle classes. Marcuse and his academic disciples—revolutionists with tenure!—are not mollified by the absence of mass hunger among the workers. They

4. Marcuse, *loc.* cit.

are not reconciled to the attempts by guaranteed family income and other reforms to wipe out hunger everywhere. They are not happy that Marx was proved wrong about the mass pauperization of the working class. They are actually repelled by the spectacle of mass satisfaction, by the acquisition of personal property, by the fact that having acquired a vested interest in things, the workers resent losing them through the violence inspired by calls for revolution. For all his rhetoric about universal freedom and self-determination as sanctifying revolutionary overthrow, what Marcuse finds really offensive are the life styles, the patterns of values and choices both of the majority of the population and the majority of the working class.

Nothing reveals so starkly the élitist, undemocratic bias of the New Left cult of the revolution. There is something snobbish as well as hypocritical in the spectacle of middle-class intellectuals, cradled in security and comfort, luxuriating in a standard of living dependent upon the intensive use of the latest technological refinements, hectoring the masses for aspiring to the same material benefits that most of these intellectuals are loath to surrender. To be sure, the masses enjoy their leisure differently and in the contemptuous eyes of their liberators, vulgarly. But the fact that the masses are blamed for their choice, for acquiring artificial and inflated needs, shows that they are *not* being coerced. One may disapprove of their hierarchy of values and the way they choose to spend their leisure. But they are no less free in selecting their life styles, within limits of course, than their would-be liberators.

Marcuse denies this as a liberal evasion of the facts of social coercion. He insists that the masses are being seduced by carrots where previously they had been driven by sticks—and *both* are forms of coercion.

This equation between carrots and sticks as equal forces of repression preventing the liberation of the masses is central to the political theology of the priests of the revolutionary cult. But I make bold to proclaim in opposition that the difference between the carrot and the stick—or the gun!—in eliciting consent is the key to the whole culture complex we call civilization when we use the word normatively. It may be compared to the difference between seduction and rape which that genial anthropologist, Goldenweiser, in a *jeu d'esprit* once declared marked the moral basis of civilized family life. After all where adults are concerned seduction involves an offering of carrots in the generic sense of the term. It is an exchange of sorts, conscious and risky but always undertaken in anticipation of what are believed genuine values. To be seduced is to be induced. True, we are sometimes induced by invalid arguments—the remedy is to learn to reason better. True, we may be induced by false and glittering promises—the remedy is the cultivation of skepticism, reliance on the argument from Missouri, the plain man's critical empiricism. Except in certain extreme or limiting cases—induced behavior is not morally comparable to physically coerced behavior—to the violence that brutally overrides one's consciousness and reduces the human being to the status of an animal or unfeeling thing.

The cultists of revolution have written off the class that Marx had hailed as the carrier of progressive social change.

We cannot, however, doubt for a moment that the same arrogance that would dictate to the working masses how they must live to save themselves and society would be turned against the new carriers of the revolution, the ghetto inhabitants and the New Left students, if they were to come to terms with the political forces of the environment and entered into the coalition politics of the pluralist society. They, too, would be denounced for permitting themselves to be "co-opted by the Establishment."

Actually, there was a period in the past when Marcuse doubted that the black ghetto population in the United States would and could assume the burden of revolutionary redemption. He was prepared then to condemn even their right to choose if they were to choose wrongly. This was during the years that preceded ghetto violence in which the black population was making great gains in breaking down the institutionalized prejudices of the past. At that time Marcuse dismissed the civil rights movement among the American Negroes as inconsequential on the ground that they were using their new electoral freedom pretty much as their corrupted white fellow citizens and that they were succumbing to the same consumer-oriented blandishments of the affluent society. He was then asked which state of affairs he considered more desirable—one in which Negroes remained deprived of the civil rights and freedom possessed by white citizens or one in which they used these rights to choose wrongly from *his* point of view. He replied without evasion that he would rather they had no freedom to choose than that they choose to become integrated in the corporate affluent, technological culture that had "corrupted" the organized labor movement.[5] Autonomous choice or genuine self-determination on this view is present only when it conforms to the values of the revolutionary élite—all other values are "prejudices." Being wrong means disagreeing with Marcuse and the workers have no right to be wrong. Naturally this paternalism is not likely to have a mass appeal.

One refreshing feature of this élitism and paternalism is that it is so undisguised not only in Marcuse but in Sartre and in the writings of Ché Guevara, whom they both admired, as a spokesman for the Cuban Revolution when it was free from bureaucratic deformations. Sartre admits that the so-called dictatorship of the proletariat in the Soviet Union which he had so passionately defended is and always was a dictatorship *for* and *over* the proletariat. Ché Guevara, one of the key figures in the cult of revolution, in justifying "the avoidance of the commonplaces of bourgeois democracy," by which he means free elections and a legally recognized opposition party, in the Cuban long march to libertarian socialism frankly contrasts the roles of the privileged vanguard and the masses. Members of the vanguard, in virtue of their superior insight, are "qualitatively different from the masses who see only by halves and must be subjected to incentives and pressures of some intensity: it is the dictatorship of the proletariat being exercised not only upon the defeated class but also individually upon the victorious class." The reason that free democratic choice cannot be permitted to individuals is that it may interfere with the revolutionary aspiration "to see man freed from alienation." Guevara spells out what this involves with a Latin clarity that reveals more than the Teutonic circumlocutions of Marcuse. But they mean the same thing. For the revolution to succeed, he tells us,

---

[5] This public response was made at the Conference on The Idea of the Future at Rutgers University, New Brunswick, N. J. June 1965 to the question posed by the author.

involves the necessity of a series of mechanisms, the revolutionary institutions. The concept of institutionalization fits in with the images of the multitudes marching toward a future as that of a harmonic unit of canals, steps, well-oiled apparatuses that make the march possible, *that permit the natural selection of those who are destined to march in the vanguard and who dispense reward and punishments to those who fulfil their duty or act against the society under construction.* ('Man and Socialism in Cuba,' translated by Zimmerman, in *All We Are Saying,* ed. Lothstein, N.Y. 1971, p. 365, my italics)

Neither Marcuse nor Sartre are so devoid of a sense of the political realities in the industrial societies of the West as to urge immediate action to achieve the power that the working class has refused to seize. There is no revolutionary situation. But until that auspicious moment arrives, the revolutionary opposition must be one of constant preparation—not only "radical enlightenment in theory and practice but development of cadres and nuclei for the struggle."

The devotees of the cult of revolution consider themselves neither romantics nor Utopians. Nonetheless they are far from having a realistic view of the effect of their doctrines *today* in the surcharged atmosphere of violence that prevails almost everywhere. The cultists of revolution can *inspire* reckless and extreme action; but they have no means of restraining or disciplining it. After all, despite Lenin, there are no firm criteria of an objective revolutionary situation—they depend very much on the fevered consciousness of street crowds and the audacity of the "cadres and nuclei" that are being primed and educated for revolutionary action. There was no objective revolutionary situation in France when the students launched their rebellion in 1968. Yet in the heated climate of the times, it was a near thing. Had it succeeded in sparking a revolution, the existence of an objective revolutionary situation would have been retroactively inferred. After the rioting fizzled out, Sartre and Marcuse condemned not the student rebels for their precipitate action and adventurism but the French Communist Party and the French trade unions for betraying the student movement. Despite a certain ambiguity in their judgment, their chief criticism of the students' rebellion was *not* that their uprising was undertaken but that it was not thought through and adequately prepared for. But this refers to a subjective, not objective component. The moral is: try again but harder! The constant willingness is presupposed; and the readiness is not so much a function of the social-economic situation but of proper organization.

As the world is constituted today the traditional Leninist conception of a revolutionary situation no longer appears valid in face of the trigger readiness of so many groups to resort to violence and terrorism to enforce nonnegotiable demands. It should be noted that it did not apply to the Cuban Revolution. That was launched, Ché Guevara to the contrary, not as a socialist revolution to free man from his alienation but to restore simple democratic political freedoms, and conduct the free elections Batista had banned, and which Castro has never held.

In pure logic a social revolution engineered by a minority may be nonviolent but where the liberation of society is to be carried out by "repressive tolerance," to use Marcuse's phrase, the resort to revolutionary violence and terror necessarily becomes the order of the day when the moment to strike arrives. An affluent society has enormous latent powers of resistance. It must therefore be taken by surprise. The cultists of revolution must be on the lookout, really on the lurk, for opportunities to head and guide spontaneous outbursts of violence directed against the system. They cannot reasonably expect victory by any one act but hope through a series of acts that generate a continued chaos to ride to success. Despite their occasional disclaimers, in their hearts they cannot condemn any violence that erupts against the system. For not only do they regard the instigators of violence as victims, they nourish the wild hope that the whole fabric of society may catch fire from the eruption. When violence fails, the odium of the failure must therefore always be placed on those who have put it down not on those who have initiated it.

The espousal of revolutionary overthrow of the existing social and political system does not take place in a vacuum. In the

United States, incitements to violence are no longer prosecuted, and even many acts of violence go unpunished. The very system denounced as repressive by the cultists of revolution gives them a platform and an audience through its public media, in quest for the sensational and extreme, which they could never reach by their own means, or command in virtue of the intrinsic merit of their ideas.

It would be absurd to attribute to the cultists of revolution primary responsibility for the tidal wave of violence that has engulfed almost all areas of American life in recent years. But it is not absurd to attribute to them, in a considerable degree, the growing acceptance of domestic violence, its social and intellectual respectability in American society. At the time of the ghetto riots one of the chief theoretical organs of the New Left with a wide circulation in the universities not only carried an illustration of a Molotov cocktail but instructions on how to make one. What is perhaps more serious, the glorification of "the creative function of violence," and the rationalizations to which it has given rise, has lamed the critical functions of our colleges and universities in dealing with the violent excesses of the student movement. Even Marcuse has shrunk from the spectacle of organized violence in the university which has given him a haven and protection from the fury of those who would turn his own principle of repressive tolerance against him and treat him as he himself advocates that others be treated. If, as he believes, the university is an integral part of the beaurocratized Establishment, and its destruction contributes to the radicalization of the student young, so necessary if the social revolution is to have a chance of success, the Cohen-Bendits and other leaders of extremist students are not altogether wrong in taxing Marcuse at this point with inconsistency.

There are some who regard concern with the verbal hysteria of violence as itself an hysterical expression of a fear that takes the shadow for the substance of danger. It is only *actions*, they say, that we need trouble ourselves about, and the social causes out of which they grow. The rest is ideology or mythology that functions as a rationalization for behavior that is *not* determined by ideas or words. This is a half truth. One would have imagined that the effects of mythological beliefs about race in our century would have taught us what practical effects ideas, even mistaken ideas, can have. Not only have ideas consequences, words have consequences, too. Auden may have been right when he wrote: "Poetry makes nothing happen" but he can hardly believe it of prose, even bad prose. Were Hitler's ranting speeches without effect?

All political movements have their peripheries of the psychotic and semipsychotic. That is why the terrorism of the word often inspires a terrorism of the deed for which the wordmongers of terror are responsible even when they find it politic to disavow the deeds. More dangerous is the growing tendency of cultists of violence to portray those who have been guilty of crimes of murder, assault, and theft as political prisoners, to glorify criminal elements in the population as revolutionaries, and to hail their prison revolts as part of the movement toward liberation. Where criminal violence can be interpreted by malefactors as a blow for collective freedom, it provides absolution in advance for the most callous kind of inhumanities. The thief becomes a freedom-looter who does not steal property but liberates it. If he kills in the course of his piecemeal expropriation of the oppressor, it is no longer murder but a symbolic act of protest against the systematic injustices of society. The revolutionary exploitation of prison violence since the outbreak at Attica, New York, has become more pronounced. In the long run it is self-defeating in any civilized society to link revolutionary movements with prison breaks by hard criminal offenders. But its short run impact may be a greater surge of violence, and inescapable counterviolence.

It has long been noted by students of crowd behavior that few individuals when alone commit, or are even tempted to commit, the bestial acts they find themselves doing as members of a lynch mob. The reason for this is in part that the mob is united by a common passion or idea that takes the individual out of himself. When the individual member of a crowd is caught up in violence, he tends to think of himself as a disinterested even an unselfish agent of a collective will. The inhibiting bonds of existing moral tradition are loosened not out of naked self-interest but by the authority of a cause which ennobles every vicious desire and impulse hitherto suppressed. That is why violence in behalf of an ideology or cause is apt to take more horrible form than ordinary criminal violence. This is not to equate crime with revolution. It explains only why the violence that results from the cult of violence is often so much worse than the violence of ordinary crime.

In their reflective moments the cultists of revolutionary violence insist that they, too, detest violence and desire to eliminate it from human life. To oppose violence, they admit, is not so much a sign of one's humanity as of one's sanity. It is intrinsically evil but when its use is necessary to avoid a much greater evil or promote a very great shared good, it is morally justified. Again, one can agree with these abstract considerations but if adduced to justify revolutionary resistance today they are completely question-begging. Most of those who talk this way are completely and avowedly ignorant of what the costs of revolution would be, and they refuse to examine carefully the human costs of the revolutions of our time. Instead they fall back on general considerations to present a persuasive case in justification of revolutionary violence. In succeeding chapters we shall examine the costs of revolution and the ideologies of violence. Before concluding discussion of the cult of revolution, some cautions are in order that may be overlooked when fear and revulsion grip the community after some unspeakable atrocity has been committed by the self-denominated "vanguard" of liberated humanity.

There are two great dangers. One is that the genuine evils and injustices of society which have spurred idealistic fanatics into a mad impatience will remain unmet even after the violence is put down, or that if they are being met, they are not being seen as met. One of the reasons why the cult of revolution has fallen on deaf ears among the workers in Western democratic countries is that they have had visible and continuing evidence of the relative improvement of their estate. But the economic improvement is still insufficient and uneven, and acute problems, in some countries racial, in others religious, cut across class lines. *The ineptitude of the language and barbarity of the methods used by revolutionary cultists should not blind us to the existence of these problems and the moral necessity of grappling with them in order to expand the area of human freedom.* There are some who claim that the true "permanent revolution" is to be found not in any self-proclaimed revolutionary state today but in the processes of continuous democratic social reform. I think it is a confusing use of the term "revolution." At any rate democratic welfare states do not guarantee this permanent revolution. They only make it possible.

The second danger posed by the phenomenon of violence is that the methods used to counteract, suppress, and punish those who initiate it may themselves be so extreme and indiscriminate as to awaken sympathy and support among elements of the population not previously infected by the contagion of violence. The problem is extremely difficult. It has never arisen in the past in the same fashion that exists today.

The *forms* of violence we find today, whether they are assassinations, kidnappings, fire-bombing of innocent civilians, the seizure of hostages, even self-immolation are an old story. What is new is the strategy of violence of urban guerrillas in many countries who hope by senseless acts of terror (like the murder of kidnapped hostages who may not even be citizens of the country) to provoke measures of repression that by falling on guilty and innocent alike tend to discredit those who are defenders of public order.

This strategy has been described by Carlos Marighella, one of the ideologists of Brazilian terrorism, in frankest terms.

"It is necessary," he says, "to turn political crisis [always at hand in some countries] into armed conflict by performing violent actions that will force those in power to transform the political situation in the country into a military [or police] situation. That will alienate the masses who from then on will revolt against the army and police and blame *them* for this state of things" (my italics, quoted by Robert Moss in *Urban Guerillas in Latin America*, Conflict Studies, 1970, p. 7).

This strategy can be very effective when implemented by suicidal acts of terrorism and atrocity. It makes it all the more essential that the guardians of public order act intelligently, and even when they have to react firmly against extreme provocation, do so in a civilized way. In crisis situations this may appear as a counsel of perfection to those whose lives are at stake on the firing line. But these crisis situations must be prepared for in advance. This is a lesson that applies just as much to violent campus disruption and prison revolt as to hit and run tactics of political terror. All the appropriate resources of the community must be brought to bear on the situation with vigor and promptness, with the promise of justice but rarely, if ever, of amnesty. And when force must be deployed, it should never be excessive.

CHAPTER SIX

The Human Costs of
Revolution *

I

To speak of the human costs of revolution already presupposes that revolutions are not merely natural events. For although natural events like earthquakes and storms may take a great toll in human life and suffering, we do not reckon these consequences as costs. Costs are the result of human actions. Although we may not be aware of the costs or ignore them, they flow from intended actions—individual or collective.

That is why it is perfectly intelligible to raise questions about the validity and justification of revolutions, social or political—the more so when theories of revolution abound, designed not merely to explain revolutions but to bring them about. Reflections about

* This chapter was written in the fall of 1967 at the time of the 50th Anniversary of the October Russian Revolution.

150

revolution, therefore, are not like reflections about chance, love, death, and other tragic happenstances of experience which are unaffected by whatever conclusions we reach about them. They contribute to a climate of opinion that may have fateful consequences for the living and the still unborn. To be sure, individuals, even an entire generation, may be caught in a revolution just as they may be caught in a storm in whose making they have had as little to do. But until the weather is brought under control, it remains a natural happening in a way that no revolution is. For revolutions are made by men even if not by all men who are affected by them.

The fiftieth anniversary of the Russian October Revolution is an appropriate occasion for an assessment of the rationale of social revolution, of the gains and costs of those measures of revolutionary violence undertaken to bring about not the Bolshevik program of a socialist society, for this is still in the limbo of the unrealized, but incontestable complex social changes that differentiate prerevolutionary Russia from the Soviet Union today. Such an inquiry is difficult but not impossible to make. The questions related to it certainly make sense. We ask similar ones about many different things. Looking back on the past we assess important actions in the light of what is presently known not in order to determine whether we would perform them again if time were reversible, but to determine whether, assuming that they were not inevitable and were genuine choices, they were justified by their consequences—whether, in short, the gains or the glory or the freedoms won were worth the pains or the agony or the freedoms lost. An experience may be justified by its consequences even though we have no desire to live it over again. Unless such judgments can be validly made there can be no such thing as wisdom in human affairs. Or foolishness for that matter. Regret about the past may be vain particularly if it has no bearing on future conduct. But *judgment* about the past is so much a part of the business of living that whoever foregoes it has lost all sense of direction or purpose or has become a creature of other people's purposes.

What is true of the small crises in personal experience is also true of the great crises in history. Only those who regard the world of historical events as completely irrational or in Hegelian fashion as a pattern woven by the Cunning of Reason can forswear judging it.

With respect to the Russian Revolution we can nonetheless rule out as illegitimate the negative judgments that stem from three different sources. There is first of all the class of judgments that condemn the October Revolution on grounds of pacifism or opposition to all war and *a fortiori* to civil war, which is usually the most barbarous kind of war. The pacifist is usually on solid empirical ground when he argues that the costs of war are too high to justify any of its alleged benefits. But he overlooks the very real possibility that a revolution may be undertaken to prevent war. To the extent that it succeeds in forestalling a major war without precipitating bloodshed on as great or greater scale in a civil war, a revolution would be pragmatically justified—other values for the moment taken as being equal. If all the Bolsheviks had done was to take Russia out of the First World War (and Kerensky now believes his great mistake was not to do so after the Kornilov revolt), it would be hard to find a reasonable ground of condemnation for October, especially if their separate peace had been upheld in a national referendum and they had abided by the results of the elections for the Constituent Assembly. It is one thing to charge the Bolsheviks with *unintelligent* and *unnecessary* use of violence in consolidating their power, in industrializing the country, and in collectivizing agriculture. It is something else again, and far from legitimate, to condemn them *a priori* for the use of violence, since a similar condemnation would have to be made of any and all their political rivals. It would have required violence, even if not very much, to prevent the Bolsheviks from seizing political power violently.

The second type of negative judgment which must be disallowed comes from those individuals who have suffered an inconsolable loss as a result of the revolution. Most human beings are prepared to count the world well lost for the sake of loved ones. And if among the faces of the dead are the faces of those who have been loved, this is sufficient in the scale of personal values to condemn the social action that precipitated it. We cannot expect detachment in such situations, although we should praise it highly whenever it is found. The survivors of a revolution are not the best judges of its social justification even when they bring authentic testimony of the weight of its human costs. We recognize this in other areas. The grieving parents of a child raped and slain by an ex-convict with an unsavory record are not the best judges of a parole system or of the wisdom of capital punishment. By the same token, the beneficiaries of revolutionary change cannot expect us to judge the events *merely* by the change it produced in their social status without considering other social costs and especially whether this change of status might have been achieved in less costly ways.

The third class of negative judgments about the October Revolution which must be ruled out as *a priori* are those derived from acceptance of the premises of orthodox Marxism. This may appear surprising to those unfamiliar both with doctrine and with the form of the question posed to which we are seeking an answer. The question posed is whether the industrialization and modernization of the Soviet Union which followed the October Revolution required the totalitarian system established by Lenin and Stalin and its various degrees of terror. One increasingly popular answer is that those costs are comparable to those paid in England, Japan, Germany, and other European countries for *their* industrialization and modernization. And since these costs are accepted almost as a matter of course by liberals, it is the veriest sentimentalism to indict the Soviet Union and other Communist countries embarked on the same social program of modernization for moral callousness and the systematic brutalization of man.

The Marxist rejects the whole question out of hand as irrelevant to the problem: when is a revolution justified? For according to him this problem has *actualité* in modern society only when industrialization, and the phenomena integral to it, already have occurred. For Marxists the political revolution which marks the development from capitalism to socialism already presupposes that the industry and technology, without which socialism spells merely the socialization of poverty, have developed. To the extent that the costs of revolution are calculated, in the eyes of the Marxist they refer only to the advisability of the immediate political action of taking and keeping power. The question for a Marxist is *not* whether the costs of revolution are to be weighed against the benefits of industrialization, but only whether the existing forms of industry are to be socialized through due legal process or by the extralegal act of revolution.

This way of posing the problem begs all the important questions. It ignores the fact that the orthodox Marxist dogma, according to which no social order disappears until all the potential productive forces within it have been actualized, has been proved to be a myth. The Bolshevik-Leninists succeeded precisely in doing what the theory of historical materialism declared to be impossible. The industrialization of the country did not prepare the way for the revolution; the revolution prepared the way for industrialization. By jettisoning Marx, the Bolshevik-Leninists gave sense to a question which had no significance on Marxist premises. It is a question that has become focal in every underdeveloped country striving to modernize itself and tempted to adopt totalitarian methods to achieve that modernization. It is a question that did not exist for Marx because for him no underdeveloped country could be ready for socialization. Underdeveloped countries could only become less underdeveloped by following in the path of the more developed which showed them the face of their future.

Leaving aside the context of Marxist presupposition, the problem is a genuine one for any country convinced of the desirability of industrialization and aware of alternative routes and costs by which it may be reached. It is in connection with this problem that the discussion of the costs of the Russian Revolution has acquired an additional interest. Some of those who have been critical of Soviet developments have argued that these costs have been of a dimension which renders any attempt at a rational assessment of this period grotesque. Others who have been critical believe that a rational assessment can be made, and that in the light of the costs of industrialization in other countries, as well as the alternatives open at various times to the Communist leadership of the Soviet Union, these costs were much too high. Both forms of criticism have been rejected on several grounds by writers who claim to be not altogether sympathetic to communism.

It has been argued that the costs of industrialization in the Soviet Union are comparable to the costs of the industrial revolution in Great Britain, Japan, and Germany. The inevitable references to the conditions of the English working class as discussed both in Engels's early work and in Marx's *Capital* are introduced. It has also been argued that the costs of revolution have been unfairly computed insofar as the costs of normalcy and the status-quo, and even of reform and gradualism, have been ignored. If millions have starved under a given régime and are expected to starve if it is preserved, it is morally inadmissible to indict a revolution designed to change the system that permits starvation on the ground that the victims are counted in their hundreds of thousands. Finally, it is pointed out that there is an historic injustice in condemning even the excesses involved in implementing the program of social revolution in the light of the excesses committed in the past in the name of freedom and even of tolerance. It is asserted that there is a legitimate sense in which the red terror is an answer to a white terror. The latter, even if not so intense and dramatic as the former, has endured for a longer time. What are these considerations worth, especially in their bearing on the assessment of the Russian Revolution or of any other revolutionary transformation of an underdeveloped country by violent, dictatorial, and terrorist methods?

II

The first striking but pervasive confusion in computing the costs of social transformation in the Soviet Union is to speak of the terror under Lenin and the horrors of the Stalin régime as if they were necessarily involved in the processes of industrialization and collectivization. The costs of the industrial revolution in England and other countries are measured in terms of crowding, lack of hygiene, disease, malnutrition, physical discomfort, long hours, child labor, and other privations of a similar order. These costs were the object of bitter criticism. A great deal of the data dramatically used by Marx comes from the reports of the official factory inspectors. The alleviation of these hardships of the industrial revolution became the active object of parliamentary and trade union activity. Before Marx's death many of them had disappeared. There were no mass purges, deportations, executions, and forced labor concentration camps for millions.

The costs of the industrial revolution in the Soviet Union were to some extent already paid for in the prerevolutionary régime, whose social welfare legislation was in some respects in advance of some Western countries. But the dislocation of the population after the civil war, the government monopoly of employment and housing, and the absence of free and militant trade unions restored some of the old conditions and introduced others. Nothing comparable to the phenomenon of the *Bezprisorni*, the hordes of wild children, resulting from the deportation of their parents, which I myself observed in Moscow in 1929, developed in other countries as incidental to their industrial revolution.

But all of these costs of the expanded industrialization of the Soviet Union were as nothing compared to the political excesses of the régime. The millions of casualties of the continued civil war waged by the Kremlin against the Russian population had nothing to do with the processes of industrialization *except to hamper them.* The claim made by some Western apologists, including the Webbs, that the organized terror by the régime was necessary for the expansion and functioning of industry—that the Russian workers had to be driven to a modernized economy against their own will—not only violates the assumptions of every democratic variant of Marxism but sets on its head the simple truths about the prerequisites of industry. During the purge years when hundreds of thousands were sent to death camps on grounds of industrial sabotage, it was clear that the régime was equating industrial errors and mistakes with crimes, and particularly crimes against the state—in short, with treason. As subsequent revelations have confirmed, under such circumstances hardly anyone could be found who was willing to take the initiative, to assume the chance and risk of fresh and original judgment. Almost everyone played it safe, marked time while he protected himself behind a barrier of documents that spread the responsibility and shared it with others similarly engaged in a protective avoidance of industrial leadership. If anything can make the political terror worse than it was, it is the fact that it had no industrial rationale whatsoever. It involved the sheer and immense waste of human and material resources.

All one need do to test this is to select some of the specific outrages committed by the Communist high command, especially Stalin, and to inquire what industrial purpose it served. If a victim of the Moscow Trials confesses that he organized a group to sabotage machinery or to put glass or tacks in butter, what possible effects could his punishment have on those producing machines or butter except to limit production by more conscientious effort to avoid furnishing any pretext for the charge of sabotage?

What possible bearing on the costs of industrialization did myriads of crimes have from the Katyn massacre to the murder of Ehrlich and Alter, leaders of the Jewish Bund, as agents of Hitler? Not a single one of the incidents reported by Khrushchev in his speech before the Twentieth Congress of the Communist Party as indicative of the type of "breaches of legality" of which Stalin, in complicity with his opportunistic detractors, was guilty, in any way furthered the industrialization and modernization of the Soviet Union. In no other country of the world was political murder on such a vast scale among the methods by which the industrial revolution was brought to pass.

III

There is something odd about the comparison of the costs of industrialization in the Soviet Union and other Communist countries with the costs of industrialization in Western countries. What is odd about it is that a series of events which no one agency or institution willed is being compared with a series of events which was the result of a deliberate program or policy. Although the events that constituted the industrial revolution in the West were voluntary, their costs were unintended in the sense that no one agency or institution *initiated* the industrial revolution. The costs of industrialization in the West were not any less for not being willed. But the moral responsibility was less: it was limited to the range of actions open to the community when the unintended consequences of the unintended industrial revolution unrolled themselves in time.

The industrialization undertaken in Communist countries was a consequence of deliberate decision. It was willed, together with its costs, in the face of various alternatives ranging from postponement of the execution of an overall plan to plans of a more modest scope and pace of realization. An intelligible choice, aside from its wisdom, is a choice made among viable alternatives in the contemporary spectrum of realistic possibilities. Its justification must be grounded on the differential consequences of pursuing one course of action rather than another. A policy that requires a reign of terror to implement it, if justified, can be grounded only on the evidence that this is the only way to avoid what is sure to be a greater reign of terror. But by no stretch of common sense can it be justified on the ground that some state of affairs like the industrial revolution in England, which was not the outcome of a policy, had led to an equal or greater amount of suffering and evil in the past.

There is a surprising moral callousness in some of the assessments of the costs of the Russian Revolution which stems from a failure to realize that any social action that is willed carries with it a degree of responsibility that cannot be ascribed to actions that are not willed. The question is not one of miscalculating the effects of a specific policy. The error consists in what is being taken as the basis of the calculation. In discussing the calculus of revolutionary violence, Mr. Barrington Moore, Jr., writes:

> . . . one has to weigh the casualties of a reign of terror against those of allowing the prevailing situation to continue, which may include a high death rate due to disease, ignorance—or at the other end of the scale, failure to control the use of

powerful technical devices. (The 40,000 deaths a year in the United States due to automobile accidents come to mind here. What would we think of a political régime that executed 40,000 people a year?) [1]

Presumably, the author believes, in answer to his question, that we would think equally poorly of such a régime. Presumably, if the political régime executed only 20,000 people a year it would be only half as bad as if it executed 40,000, and half as bad as a régime which has 40,000 traffic accidents! Accidents and executions are put on the same moral plane!

But this is absurd. Its absurdity can be brought home by considering the parable of the magic carpet. Suppose we were offered a modern version of a magic carpet which required neither oil nor gas to take us where we will at speeds of our desire. It could be rolled up and stored in a closet, accident-proof and unaffected by technological obsolescence. Compared to it our automobile would be a very crude contraption. All the ingenious inventor wants for it is the lives of 10,000 people. Having read Mr. Moore, he argues: "If you are prepared to pay the price of 40,000 lives for such an inefficient and costly machine as the automobile, why do you hesitate to pay me my resonable price of 10,000 lives? "

The answer is obvious. Even if the accident rate is not likely to diminish in the future, we would not regard ourselves as benefactors of mankind if we paid the asked-for price for the magic carpet, but as murderers, because it would be our deliberate decision that would make us responsible for their deaths. There are many other reasons on which to ground our refusal to cancel out the distinction between accident and murder, but this one is sufficient. The assumption that our action is limited to a choice between accepting the accident figures of the past and deliberately destroying human beings in order to avoid future accidents is, of course, one that is easily challenged. Once we permit assumptions of this grim kind to stand, then the door is open to any

1. Wolf, Moore, Marcuse, *A Critique of Pure Tolerance* (Boston, 1965), p. 76.

fanatical savior or wilful political adventurer to try to introduce a reign of terror in order to eliminate the errors and accidents and evils that are bound up with ordinary human bungling. In the world of historical reality, of course, there is no guarantee that accidents and wars would be less when freedom, and especially freedom of criticism, was sacrificed on the altar of efficiency. Some of the greatest follies of past dictatorships, often fatal to them, could have germinated only in an atmosphere where the cults of efficiency or personality or party infallibility silenced dissent.

IV

There is another point of great importance ignored by those who compare the evils of the industrial revolution in the West with the evils of industrialization in Communist countries. This is the difference which the presence of political democracy makes. It was because of the processes of political democracy that the costs of the industrial revolution in Western countries were exposed, diminished and controlled, and some of its greatest evils abolished. The reports of the English Factory Inspectors, to whose moral integrity Marx paid a tribute his own theory of morality cannot account for, led to the social welfare legislation that brought the excesses of the industrial revolution to a halt. And that they were excesses can hardly be doubted. The reports naturally centered around illustrations that were extreme rather than typical. A free press, a free literature, and an unmuzzled Parliament proclaimed the evidence of industrial inhumanity to the entire world.

The actual costs of the industrial revolution in Communist countries have gone largely unreported, partly because there were no agencies independent of the government to describe them or facilities for distributing eyewitness experiences and partly because the outrage of the political terror dwarfed the sufferings and privations of ordinary life. There were no reporters on the scene to write up what happened to the hands of the child silk-workers in Tashkent or to give an account of the lives of those "lumber workers" in the Northern forests, except escapees and refugees whose revelations were discounted or dismissed as prejudiced judgments reflecting only their personal experiences.

Even if there were some way of making an objective estimate of the sufferings of human beings in the past and in the present, there is something absurd in justifying the evils of today by reference to the allegedly equal or greater sufferings of yesterday. Comparisons of this kind are worse than useless to the extent that they distract us from recognizing that intelligent choice is always between the evils of alternative courses of action in the *present*. Whatever the evils of yesterday were, they are beyond our control.

To make comparisons with evils of the past, and to attempt to guide present action in their light, sometimes leads to an acceptance of the dogma of collective responsibility in its most pernicious form. It is bad enough to hold all members of a group collectively responsible for actions of some individual members of that group unless the members of the group were aware of those actions and in a position to control them or at least condemn them. But it is monstrous, and a source of great and continuous cruelty in world history, to hold a present generation responsible for the sins of omission and commission of its ancestors.

This cruelty is sometimes concealed in the echoes of rhetorical denunciation of the evils of the past. Thus even Mark Twain, misled by some French historians, in speaking of the excesses and cruelties of the "red terror" of the French Revolution declares that they were nothing but a reply to or a consequence of the "white terror" which began with Louis XIV and which continued for a longer period and with a greater loss of life than the terror of 1793–95. But Louis XIV and those of his courtiers who counseled him had long since mouldered in their graves when Marie Antoinette and her entourage, as well as thousands of French workers and peasants, were guillotined.

The very doctrine of collective responsibility and/or guilt is self-defeating in its moral absurdity, since the descendants of the victims of any action justified by the dogma can invoke it to initiate a contemporary massacre. This can only set up a never-ending cycle of hatred and bloodshed. Some Irish terrorists are still revenging themselves upon the English for the crimes of Cromwell. This makes as little sense as would an apologia for Cromwell's excesses on the ground that the Irish are not without guilt since, after all, they wiped out the indigenous population of Ireland.

In an attempt to find a rationale for the appeal to force and violence in the settlement of complex contemporary problems, some American demagogues have argued that the alleged "genocide" of the American Indians by the settlers provides a warrant for direct action against the descendants of the settlers. The latter presumably have no moral standing in history to protest against such revolutionary violence today, since they have benefited from its exercise in the past. Actually, even those who invoke this argument have also benefited by it whether they are white or black or red. Where would they be, what state would they be in if America had not been colonized? There are probably more Indians alive now than when the American continent was discovered. The rights and wrongs of the policies of the settlers cannot be discussed here—the wrongs far outweigh the rights—but these wrongs were compounded on *both* sides by the immoral doctrine of collective responsibility which made one Indian village or white settlement guilty for actions committed by other villages or settlements.

It is this concern for past rights and wrongs which bedevils so much of contemporary history and prevents an intelligent approach and resolution of problems *in the present.* The legacy of the past and the consciousness of the past weighs too heavily on the whole complex of Israeli-Arab problems. And not only in the Near East. One can mention the Far East and Central Europe as well. Wisdom requires an adoption of something like a statute of limitations upon the drive for absolute historic justice, and the substitution of a policy of limited peaceful gains. There is no such thing as absolute justice in this world. The evils Hitler, and not only Hitler, did the Jews in Europe will never be atoned for or repaid, and the only good reason for remembering what he did is to avoid in the present and future the kind of thought and action that led him to his unspeakable barbarities.

From this point of view, the assessment of the Russian October Revolution, as of all other revolutions, must be primarily in terms of the possibility of other alternatives that could have been considered and taken. The misdeeds of Ivan the Terrible and the cowardly weakness of Nicholas II do not mitigate the actions of Lenin, Trotsky, and Stalin. The only justification of their purges and terror, based on the unlimited rule of force, was that there were no other alternatives that could be taken. Although one can establish this for some phases or some actions, by and large every decisive turning point in the history of the Soviet Union—from the forcible dissolution of the Constituent Assembly to the forcible collectivization of agriculture, to the Moscow Trials, the Nazi-Soviet Pact, and the resumption of the cold war against the United States and the West—could have been avoided without any threat to its justifying principles of freedom and welfare. The incontestable fact remains that the working masses of the Western democratic world have secured for themselves a greater freedom and a higher welfare at a far lesser cost than "the blood, sweat, and tears" paid by their Russian brothers for their present lot.

CHAPTER   SEVEN

Evolution in Communism? [1]

Recent events in the Soviet orbit, dating from Stalin's death in March 1953, have posed the problem of what may be termed "liberation by evolution," that is, the gradual transformation, within the ideological tradition of Marxism-Leninism, of the totalitarian system of communism into a libertarian culture in which the strategic political and cultural freedoms of an open society are legally recognized and *in fact* realized.

Obviously it is impossible to predict if or when such a transformation actually will occur. This depends upon many factors outside the scope of the present discussion. The purpose of this

1. This was written in 1957 after the abortive Hungarian and Polish opposition to their local Stalinist regimes as a contribution to a discussion of the possibilities of evolutionary development in Communist countries. The question was: ruling out the possibility of war, what internal ideological developments could lead to a relatively free culture? The dim prospects of any such evolution were extinguished in 1968 when the Soviet Union invaded Czechoslovakia and declared that no satellite Communist state would be permitted to transform itself, however

essay is simply to raise the question of whether such a transformation is *possible*, and if it is, to determine which elements in the traditional Marxist ideology and which in current Communist theory and practice would lend themselves to such a development.

Of course, the ideology of Marxism and Leninism cannot so simply be assimilated to the ideal of human freedom. Yet anyone acquainted with the history of ideas knows that the same generic terms and doctrines have encompassed the widest variations in personality, belief and practice. Communism as a secular religion has often been compared with Christianity, and identified by Toynbee—mistakenly, in my view—with one of its sects. But how vast and full of incompatible elements is the spectrum of beliefs called "Christian." The development of Christianity is largely the history of radical changes, both in doctrine and in practice, by those who claimed to be doing no more than returning to the pure essence of the doctrine.

What is true of religious movements is also true of other fields of human experience. Whether we consider the actual content of the slogans "the return to Christ" or "the return to Kant," the "return to Rome or Jerusalem"—we will find that these returns always mark an original departure in doctrine and movement, sometimes in opposition to the actual intentions of the innovators.

What is for present purposes more to the point, is that even Lenin's slogan "Back to Marx," which he borrowed from Rosa Luxemburg, marked a tremendous revision in what until then had been understood as Marxism. Lenin's extremely voluntaristic *What Is to Be Done?*, although perhaps too simply characterized by some critics as spawned under Bakuninistic and Blanquist influence, was certainly not the Marxism of Kautsky and Plek-

peacefully, into a democratic socialist state. Since then most of the measures Khruschev half-heartedly took to liberalize culture in the Soviet Union have been reversed. Comparable reactionary tendencies are observable in Yugoslavia. Nonetheless if and when any outstanding leader or group were ever moved to liberalize their regimes—an unlikely event in the foreseeable future—the considerations developed in this chapter would be relevant.

hanov. What Lenin did to Marx in the name of Marxism, Stalin in lesser measure did to Lenin in the name of Leninism. This raises the question of the extent to which it will be possible in the current atmosphere of ambiguous devaluation of Stalin to initiate in other Communist countries even more far-reaching departures in Communist theory and practice by "returning to Marx."

1. ROADS AND INROADS

Communist theory and practice hang together more closely than in other ideologies, but it is possible to exaggerate their monolithic unity. Although adherence to a set of doctrines is, and always has been, *de rigueur* for all Communist parties affiliated with the Kremlin, some variations were permitted in the road to power—especially if they proved successful and were not taken in defiance of the Kremlin's orders. Stalin explicitly condemned the American Communist theory of exceptionalism—which simply asserted the banal proposition that each Communist party must take note of the distinctive peculiarities of national political history and geography—primarily in order to replace one faction by a more compliant one. Yet when the opportunity presented itself after the war, he heartily approved of the manner in which the Czech, Yugoslav, and Chinese Communists seized power, even though in one case it involved making the peasantry, not the proletariat, the basis of the Communist movement (China), and in no case did it involve the use of soviets, in whose name the Communist Party had seized power in the Russian October Revolution.

When we turn from the consideration of "different roads to power" to "different roads to socialism" we find the variations in the practices of Communist states just as great, but enormously more significant. Different roads to power are comparable to different roads leading to a city. The city is the same irrespective of the way we reach it. But different roads to socialism, about which the classics of Marxism really say little, may be compared to different ways of building a city. The different ways of building a city result in substantially different cities because the means used are not like the scaffolding torn away when the building is constructed but are like the bricks and mortar, the steel and glass which become intrinsic elements of the finished construction. The architectural metaphor serves admirably to drive home the logic of the means-end relation. If it is true that not pious words but means determine ends, then the adoption of different means of constructing socialism involves the very real likelihood of different kinds of socialism, unwelcome as this may be to the leaders of the Communist movement.

Today under the name of communism and Marxism, we find considerable differences in the theory and practice of "socialist society" in four different regions—the Soviet Union, China, Yugoslavia, and Poland. Some of these differences reflect, so to speak, the historical and geographical landscape and the accidents attendant upon origin. The differences may turn out to be even more momentous because to the extent that theory is a guide to action—and it is often only a rationalization of action—differences in doctrine can lead to the intensification of differences in social, economic, and cultural behavior. Thus, when Mao Tse-tung says that socialism is a garden in which many different theories can be permitted to grow, he has said something of which Khrushchev cannot approve without the danger of letting the "thaw" get out of hand. Even though, as seems likely, Mao Tse-tung will destroy as a "poisonous weed" any doctrine he does not like, his words *may* meanwhile inspire programs of liberalization in other countries—programs hesitant and tentative, to be sure, but still possible bases for further development. Even more significant, when Gomulka proclaims (in his speech to the Eighth Plenum in October 1956) that "the best definition of the social contents inherent in the idea of socialism is contained in the definition that socialism is a social system which abolishes the exploitation and oppression of man by man," and that "what is immutable in socialism can be reduced to the abolition of the exploitation of man by man," these pronouncements constitute a more radical revision of traditional Marxism-Leninism-Stalinism than do Titoism and Maoism. For it follows at once that socialism, according to *this* definition, is absent in the Soviet

Union and the "people's democracies"—since it is not difficult to show that their populations, as they very well know, are exploited and oppressed economically, culturally, and politically. It follows from this definition that even a Jeffersonian community of small landowners who till their own soil and one of individual craftsmen who own their instruments of production, who do not employ others and hence cannot exploit their labor, would have to be called socialistic!

The very conception of "different roads to socialism" gives rise naturally to the notion of "national communism" so much feared by the Kremlin and therefore even by Tito and Gomulka. For "national communism" is just as much a departure from the classic views of international communism as "national socialism" is from the socialism of the *Communist Manifesto*. And in a genuine sense the first expression of national communism is to be found not in Titoism but in Stalinism, under which the concluding line of the *Communist Manifesto* was in practice made to read: "Workers of the World Unite—to Defend the Soviet Union."

2. PROPERTY AND POWER

The question here raised is whether, in terms of the official ideology and in the light of incontestable realities, the totalitarian integument of Communist doctrine can be shattered by uncovering, developing and reinterpreting the rich legacy of ambiguities in the intellectual and social movement of Marxism. The existence of these ambiguities is revealed in the accounts given by former ideological functionaries of Communist parties, such as Wolfgang Leonhard, of the process by which their difficulties developed into cancerous doubts, Stalin gradually rejected in the name of Lenin, and Lenin finally rejected in the name of Marx. I am not raising the question of whether any profound institutional changes can take place by way of doctrine alone, for this seems very improbable. Economic and international political factors are usually more weighty. I am asking only whether in the struggle for freedom any aspect of the Marxist tradition can be refashioned and sharpened into a serviceable weapon in the cause of liberation—a liberation not only from foreign but from domestic despots.

Let us look at some key Marxist concepts in this light.

There are two conceptions of property in Marx and the Marxist tradition, one of which provides the basis not only for the critique of capitalism but even more powerfully for a critique of what passes for "socialist economy."

The first conception of property is substantial and legalistic. It defines property in terms of legal relations where the law is construed as a decree certifying title of ownership. The development of modern economy in the West has limited the usefulness of this concept by separating title from actual economic power. The second conception of property in Marx is functional and sociological. It is bound up with the Marxist ethical critique of capitalism. According to this conception, property is a form of power—the power not so much to use or abuse instruments, goods, and services (since this is always limited) *as the power to exclude others from using them.* Wherever property in land and instruments of production gives power to exclude individuals from the land and from access to instruments of production, it gives definite power over the personal lives of these individuals.

Where legal title to property has been abolished, the continued *de facto* power to deny others access to goods and services, and especially access to the means of livelihood, in effect gives those who wield this power most of the traditional rights of ownership under classical capitalism. This cuts right to the heart of the fiction that collectivized or nationalized industry, since it is no *one* man's individual property, *eo ipso* automatically spells the end of exploitation. Under any system of socialization, where the institutional framework makes it possible for workers to be systematically denied access to the means of production, *i.e.*, to their means of livelihood, it is a mockery to speak of the workers' ownership of the productive plant.

The same applies when it is said that the property in question is *state* property. For this merely pushes the question farther back. To whom does the state belong or who controls the state? If a group is excluded from effective political participation, what sense does it make to say that the state belongs to that group? In the Soviet Union and in most of the satellite countries the juridical change in proprietorship transferred title from capitalists and landlords to the collectivity. But the collectivity is a legal fiction whose actual content, according to sound Marxist principles, depends upon how it is actually organized, how it functions, and the different rôles played by different groups in the actual processes of production. Almost from the very beginning, the Communist rulers had absolute power to deny any peasant or worker access to farm or factory, to decide what should be saved, spent, and how, and to determine the conditions and rewards of work as well as everything else connected with the use of the industrial plant, natural resources, etc.; this power was in no way susceptible to control by those whom its decisions so fatefully affected. In effect, then—and again according to legitimate Marxist categories—the instruments of production belonged to the Communist Party hierarchy, giving it all the traditional privileges of ownership except the right to buy and sell and the right of testamentary disposition. Under such a setup, workers can be and have been exploited more intensively, *i.e.*, more surplus value has been sweated out of them, than under other forms of legal ownership since the early days of the industrial revolution.

Despite the semantic outrage of referring to the Soviet Union or any other Communist economy as a "workers' state" and to the productive plant as "state property," the facts were really not in dispute. When Lenin brutally proclaimed to the Eleventh Congress of the Russian Communist Party, in 1922, "We are the state," he might as well have said, "We are the owners of the economy." [2] Insofar as Marxism is a critique of the economies of exploitation, it can be used more legitimately and with greater devastation in present-day Communist countries than in most of the present-day democratic capitalistic countries of the West.

2. V. I. Lenin, *Selected Works* (Moscow: Foreign Languages Publishing House, 1951), Vol. II, Part 2, p. 644.

It is obvious when we look at the economies which are called socialist in countries like the USSR, China, Yugoslavia, Czechoslovakia, and Poland that there are considerable differences in practice. When we examine Marxist theory we can detect even greater potential differences in meaning—a democratic *or* totalitarian variant. Because Marxism is primarily a critique of capitalism, it provides no specific directives but only general guides as to how to build socialism. These guides are more social, political, and moral than economic in nature, because Marx assumed that the processes of accumulation would have progressed to a point where there would be no problem of having to construct capital goods industries. The ambiguities in Marxism are aggravated by the Bolshevik success in refuting (or revising) Marx in their attempt to lay the foundation of socialist economy by political means in industrially backward areas—something presumably ruled out by historical materialism.

There is no historical necessity in the way in which socialism is to be built, otherwise we could not speak of different paths to socialism. No matter what the objective economic conditions, other factors enter into the situation. Among them an important—though not necessarily decisive—factor may be the way in which traditional Marxist principles are interpreted and developed. The direction in which "socialist" economy and society will develop may depend, for example, in some countries upon how the principle of "workers' control," stressed in pre-revolutionary times by both syndicalists and Marxists alike, is understood.

3. WORKERS' CONTROL

There has always been an ambiguity about the nature and function of "workers control" in socialist theory. The utopian theory of Marxism, according to which some day the state will disappear, made the organs of workers' control on the level of the factory the administrative unit of society which would function without coercion by the voluntary cooperation of an historically new species of man. For purposes of revolutionary struggle, "workers' control" was stressed as a means of heightening the pitch of a revolutionary situation. All tendencies within the socialist movement declared themselves for workers' control but few seemed clear about what it meant. All agreed, however, that workers' control was something exercised for the workers by a political group monopolizing power or, on the other hand, that it was something exercised by the workers themselves, following whatever leadership they chose.

In the early days of Bolshevism, on the eve of taking power and shortly thereafter, the Communists stressed in the most emphatic way the desirability of workers' control in every factory. Before long, however, the control of the Communist Party asserted itself so forcibly that the phrase "workers' control" became a transparent piece of terminological hypocrisy. Lenin himself led the fight against "the workers' opposition," a group in the Communist Party which took the earlier agitational and propaganda slogans seriously, as an anarcho-syndicalist deviation.

The Yugoslav Communists who speak today of "workers' control" imply that Stalin revised Lenin's position on this question while they are following the Leninist pattern. This is a misleading over-simplification. It results from confusing decentralization of industry and planning, which permits greater autonomy to the individual plant, and which the Yugoslavs have carried out, with independent workers' control in the decentralized plants, a control which the Yugoslavs only promise. And if they follow Lenin, they will never deliver on their promises. For even in the most liberal period of Soviet economic life, Lenin insisted that in the interests of rapid construction of large-scale industry "it is absolutely essential that all authority in the factories should be in the hands of the management." [3]

It need not be pointed out that management in the so-called capitalist countries has much less power over workers than management in socialist societies, while trade unions in the former enjoy far more control in actual practice than do workers' councils in theory. Lenin recognized the limited role of the trade

3. Ibid., p. 648.

unions in correcting "the excesses and blunders resulting from the bureaucratic distortions of the state apparatus," [4] and this stand was of tremendous importance in that it provided a justification of the right of the workers to strike in the so-called "workers' state"—to strike in all state enterprises. That this right was hedged in by all sorts of restrictions and qualifications, that it was more honored in the breach than in the observance, does not detract from its significance and its use as a rallying cry in the present and future. It was this truncated right which was lost under Stalin and in all Stalinist régimes. It was a grievous loss, for the abolition of the right to strike means in effect the existence of a system of forced labor with all its multiform kinds of exploitation and aggression.

In Yugoslavia today a very limited kind of workers' control through workers' councils operates in conjunction with a largely decentralized industry planned to meet the market needs of local regions. This system came into existence more because of economic necessity than because of political virtue.[5] And however limited the control, Soviet critical reaction has not been the less severe. What is interesting is the theoretical justification of these institutional deviations from the Soviet pattern expressed by Kardelj and other Yugoslav Communists in grandiose ideological terms.

Edward Kardelj, the leading Yugoslav theoretician, in his speech of December 7, 1956, before the Yugoslav People's Assembly, frankly accepts the theory of exceptionalism, but he claims Yugoslavia to be exceptional in being most faithful to the conceptions of Marx and Lenin.[6] The development of socialist industry, he asserts, must take place concomitantly with a progressive democratization of all social relations. "Human beings

4. Ibid., p. 646.
5. For a discussion of the origin and functioning of Yugoslav workers' councils, see E. Halperin, "Is Russia Going Titoist?" *Problems of Communism,* September-October 1956.
6. *Borba,* Belgrade, issues of December 8 and 9, 1956. A German translation appears in *Ost-Probleme,* Bonn, March 8, 1957.

should not in a socialist system become the slaves of a state machine in the name of any higher interests whatsoever." To achieve independence from the state machine, the social and economic position of the worker must be secured by strengthening the democratic control of the workers in the factories and in their communities. Only in this way can the state wither away in Marxist fashion instead of becoming an all-devouring Frankenstein monster.

For Kardelj, the key issue is to avoid the bureaucratization of socialism. This is inevitable, according to him, unless there is "active, direct and increasing participation of the producers in the direction of state and industry." Those who, like the Soviet Russian apologists, interpret this as undermining the dictatorship of the proletariat are indifferent, he says, to the fact that "the dictatorship which they characterize as 'proletarian' can be anything else in the world except proletarian, precisely because it is not filled with a democratic content."

The motivation of this theoretical departure from Stalinism, the extent to which it is actually embodied in Yugoslavian practice, and the political uses to which it is put are irrelevant issues in this discussion. Tito, for example, although professing to blame the Hungarian Stalinists for refusing to follow the lead of the Hungarian workers, inconsistently supports the Soviet suppression of their councils. Considerations of *Staatsraeson* obviously determine the official reactions. But once launched upon the world, ideas, although not independent, may develop a life and an influence of their own. It is the direction of the Yugoslav heresy which is important—not only its nationalism, its claim that all Communist states are equal in dignity in a common cause, but its emphasis upon a conception of workers' democracy which *might* turn out, once material conditions are favorable to it, to be an ideological hydrogen bomb.

The most significant thing about the ideological position of the Yugoslav régime is that, if it is taken seriously, it spells the end of the political monopoly of the Communist Party. A "workers' control" which is in turn controlled by a party faction with the secret police behind it collapses of itself—it dies of boredom and disinterest, like the Russian soviets and local trade unions. Some semblance of power, no matter how fearfully guarded by the party watchdogs, must be given to the workers. This power in time either grows from what it feeds upon or becomes atrophied. It is the natural form through which, where it exists, opposition can be "legitimately" channeled.

That Kardelj, for all his lack of clarity, his inconsistencies and backtracking, is on the right road, from the point of view of intensifying the struggle between the democratic and totalitarian potentials of socialism, is evidenced in part by the character of the embittered reply made to him by a Soviet writer, by name Rumiantsev, in the chief theoretical organ of the CPSU, *Kommunist* November 18, 1957. As Rumiantsev recognizes, Kardelj in effect is charging that the Soviet Union is a new form of class state in which, although the legal title of ownership has been transferred to the workers and peasants, the latter are in fact being exploited by the state apparatus, its functionaries and pensioners, and that consequently the class struggle is still being waged in the alleged socialist society, not between nonexistent capitalists and landlords, on the one hand, and the toiling masses, on the other hand, but between the latter and the new class of Communist officials, managers, and their retainers. Rumiantsev attempts to toss this off with a laugh as a *reductio ad absurdum* too ridiculous to require refutation—and then attempts one anyhow. If the workers by definition own the instruments of production, he asks, how can they be said to exploit themselves? He is oblivious to the possibility that there may be something wrong with his definition, and that to resort to it in the face of the glaring facts of political and economic inequality is merely to fall back on a question-begging definition.

Gomulka's discussion of the function of the workers' councils is something else. He sees their development as one of the three main elements in the "Polish road to socialism." In his speech before the Ninth Plenum of the Party Central Committee (May 1957) Gomulka outlines seven chief tasks of the workers' councils which if taken literally would make them masters of the factories and, therefore, of all of industry. He warns against regarding the councils "as organs of political power," but at the same time is fearful lest the political leadership of the Communist Party fractions be displaced. He wants workers' councils to be autonomous and at the same time seeks (in vain, it seems to this observer) to limit their functions to purely industrial issues. Because of the nature of the Polish economy, he is undoubtedly sensible in cautioning the workers' councils against a too near-sighted and too decentralized view of the needs of production. But if they are actually given the right to make mistakes in these matters, they are being given very real powers indeed. And he is quite forthright in acknowledging the right of the workers to strike, although he does not regard this as the best way of rectifying grievances.

Gomulka's ambiguous feelings about increasing the power of the workers' councils stem from his fear that they may work free of the influence of the Communist Party, whose leading position he regards as essential to the building of socialism. As if aware that all the elements which define the Polish "road to socialism," if given their head, may carry Poland out of the Kremlin's orbit, as if to reassure the uneasy Russians, he delivers even stronger attacks against those he calls revisionists, and who really are democratic socialists of the Western type than against the Stalinist dogmatists and conservatives. Gomulka taxes the revisionists with believing that socialism can be built without any class struggles. The accuracy of this characterization can be regarded as very questionable. The difficulty is to know what kind of class struggle can be waged after the capitalists and great landholders disappear. Struggles still go on, but if they are class struggles they are of the kind that Kardelj describes—between the toilers, the workers and peasants, and the state and party officialdom. More accurate is Gomulka's charge against the revisionists that they are opposed to the dictatorship of the Communist Party. This is true. But it is also true of Marx.

4. THE DICTATORSHIP OF THE PROLETARIAT

It is perfectly clear by now that "the dictatorship of the proletariat" as interpreted by Lenin and Stalin is substantially the dictatorship of the Communist Party over the proletariat and all other social groups. That this represented a radical departure from the meaning Marx gave to the rarely used phrase in his writings can scarcely be doubted. Marx and Engels pointed to the Paris Commune as illustrating what they meant by "the dictatorship of the proletariat." The Commune was one in which several different political groups or parties participated, and in which the followers of Marx were a tiny minority. In the *Communist Manifesto,* Marx had said that Communists "do not constitute themselves a special party over and above other working-class parties." Before he died Engels claimed that the dictatorship of the proletariat could be realized within the framework of a parliamentary democracy.

The "dictatorship of the proletariat" in the corpus of Marx's writings is not primarily a political concept but a social one. The opposite of the phrase is the "dictatorship of the bourgeoisie." Since, according to Marxist theory, a "dictatorship of the bourgeoisie" is compatible with many political forms ranging from monarchy, Bonapartism, and other expressions of dictatorship through an entire spectrum of parliamentary democracies, it is clear that the economic and social content of the dictatorship of the proletariat, in theory at least, is compatible with the existence of one or more political parties and with political structures ranging from dictatorship to democracy.

Socialism declares itself opposed to all forms of exploitation and oppression, to any kind of class society in which coercion, open or veiled, is present. Marxism recognizes, however, that every dictatorship, even when it is considered progressive with respect to expanding the forces of production, is a form of oppression. If one takes Marx literally, the elimination of all coercion from human relations, the complete withering away of the state, is a Utopian ideal—but pragmatically it can be interpreted as an *ideal* of diminishing coercion and exploitation of human society.

If one reads Marx in the light of modern sociology, one understands that classes will continue to exist, class struggles will continue to be fought, even though the role of classes will differ when different social relationships are introduced. A strike under socialism is a struggle even though some terminological purist may balk at calling it an expression of class struggle. In either case, or in either interpretation, there is an immanent dynamic toward greater democracy in the Marxist ideal, toward a permanent revolution against whatever series of evils the social process generates.

Marxism is a philosophically primitive system, but it never identified the social system of the future with the end or process of history itself in the way in which Hegel identified the Absolute Idea or the Way of God with some features of the Prussian state. Because communism is a disease of idealism, if only it does not harden into the fanaticism which makes a fetish of the instrument—the instrument of the Communist Party—it may prove to be susceptible to the virus of political liberalism.

Historically, in Russia the Bolsheviks took power with the Left Social Revolutionists as a cover. They permitted other socialist parties to exist for a time in a tortured way. On paper, but only on paper, bourgeois parties could exist. On occasion, in order to bring home the distinction between the dictatorship as a social and economic instrument and dictatorship as a political weapon, Lenin maintained that it is "quite conceivable that the dictatorship of the proletariat may suppress the bourgeoisie at every step without disenfranchising the bourgeoisie; . . . while it is essential to suppress the bourgeoisie as an [economic] class, it is not essential to deprive them of their suffrage and equality." [7]

What this meant with respect to bourgeois parties, and later all other parties, is that if they agreed not to oppose the program of the Communist Party in any way whatsoever after the latter seized power, they would be permitted to exist, although it is not clear what the point of their political existence would be. With respect to other working-class or socialist parties, Bolshevik fanaticism led to the same result. For the Bolsheviks believed that any serious disagreement with the Communist Party by *definition* had counterrevolutionary objective consequences.

The Communist régimes in the Soviet Union, Yugoslavia, and some of the satellites are unabashed one-party dictatorships. In

7. Lenin, op. cit., p. 169.

China, Poland, Czechoslovakia, and East Germany the Communist Party rules with the device of spurious coalition parties. The existence of these parties is in part the price the Communists pay for their hypocritical pretenses to democracy, but under a favorable conjunction of circumstances, especially in the satellite countries, where aspirations to national independence are strong, conditions may compel them to pay a higher and higher price in granting political rights to other parties.

In this connection, of course, Gomulka's régime is unique. Since he is trying to do the impossible, to keep the dictatorship of the Communist Party and to encourage the independence of the Peasant Party, Gomulka must fail. But he and those who support him can fail in two ways—fail in encouraging other political parties or fail in being good Bolsheviks. In the view of democracy, the latter failure is of course preferable. When Gomulka proclaims, "It is a poor idea to maintain that only Communists can build socialism, that only peoples holding materialistic social views can do so," he should certainly be applauded, and even more so when he characterizes socialism in ethical terms as "the system of social justice."

When with this conception of socialism he urges "competition between our party and the Peasant Party as well as between all those in favor of strengthening the socialist system," he has taken a longer stride away from the Leninist and Stalinist conception of the political dictatorship of the minority Communist Party than he is aware of. When he also calls for the revitalization of the *Sejm* (parliament), its assumption of greater legislative tasks, and control over the work of the government and state organs, when he proclaims that "in my opinion Sejm control over the executive organs of state power should be exercised by an institution subordinated directly to the Sejm and not to the government as has been the case up to now," who can fail to hear with his inner ear, despite the uncertain words and reluctant tone, the voice of parliamentary democracy? [8] If only Gomulka really meant what he said!

Many of the moves away from total or extreme collectivization

8. All quotations from Gomulka's speech before the Eighth Party Plenum, October 20, 1956.

and the more conspicuous forms of party terrorism in Communist countries are motivated today by considerations of political strategy. They may be reversed overnight. Nonetheless they are all points of ideological and institutional infection in the Communist body politic. *If* these heretical germs get into the Marxist blood stream, they may produce fevers in the short run and languors in the long run, resulting in profound organic changes in the system.

Recent events behind the Iron Curtain have shown that socialist humanism, despite its exaggerated claims to novelty, has a greater continuity with traditional forms of Western humanism than both its official spokesmen and its hostile Western critics imagined. The new Soviet men, the new Communist men with new criteria of the true, the good, and the beautiful, of whom Stalin boasted and whom the West feared, are a myth. Despite the principle of "partiinost" or partisanship in dialectical materialism, Communist intellectuals, whether scientists or historians, know the difference between truth and lies, facts and fiction.

Things can never be the same again after the fumbling attempt of Stalin's accomplices to destalinize, after the Polish declaration of independence, after the heroic spectacle of the Hungarian nation in arms against the Soviet occupation. Even without war or foreign intervention, even without violent revolution, the intellectual élite of all Communist countries will produce in each generation, and in every social group or class, critical spirits nurtured on the ideals of freedom expressed in the classics of Marxism as well as in those of the humanist tradition, well aware of the discrepancies between Soviet promise and performance, and of the Communists' betrayal of almost all the liberating ideals which inspired the socialist movement. Their presence, whether articulate or eloquently silent, will constitute a permanent opposition to cultural and political tyranny.

Given the history of the twentieth century, once a "thaw" sets in in any aspect of culture in a totalitarian society, it has a tendency to extend not only into neighboring cultural fields but to take political form as well. The chagrin and rage of the Soviet Communist leaders at the Hungarian and Polish intellectuals is due to their realization that the heretical cultural ideas of these men will prove in the long run politically infectious. The logic of the situation is such that every concession made to artists, writers, or scientists carries with it consequences that call for further concessions, which when denied put into question the sincerity and genuineness of the first concession. History often shows that changes are more rapid when things begin to get a bit better. Despair paralyzes the will to action, especially risky action; hope inspires it. We can be sure that the slight taste of the freedoms which the peoples of the satellite countries have been given, after being deprived of them for almost a decade, will generate an enormous appetite for more—and perhaps this hunger will spread to the Soviet Union itself.

CHAPTER EIGHT

Rethinking the Bolshevik Revolution

The tides of interest in the past often depend on events in the present. The conjunction of the diplomacy of détente and the recent fruits of scholarship has brought to the fore issues that were the obsessive concern of Communist political factions a half-century ago. The publication of three massive biographies of Stalin within the space of a year and the first comprehensive political biography of Bukharin together with the world clamor over the revelations of Solzhenitsyn's *The Gulag Archipelago* have made the nature, development, and justification of the Russian October Revolution a topical question once more. Almost all considered reviews of these works raise the problem of the relation between the thought of Lenin and Stalin, and of both to the thought of Marx.

Were the Bolsheviks the true heirs of Marx? Was the success of their seizure of power an historical fluke or a rational move under the circumstances? Was the fateful development of the Soviet

Union implicit in a situation resulting from the failure of revolutionary movements in Western Europe to materialize, whose expected outbreak was among the premises of the October action? Or was the transformation of a technologically backward, agricultural country into one of the most highly industrialized the consequence not of the historic or economic logic of the situation but chiefly of the genius—evil or not—of a great leader? Must we acknowledge the presence not merely of one event-making personality in history, Lenin, whose heroic and indispensable role in forging and preserving the October Revolution even a doctrinaire Marxist like Trotsky was ultimately compelled to admit, but of two—Stalin as well? However we assess Stalin's personal capacities, whether as a "grey blur" (Sukhanov) that insidiously spread until it absorbed the whole political landscape or as a "marvellous Georgian" but intolerably "rude" party secretary (Lenin) or as "a mediocrity" (Trotsky) fashioned by the bureaucratic machine to serve its interests in the ebb tide of the revolutionary spirit or ". . . a genius, no less so, perhaps, than a Mozart or Einstein . . . in his own highly specialized and destructive field . . ." (Hingley)— was Stalin Lenin's genuine political disciple, as he himself always professed to be, or his historical nemesis who destroyed his legacy and transformed Lenin's vision into a nightmare? And regardless of the personal differences between them, their cultural and intellectual disparities, was the terror that Stalin unleashed his own creative improvement on Lenin or was he applying to a new situation the lessons he learned from his master?

Any one of the biographies of Stalin referred to above (by Tucker, Ulam, and Hingley) can serve as a point of departure in considering these questions. But the biography of Stalin's most formidable victim (after Trotsky), Nicolai Ivanovitch Bukharin,[1] by Professor Stephen F. Cohen, seems to me to provide the freshest challenge to those who wish to reconsider the tangled issues. And this for several reasons. First, to those who are not professional students of Soviet and Communist affairs it contains more new information about Bukharin, his rise and fall, than is

1. Stephen F. Cohen, *Bukharin and the Bolshevik Revolution. A Political Biography, 1888-1938* (New York: Knopf, [date]).

available in the other studies in the context of a fascinating, eminently readable account of the Russian Revolution. Second, it is written with a sympathy and compassion for Bukharin as a human being that transcends the author's political differences with him. The human and personal costs of revolutionary statecraft are never glossed over. Third, and most important, it takes a clear stand on all the basic questions posed above.

According to Cohen it is Bukharin not Stalin who is the true interpreter of Lenin's legacy. And of special significance is the nature of that legacy. It is not to be found in the corpus of Lenin's prolific writings nor in the great deeds of his life work but in the last few articles he penned or dictated as he lay ill and dying. In them and in conversations with Bukharin, who was very close to him after he was stricken, Lenin disclosed his final views of the way to the ultimate socialist goal. Appalled by the growing careerism and bureaucratization of Soviet society, he reversed the grand strategy that had brought the Communist Party despite its triumphs to a despairing impasse. He outlined a way of growing into socialism not by class war, however moderated, between workers and peasants but by class cooperation, not by planned rapid industrialization but by gradual, balanced growth in which the needs of the consumers, if not central, would always be regarded as important, not by abandoning the New Economic Policy, originally introduced as a breathing spell and which appeared to "infantile Leftists" to be getting out of hand, but by expanding and transforming it. All this was to be accomplished in a spirit of civil peace, without any resort to the "extra-ordinary measures," a euphemism for brutal coercion, of war communism, or to any extralegal measures. In words more recently current, Lenin had become a partisan of "socialism with a human face."

Abandoning his own earlier views about the economics of the transition period, Bukharin became a convert of the revised gospel to which he was emotionally predisposed by his genial, sunny nature. He preached it strongly first against Trotsky and then falteringly against Stalin, who slyly used him to destroy Trotsky and then defamed and murdered him. On this reading of the development of the Russian Revolution, both Trotsky and Stalin departed from the position that Lenin embraced with characteristic fervor before he died, and for which Bukharin was martyred.

The linchpin therefore of Professor Cohen's fascinating and brilliant interpretation of Bukharin's last stand for his principles and his life in his contention that Lenin himself had experienced a profound change of heart shortly before he died. He rethought his "first principles" not with respect to the socialist ideal or Marx's basic theories but as they bore on the strategy of practice in approaching them. Presumably he was moved to do this by frustration over the conditions of the country—five years after the heaven-storming events of October, by fear of deteriorating developments for the future, and by deep dissatisfaction with the character of the Party he had forged. No longer sanguine about the imminent revolutionary outbursts from the West, he espoused for the long haul, not for the short run, domestic policies more peaceful, conciliatory and humane than any previously envisaged. In this he carried Bukarin with him, the leading theoretician of the Party until then noted for his left-leaning tendencies and doctrinal intransigence.

Needless to say this is a very appealing thesis to those who regard Trotsky as a revolutionary firebrand whose program would have imperiled the survival of the Soviet Union and to those who see in Stalin not the legitimate executor of the social and political testament of October but its bloody-handed executioner. It has also recommended itself to some distinguished scholars of Russian history who have no political ax to grind.

Before considering this central issue together with the related question of the responsibility for the role of terror in the Soviet Union, something should be said of the personality of Bukharin as it emerges from Professor Cohen's masterly study. Bukharin seems to have been the most likeable and attractive individual among the Bolshevik leaders, more interested in finding common ground in conflicting positions, much more aware of currents of thought in the non-Marxist world, friendlier to the multihued variety of socialists with whom he disagreed (he was the only outstanding Communist whom the Menshevik leaders in exile spoke of without bitterness), and in general much more humane than the dour and morose Stalin, the envious Zinoviev, the intellectually arrogant Trotsky, and the fanatically intolerant but personally modest Lenin. Doctrinally and organizationally, Bukharin was no less a Bolshevik than any of them until Lenin's death. In the turmoil of events, doctrine is more likely to have a greater significance than mere nuances of personality except where we are dealing with a truly forceful personality who can rise above customary doctrine in the name of a higher sanctifying ideology. Bukharin was not a forceful personality on the plane of Lenin, Trotsky, or Stalin. With respect to his subsequent differences with Trotsky and Stalin, a democratic socialist would certainly have preferred his social and political line to triumph rather than theirs. But with all their differences, he still shared more in common with them than with any of their political opponents. He was no democrat. He was just as much committed to the fateful dogma that the dictatorship of the proletariat was substantially the dictatorship of the Communist Party as the other leading spokesmen for October. He was an apologist not only for the seizure of power and the forcible dissolution of the Constituent Assembly but for the excesses of war communism. "Civil war," he proclaimed, "lays bare the true physiognomy of society. . . ." He justifies "proletarian coercion in all its forms, beginning with shooting and ending with labor conscription," as a method of creating a new communist man. His views on the role of coercion in his *The Economics of the Transition Period* were approved by Lenin with fervor. Cohen for all his sympathetic approach offers no holding brief for Bukharin. He is scrupulously fair in presenting evidence that can lead to judgments less generous and tempered than his own. He cites some gruesome utterances of Bukharin endorsing Bolshevik violence, not only about the necessity of breaking eggs to make an omelette which anticipated Goering's *bon mot* in the 1930s when another type of omelette was being prepared, but of "cracking skulls." He referred to intellectually handicapped persons as "humpbacks" and says of them that they "are only cured by death." Cohen hastens to add, however, that "Personally Bukharin had little taste for cracking skulls," which apparently is true. He left that to others. There is some excuse for a surgeon who can't stand the sight of blood to lecture on radical surgery to help his brethren. With the use of terror as a political instrument the moral case is different. It is arguable that a terrorist who does not offer an apologia for terror acts on his party's program as a simple soldier is less culpable than an eloquent apologist for terrorism who hasn't the nerve or guts to pull the trigger himself. He is certainly less dangerous in a world in which ideas and even loaded words have consequences.

What cannot be gainsaid is Bukharin's personal popularity among his party comrades and nonparty intellectuals within the Soviet Union. Lenin was the father figure of the party and was glorified before he was deified. No significant comparison can be made between them. Lenin's attitude to Bukharin was avuncular; he overlooked a certain softness in him. He was not impressed by Bukharin's erudition. What he regarded as a dialectical weakness in his Marxism was Bukharin's sensitiveness to argument and evidence in controversy with opponents. There is no doubt that he could live more easily with ambiguity than any of his fellows. And *up to a point* he could accept dissent within the party without appealing to administrative measures.

The sticking point for Bukharin was any serious threat to party-unity and the danger of a split. Where he believed that the unity of the party was at stake he countenanced stern disciplinary measures against dissenters. At the same time he silently ac- quiesced to the most outrageous abuses by the party leadership whenever he feared that public opposition would endanger the unity of the party and precipitate a split. This explains why long before the systematic bloodletting began he made no public pro- test against the cruel and unjust treatment of Trotsky and his followers at the hands of Stalin, the degrading details of which could not have been unfamiliar to him. He made a fetish of party unity in a way that neither Lenin nor Trotsky ever did. Although it was later argued that it was awareness of Hitler's planned crusade against the Soviet Union that produced Bukharin's fear of a party split, his behavior was no different long before Hitler acceded to power.

The pattern of Bukharin's subsequent behavior is simply unintelligible without reference to the controlling influence of his fetishism of party unity. Why, for example, after characterizing Stalin in secret talks with others whom Stalin had already victimized as a "Ghengis Khan" and "a devil," did Bukharin return from the safety of Western Europe to the Soviet Union? A fierce attack on him in *Pravda* had already signaled his fate. André Malraux reports that at that time Bukharin confided to him his certainty that "now he [Stalin] is going to kill me." His young wife in exchange for whose life, it is alleged, he later confessed was at that time with him abroad. Bukharin could hardly have believed that his other relatives would escape Stalin's devilish vindictiveness once he became an official victim.

Singularly unconvincing therefore is Professor Cohen's explanation, shared by other eminent scholars, of why Bukharin confessed. Although he apparently was not tortured as were some of the other Moscow defendants, he acted out his assigned role to save the lives of his wife and child. Then having agreed to this bargain, he skillfully makes nonsense of his own confession and testimony. By the use of Aesopian language, he refutes the criminal charges against him and indicts Stalin for destroying the party of Lenin.

The implausibility of this interpretation stares us in the face. If Bukharin believed only a fraction to be true of what he said to Kamenev, Nicolaevsky, Dan, and others, why should he have trusted Stalin to fulfill his promise? There is no evidence that the dependents of those who did not confess suffered a worse fate than those who did. The same threats were probably made to all. And if Bukharin really banked on Stalin's or Vyshinsky's promise, why should he then have attempted to deceive them by his testimony? After all, he was dealing with two of the most pathologically suspicious minds in Russia, with individuals who were capable of suspecting a person of being a Trotskyist on the ground that his denunciations of Trotsky quoted him at too great a length. Stalin and Vyshinsky may have been "devils": they were no fools. They knew all about Aesopian language. People were being jailed and executed for its use. Their very awareness that they were concocting an elaborate and fantastic hoax, the fabricated details of which had in part been exposed from afar by Trotsky, would have made them extremely distrustful of Aesopian contraband in prearranged texts of confession. If the lives of his wife and child meant so much to Bukharin why would he risk them by a macabre game that would furnish Stalin with a pretext to destroy them? As if Stalin required one!

Nor is it clear that Bukharin was secretly communicating to the world his innocence and Stalin's guilt any more than Radek did in some of the passages and asides of his confession. Had Bukharin acted like Krestinsky who recanted his confession and then recanted his recantation after the court in angry confusion adjourned to permit him to be "requestioned," much more dramatic and effective doubts would have been generated. In a culture in which the alleged "objective consequences" of a person's words or ideas or acts, if considered harmful to the State or Party, regardless of his subjective intentions, were often evidence of a capital crime, Bukharin's confession served Stalin's purpose more than adequately. "I plead guilty," he declared, "to the sum total of crimes committed by this counterrevolutionary organization, irrespective of whether or not I knew of, whether or not I took a direct part in, any particular act." Cohen maintains that "the second half of this statement makes nonsense of the first." I fail to see this—especially if the emphasis falls on the word "particular." Even by the canons of Western jurisprudence, a person who organized and inspired a group of bank robbers could truthfully say this. One can also participate in a conspiracy without having knowledge of, or participating in, any particular actions. The chief principals may not have been informed of them before their occurrence.

One can only guess at why Bukharin said some things and not others. It is to his great moral credit that he refused to plead guilty to the degrading specific charges of treason and attempted murder. He knew that the eyes of the world were on him, and so did Stalin. In a sense had he confessed in a spiritless way to the entire litany of absurd charges the trial would have appeared even more of an extravaganza than it did. The most rabid of the American apologists for Stalin and the Moscow Trials, like Malcolm Cowley, seized on the fact that the defendants did not confess to everything and that judgment might therefore be suspended concerning their guilt on these points, as evidence of the authenticity of the trials.

Why, then, did Bukharin confess? Cohen, as well as others, dismisses as sheer fantasy Arthur Koestler's literary reconstruction of Bukharin's psychology. Despite his hatred of Stalin, Bukharin confessed out of a desire to perform a last act of loyalty and piety to the Party. Although one cannot claim verisimilitude for the details of *Darkness at Noon,* Koestler's imaginative insight into Bukharin's motives seems to me to penetrate more closely to the truth than any other hypothesis. And it is Professor Cohen's impressive scholarship that provides ample evidence for it although he himself does not recognize the cumulative weight of the facts he cites.

Bukharin confessed for the same reason that he chose to remain publicly silent from the very day he suspected the existence of Stalin's murderous plans against his opponents within the party; for the same reason that led him, after his suspicions were confirmed, to charge the left-opposition with complicity in Kirov's assassination; for the same reason that accounts, as we have seen, for his sacrificial return to doom from the comparative safety of Western Europe—to wit, his fetishism of party unity, his fear that the Soviet régime would be imperiled by public factional strife in the party hierarchy.

Step by fateful step, Bukharin's fetishism of the party and the necessity in his own mind of preserving the public appearance of unity, led to his own undoing. In 1926 he pleaded with the left-opposition: "Hold to your own principles, defend your opinions, speak at party meetings . . . but do not dare form a faction. Argue but after decisions are made, submit!" Why? Because "if we legalize such a faction inside our party, then we legalize another party and . . . in reality . . . slip from the line of the proletarian dictatorship." Later in the same year, to Stalin's plaudits and admiring comments, he changes tune. He no longer wants the left to hew to their own principles. He demands repentance: "Come before the party with head bowed and say: Forgive us for we have

sinned against the spirit and letter and very essence of Leninism. . . . Say it, say it honestly: Trotsky was wrong. . . ."
By November 1928 despite the evidence that his position had considerable support within the party and even more outside, as apprehension began to spread among the peasantry, instead of carrying the fight against Stalin to the party at large and the country, Bukharin resorts "to the preposterous manoeuvre" (the phrase is Cohen's) of personally drafting the resolution of the Central Committee Plenum concerning "right deviationism" —and this, after Stalin had stigmatized Bukharin as a "rightist." Why?

By January 1933 Bukharin, who was personally friendly with Yagoda, had certainly learned of the excesses of Stalin's enforced collectivization program whose horrors surpassed his wildest fears. Nonetheless he repents once more before the Central Committee. He speaks of *his* guilt, not of Stalin's, and characterizes the stand he took in 1928–29 which events had clearly vindicated as "absolutely incorrect." Why? Not out of personal fear but once more out of exaggerated concern for "party unity, party discipline"—a refrain that reappears again and again in moments of party crisis. Through thick and thin Bukharin adheres consistently to this principle of Party supremacy even after the party became the pliant creature of Stalin's will. Although in a position to deploy a not inconsiderable intellectual following strategically placed in communication and publication centers, Bukharin refuses to do battle. He speaks up only in camera, and allows Stalin to keep the struggle confined to the topmost echelons until, as Smilga phrased it, Bukharin could be "strangled behind the back of the party."

Cohen cites the evidence that Bukharin was tempted to speak out, that he was aware of the agonizing predicament of risking a party split or abetting by his passivity Stalin's criminal policies. His courage cannot be impugned; his political leadership and judgment can. Undoubtedly his fetishism of party unity was strengthened by the series of crises that consistently seemed to threaten at key junctures the stability of the régime—peasant revolts, famine; Western intervention, Hitler's accession to power. Rationalizations for showing a united face to the enemy, even when it seemed to Bukharin that Stalin's policies were helping the enemy, were easy to find. Cohen at one point expresses the view that after 1925 Bukharin "succumbed to the potential logic of single party philosophy." Perhaps, but temperament in his case played a more decisive role than political logic. In comparable situations neither Lenin nor Trotsky, who subscribed just as much to the logic of a single party philosophy, would have been deterred by it from public opposition come what may. For with unshakeable confidence they assumed that where they stood, there stood the true party.

I

In the long perspective, more important than Bukharin's tragic fate is the significance of his social and economic program. It goes without saying that no matter what program was offered to or adopted by the Communist Party after Lenin's death, it would be fathered on him. All the contestants for the succession ransacked his writings for quotations to buttress their positions. Bukharin was not a contestant for power. He undoubtedly believed that his proposals were perfectly compatible with Lenin's final views. Nonetheless it seems to me an historic injustice to him to attribute, as Cohen and other scholars do, his conception of growing into socialism to Lenin, to underestimate his own contribution in going beyond Lenin in outlining a more moderate and humane view of Soviet development. Natural piety as well as political safety would have prevented him from making any such claim even if he believed this to be true. Just as in the theological disputes of the Middle Ages contenders for the mantle of orthodoxy sought to clinch the invalidity of opposing views by showing that they led to atheism, so in the party disputes of the time it was sufficient for any position to be plausibly charged with having anti-Leninist or even non-Leninist implications, to rule it out of consideration.

The New Economic Policy was introduced by Lenin as a strategic retreat. It was adopted after the bankruptcy of War Communism, the Kronstadt revolt and a series of peasant uprisings. The policy was never intended to be permanent; it was to provide a breathing spell to an exhausted country. Future developments were not spelled out clearly. The new policy was designed to give the party freedom of action to move toward its original goals at a pace and in a manner dependent upon the international situation, possible revolutionary developments abroad, so long delayed, and domestic recovery. It was Bukharin's great merit that *he* proposed to make of the NEP a fundamental revision of the Communist road to socialism. It is *he* not Lenin who is the father of what has come to be called the movement toward socialism with a human face.

For Bukarin collaboration, not struggle, between the proletariat and the peasant was to be the process of moving forward. In that process the security and self-enrichment of the peasantry were to be encouraged not viewed with suspicion as a return to capitalism. Despite occasional lapses Bukharin did not jettison any of the old terms and categories of Marxist Leninism, especially after Trotsky, who regarded Bukharin as more dangerous and heretical ideologically than Stalin, opened his offensive. Otherwise he could hardly count on getting a hearing. Like so many other reformers before him in the history of politics and religion, he poured the new wine into the old bottles with the old labels. Of course the class struggle or class war could not be suspended any more than the state power, which grew out of class conflicts, could be dissolved. But "struggle" and "war" now meant merely competition. Private trade would gradually be displaced or reduced in the competition of the market. Capitalist enterprises would be defeated not by expropriation, unfair taxation, requisitions, but by state and cooperative enterprises both in city and country. If enterprises in private hands proved stronger, this would not constitute a danger of a return to capitalism since the reins of political power were exclusively in the hands of the Communist Party. It would mean more or better goods for the consumer until state and cooperative enterprises became more efficient and caught up.

Bukharin's elaborate account of growing into socialism

through expansion of the small and relatively free market economy was a far cry, as modest as it was, from the marketless planned economy of Lenin's thought. Professor Cohen gives an admirable account of Bukharin's economic ideas. He also recognizes that these far-reaching changes in economic policy entailed far-reaching correlative changes in political theory and practice. After recounting the differences in political approach called for by the profound shift in Bukharin's economic position, he summarizes: "If the new economics was evolutionary, the new politics was pedagogical—paternalistic, benevolent, gentle."

The words are well chosen—"paternalistic," "benevolent," and "gentle." But is it plausible to assume that they faithfully reflect what Lenin had in mind in the light of what we know about him? Did the new economics and the new politics proposed by Bukharin really stem, as Cohen and other scholars believe, from the last five short pieces Lenin published?: *Pages from a Diary; On Cooperation; Our Revolution; How We Should Reorganize the Workers' and Peasants' Inspection; Better Fewer, but Better . . . ?*

I have pored over these articles many times on various occasions since they were published. The most important of them are *On Cooperation* and *Better Fewer, but Better.* I do not find Bukharin's program in them implicitly or explicitly.

In all of these essays the relevant passages show clearly that Lenin regards the NEP as transitional, a kind of holding action. His whole conception of cooperatives differs from that of Bukharin. His cooperatives were outright socialist cooperatives since "the land on which they stand and the means of production belong to the state, i.e., the working class." Rents for their use depend completely on the decision of government agencies as well as the continuity of their operation. There is no provision for the genuine competition that Bukharin stressed. There is really no free market since the dependence of the cooperatives for all sorts of raw materials and tools is complete. And indeed if the cooperatives were given the relative autonomy and independence to make decisions in order to meet the needs of the market, especially the peasant market, how could Soviet industry plan properly? All genuine competition involves potential waste of resources—material and human. Lenin emphasizes the importance of culturally uplifting the workers, pruning the bureaucracy, economizing on costs, retaining the working-class leadership of the peasants and winning their confidence—for what purpose? First, to "insure our resistance" in the forthcoming conflict between "the counter-revolutionary imperialist West" and "the revolutionary and nationalist East" (the reference is to Asia); and second, "to develop large scale machine industry, to develop electrification, the hydraulic extraction of peat, to finish the construction of Volkhovstroi, etc." It is not surprising therefore that Trotsky and Stalin could cite the same writings as Bukharin in bitterly contesting his proposed road to socialism by civil peace. Lenin concludes his article on the reorganization of Workers' and Peasants' Inspection with a call for vigilance against "the new bourgeoisie—the Nepman," lest their activities "drive a wedge" between the workers and peasants, split them apart, and threaten the survival of the Republic? With fears of this sort preying on his mind is it likely that Lenin would encourage the kind of competition between the private and public sector that Bukharin envisaged?

There is one compelling reason, it seems to me, why Lenin would not have approved of Bukharin's proposals had he known of them. It is a reason that must have motivated to some extent the intensity of the opposition of many of Bukharin's critics. It is reflected in the frequency of the charge of Menshevism against him. The practical upshot of Bukharin's proposals, not of course the rhetoric of his goals, would have resulted in a kind of society in large outlines not too different from the programmatic perspectives of the socialist parties that controlled the Constituent Assembly. In that case how could the agonies of the October Revolution and the civil war have been justified? Such a question could not be far from the consciousness of the Bolshevik leaders since the socialist critics of Lenin had warned against the folly of force—marching a backward country unripe for any type of socialism into the classless future. If there was any criticism to which Lenin was especially sensitive, it was precisely this one, hurled at him in a thousand variations by Kautsky, Plekhanov, and the other doyens of Social-Democracy. Like a man nursing a sore tooth whose tongue keeps touching it, Lenin reverts to this criticism again and again. In his "Our Revolution," his vexation and uneasiness are quite apparent. He repeats once more his defense of the Bolshevik *coup d'état* and jeeringly recalls the objection: "Russia has not attained the level of development of productive forces that makes socialism possible. . . . They keep repeating this incontrovertible proposition over and over again. . . ."

Lenin does not deny the truth of this incontrovertible proposition. He merely denies the political corollaries Marx drew from it. "If a definite level of culture is required for the building of socialism," Lenin asks, "why cannot we begin by *first* achieving the prerequisites for that definite level of culture in a revolutionary way, and *then* with the aid of the workers' and peasants' government and the Soviet system, proceed to overtake the other nations?" Nothing, of course, is in the way—except all the cardinal principles of Marx's historical materialism which Lenin would no more think of renouncing than the Pope the principles of Christianity. And beyond these principles are the common sense considerations of human cost, and all the historical evidence that led Marx to proclaim that "social existence determines consciousness."

How far Lenin departed from Marx is evident in his prediction that socialist revolutions could succeed even in "Oriental countries" whose social, economic, and technological conditions were even more backward and diverse than those of Russia. "Where, in what books, have you read that such variations of the customary, historical order are impermissible or impossible? Napoleon, one recalls, wrote: 'On s'engage et puit . . . on voit.'" Lenin understood Napoleon no better than he did Marx. Napoleon was referring to the outcome of the battle once one has engaged. He was warning not only against excessive caution but against overconfidence, and the easy predictions of assured victory. He himself never willingly engaged before he thought he was ready. Lenin reads him as if he was willing to engage at any time under any conditions. Marx was aware that objective conditions could be ripe for socialism and yet the socialist revolution not take place or fail if it did. His point against Blanqui, Bakunin, and other extreme voluntarists was that in the absence of those objective conditions the revolution would fail. Whether Lenin and Stalin between them proved that Marx was wrong or whether the society of which they are the chief architects, despite its remarkable achievements, vindicated Marx's insights depends on what we understand by socialism. This is a complex theme that need not be developed here.

It goes without saying that the contumely and abuse poured upon Bukharin after Stalin turned against him was as grotesque and as unmerited as that directed against Trotsky earlier. But there was some justice in the persistent accusation that his road to socialism was a variant of the Social-Democratic road, something of which Trotsky in opposition was never accused. One marked feature of Bukharin's description of the road was the absence of the element of terror in his approach to the socialist goal. It would tend to confirm the suspicion of old Bolsheviks, travel-hardened in Lenin's party, that Bukharin meant to abandon, despite his protestations, the dictatorship of the party.

II

There are two generic views about terror and its function in the consolidation of Soviet rule. The first is that under Lenin it was primarily defensive, a consequence of civil war, gradually becoming peripheral to Soviet life until Stalin abolished the NEP and began his "revolution from above." From the moment that Stalin became the dominant figure to shortly after his death, terror became central in the mechanism of Soviet rule. Stalinism is pictured as a degeneration, a corruption or a betrayal of Leninism. The second view sees in Stalin the continuation and intensification of the system of terror introduced by Lenin and justified by him. The chief difference between them consists in the fact that Stalin used the awful engines of repression not only against "the class enemy" but against Communists, too, and used them so capriciously and with a ferocity so devoid of any rhyme or reason as to raise questions about his sanity.

Obviously both views are oversimplifications. They may exclude each other but they do not exhaust other more qualified interpretations of the role of terror in Bolshevik theory and practice, and the respective responsibilities of Lenin and Stalin for the horrifying record which Solzhenitsyn has unrolled before the world in his *The Gulag Archipelago.*

Certain important distinctions are not always observed. It is one thing to discuss the logic of abstract concepts unrelated to specific contexts. It is quite another to uncover the logic of ideas in action when they are used as weapons in historical situations by passionate, and often ignorant, protagonists. In pure logic the historic guilt of a class can be distinguished from the guilt of individual members of the class; in actuality one cannot destroy a class without crushing individuals who are morally blameless for their social position. In pure logic one can sharply distinguish between evil, terroristic means and ideal ends; in the logic of action the moral quality of the means infects the moral quality of the ends when it does not determine them. In pure logic a complete collectivism is not incompatible with unlimited democracy; in actuality, so long as selfishness remains unenlightened, the allocation of material resources and human labor required for planning may involve some coercion. In pure logic a one-party state like a benign patriarch of a large family can be tolerant of differences among party members and the community at large; the logic of political experience shows that where public expression of differences of opinion are not tolerated outside of the party, they are soon suppressed within the party, lest a split develop.

Bolshevik thinking about terror was a compound of certain traditional elements of Marxism, a reading of history in terms of the inexorable "law of the class struggle," a feeling that the white terror of the past of bourgeois society morally justified the red terror of the present, and the arrogant and question-begging assertion that any resistance to the Bolshevik seizure of power, and to its draconic decrees was opposition to the will of the proletariat and the ultimate good of mankind of which the Communist Party was the guardian and executor.

Engels's view that all morality is class morality—which contradicts many other things he says that have genuine moral import—is very difficult to defend in the light of reflective judgment. Even more difficult to square with the conclusions of moral consciousness is the Bolshevik amendment that the Communist Party is the best judge of the interests of the working class, and that its survival, integrity, and victory are the *sine qua non* of realizing socialism, the objectively good society. Lenin defines the right as any action that contributes to the victory of the working class, and since only the Communist Party knows in what this consists and how to bring it about, anything is right that helps the party to achieve and retain its power. Taken together with Lenin's concept of dictatorship as "rule based directly upon force and unrestricted by any laws" it opens up some awesome possibilities.

Ideas such as these were the common premises of all the Bolshevik leaders in their rationalizations of terror—not only of Lenin and Stalin but, in a more sophisticated form, of Trotsky, and of Bukharin who indignantly repudiated the charge that Bolshevik morality was on logical par with Hottentot morality since the Bolsheviks were struggling for a new, higher classless society. "What helps in the struggle is good; whatever hinders is bad." But unless the classless society has a classless moral validity, unless there are other valid moral ideals beyond the struggle that may not be violated by the means necessary to win the struggle, then we have the law of the jungle. It is a law that can be used to justify anything. It differs from Smerdyakov's dictum "All things are permissible," only in the qualification if it leads to victory or avoids defeat.

However, just because we are dealing with a common premise, it is not sufficient to explain the differences in the behavior of those who subscribed to it, notably Lenin and Stalin. Other considerations must enter—differences in personality, differences in objective conditions, differences in the perceived or suspected danger to the Soviet state. That is why the two easy interpretations of the relationship between Lenin and Stalin concerning the use of terror must be rejected. Lenin could plead the exigencies of the civil war to extenuate his terrorist acts in a way that Stalin couldn't. This is in no way an absolution. For most of the victims of Lenin's terror were not active participants in the civil war but members of social groups and classes regarded as hostile. There were many acts of repression launched before the civil war developed on a large scale. The Bolsheviks speak of the civil war as if it were an unprovoked attack against a legitimate regime. But it was they who precipitated the civil war by forcibly dissolving the Constituent Assembly whose convocation they had demanded previously, and by outlawing a major political party as "enemies of the people" whose members were to be shot, often with their families, on sight.

There was a cruelty and ruthlessness about Lenin's behavior toward anyone he regarded as a political enemy or even as an obstacle to his goals of the moment. He openly declared, long before his party seized power, that in the event of a split—when political friends and allies become political opponents—"I shall always conduct a war of extermination" against them, and use measures "not to convince . . . but to destroy them." At the time he was out to destroy their characters and reputations but subsequently he did not hesitate to imprison them and sometimes destroy their persons. Shortly after taking power, before the civil war began, he called on every village and town to destroy as they would "noxious insects" all persons guilty of "any sort of resistance" to the Bolshevik program. Workers in the factories were required to set up terror detachments to go marauding and hunting down "speculators" and shoot them "on the spot . . . if caught with the goods." Workshops that fail to do this "will be deprived of bread cards and subjected to revolutionary measures of persuasion and punishment."

Here is a characteristic passage written December 25, 1917, before the Constituent Assembly was forcibly dissolved and the civil war began. It is well to remember that "the rich" is a very elastic category in Lenin's writings and includes all members of the family; and that by "rogues" he means "lackeys of the bourgeoisie; saboteurs who call themselves intellectuals."

Thousands of practical forms and methods of accounting and controlling the rich, the rogues, and the idlers should be devised and put to a practical test by the communes themselves, by small units in town and country. Variety is a guarantee of virility here, a pledge of success in achieving the single common aim—to *purge* the land of Russia of all vermin, of fleas,—the rogues, of bugs—the rich, and so on and so forth. In one place half a score of rich, a dozen rogues, half a dozen workers who shirk their work (in the hooligan manner in which many compositors in Petrograd, particularly in the Party printing shops, shirk their work) will be put in prison. In another place they will be put to cleaning latrines. In a third place they will be provided with "yellow tickets" after they have served their time, so that all the people shall have them under surveillance, as *harmful* persons, until they reform. In a fourth place, one out of every ten idlers will be shot on the spot. *(Selected Works* [Moscow: Foreign Language Publishing House, 1951], Vol. 2, Part I, p. 376)

These sentiments were not merely morale-building propaganda. Others acted upon them in a manner that Lenin may not have approved. But there is no evidence that he ever rebuked them. On the other hand we know that it was Lenin who formulated the paragraph of the Criminal Code, forerunner of the infamous paragraph 58 of Stalin's time, which decreed "execution by shooting" for all activities of the Mensheviks, Social Revolutionaries, etc., including simple speech, as well as to persons "capable [!] of assisting" organizations hostile to the Communist Party. After the NEP, he expressed indignant surprise that anyone should protest the execution of those guilty of the heinous offense of *saying* that the NEP was a retreat to capitalism. His surprise seems quite genuine and is an eloquent indication of how natural ruthless terror as a social policy appeared to him. It was under Lenin that Maria Spiridonova, who turned against the Bolsheviks after Brest-Litovsk, was confined to a mental hospital.

This profound indifference, if not contempt, for human beings who got in the way of his social vision by the revered leader of the party could not but have influenced the climate of opinion and helped determine the attitudes and behavior of many of its members. It could be matched by remarks of Trotsky after Kronstadt, whose whole philosophy of history reflects a callousness to the victims on what Hegel calls "the slaughter-benches" of progress. In his *Autobiography* Trotsky observes "it is certainly victims that move humanity forward." Presumably the more victims, the greater the progress.

Bukharin emerges from the pages of Cohen's biography as one who was much more aware of the human costs of "progress," by natural disposition more genial and kindly than his colleagues. Despite his doctrinal orthodoxy on the necessity of terror, he himself probably would not have initiated or executed the terrorist measures of Lenin, Trotsky, or Stalin. We know that he refused to defame the Kronstadt sailors although he apparently approved of their suppression. He was reluctant to endorse Stalin's administrative measures against the Left-Opposition. But he never had the gumption to take a principled stand against them or against the unjustified repressions under Lenin. After the attempt on Lenin's life, thousands of people who had been previously arrested on all sorts of unrelated charges and who, lying in prison, could not have been even remotely involved in the action of a half-crazed woman, were nonetheless shot without trial. No protest was ever made by Bukharin.

It is this failure to take a principled public stand against any of the terroristic practices under Lenin and Stalin that makes his obvious personal distaste for bloodshed and violence against dissenters seem to be a sentimental failing, a weakness in an otherwise tough Bolshevik. Had the Communist Party followed his moderate policies, how would Bukharin have behaved if the pace of advance dragged, if the socialist sector were getting the worst of it in the competition with the private sector? He would never have gone as far as Stalin but it is not excluded that he would publicly have gone along with the stern disciplinary measures sure to be proposed by others nurtured in the Leninist tradition.

Nonetheless even if we sharply distinguish between Bukharin and other Bolshevik leaders, we cannot regard the latter as a homogeneous group. Stalin by all odds in what we both know of his private and public life was the worst of all. He added a dimension to terror that went beyond anything that Lenin ever conceived, whose techniques and ramifications seem unprecedented in the history of man's inhumanity to man. Had Lenin lived and opted for Trotsky's line, a line that Trotsky to the end insisted was closer to that of Lenin's than any other, immense sufferings would undoubtedly have been imposed on the Russian people as well as on those of other nations but it is as certain as anything can be in human affairs that the machinery of terror would not have been turned against the Party and the security and military forces of the country. Lenin was much more intelligent and much less vindictive than Stalin. He was furious with and intolerant of error. He was content, however, with the acknowledgement of error. He was vindictive with a kind of abstract historical passion against whole classes rather than against individual persons. Although ruthless and amoral, his judgments were strictly functional. He could match anyone in loud outcries about justice and injustice, if it helped to get or keep power. And with an eye on cavilling moralists, he could always rationalize an injustice in the present by balancing it against an injustice of the past even though it was necessary to go back to the French Revolution or Paris Commune to do so, although on his class and party view of the good and the right, he was not entitled to make such comparisons.

In contradistinction to Lenin, the irrationality of Stalin's terrorism with respect to his own announced goals is so striking that like Hitler's it must be regarded as psychopathological. He was luckier than Hitler in escaping the consequences of his monumental follies and crimes—saved by a bounteous harvest at one time, by Hitler's own insanities at another, and the Japanese Army's Zen-Buddhist mentality that foreclosed the two-front war in the offing. What we know about the mad tyrants of antiquity depends largely on legend. The facts about Stalin can hardly be disputed; and those that have not yet been revealed will probably add to his guilt rather than mitigate it. If any man deserves the sobriquet "The Iago of history," it is Stalin.

In saying this it is not necessary to impute to Stalin complete and sole responsibility for the oceans of suffering he unloosed not only against the Russian people but against every other national group under his sway. For a man who sowed so much evil, who, according to Khrushchev, inspired paralyzing fear in his closest subordinates whenever they entered his presence, it is a miracle that he died in his bed. That he was able to succeed with complete immunity in his strategies of terror—his death prevented another massive purge—indicates that a considerable number of people in the Soviet Union had a vested interest in the system sufficient to deter them from stopping it. The vastness, pervasiveness, and continuity of the terror meant that for hundreds of thousands it must have been a way of life even if they did not directly bloody their hands in its operation. Perhaps the explanation of the halt in the process of de-Stalinization begun by Khrushchev and the answer to Solzhenitsyn's plaintive question why so few of the specialists of torture have been brought to justice lies in the very number of those personally involved—beyond the call of duty—in Stalin's infamies. Since none of them can claim to have been critics of what they participated in, why should they incur the odium of publicity as well as the loss of the material perquisites of their collaboration?

Lenin must answer for Stalin but not for everything Stalin did. He must answer for establishing the system that made Stalin possible. He must answer for forging a party that made Stalin "actual" as its Secretary and the most powerful man in it after Lenin himself. Finally he must answer for a mode of thought, a social voluntarism so extreme that it burst all the reasonable bounds of Marxism and which led Stalin to glorify the armed will as the driving force of social change. There are echoes of the Lenin of the October days in the famous passage from one of Stalin's minions, on the eve of the revolution from above, although Lenin's sturdy common sense would have hedged it with qualifications:

Our task is not to study economics but to change it. We are bound by no laws. There are no fortresses which the Bolsheviks cannot storm. The question of tempo is subject to decision by human beings. (S.G. Shumilin)

III

The entire discussion of the course of the Russian Revolution and the attribution of responsibility to Lenin and/or Stalin for its development presupposes that it is both intelligible and instructive to ask hypothetical questions contrary to fact. It is astonishing how often estimable historians who make skilful use of "if" questions deny that it makes any sense to raise them. Perhaps we should have posed this issue at the outset. It is appropriate to consider it at the close as we meditate on the fall of "the last Bolshevik," as Professor Cohen refers to Bukharin underscoring his continuity with the position of Lenin. Professor Cohen quite clearly believes that had Bukharin's policies been adopted by the Russian Communist Party, the whole course of Soviet history, economics, politics, and culture which we associate with the triumph of Stalinism, would have been quite different. Although the precise details of the alternative development cannot be described, the Russian people would have been spared the worst features of Stalin's régime. I agree with this but not with the judgment that Bukharin's policies were Lenin's and that he, not Stalin or Trotsky, was the true heir of Lenin's revolutionary legacy. Professor Leonard Schapiro whose writings, as distinct from those of E. H. Carr, combine in exemplary fashion scientific objectivity and insight together with compassion for the victims of historical cruelty and injustice, concurs with both judgments of Cohen's. This adds great but not conclusive weight to Cohen's thesis. Curiously enough, however, in his very sympathetic review of Cohen's book, Professor Schapiro writes:

The historian cannot say what might have been since it is impossible to assess all the consequences that would eventually have flowed from a certain course of action had it been taken at a certain moment of time. On the other hand, human reason instinctively revolts against accepting the argument that a policy involving the massacre of tens of millions of innocent people and an internal upheaval of which the traces are fully evident over forty years later can ever be regarded as either realistic or necessary. *(New York Review of Books*, 2 Feb., 1974)

Surely the second sentence contradicts the first. To deny that the massacre of millions of innocent Russians was either realistic or necessary is to assert that *if* some other policy had been adopted this horrible outcome would not have occurred. Of course, we need not claim to know with certainty all the consequences that would eventually have flowed from a certain course of action had it been taken at a certain moment in time. All we need claim is that with respect to some important consequences that they probably would not have occurred and that some other consequences probably would have occurred if another policy had been followed. Indeed, an historian or any person delivering a considered judgment cannot make a causal attribution to any event or individual without implying at the same time what would have resulted if the event or action had *not* occurred. For to say that x is the cause of y is to say that in the absence of x, y probably would not have occurred in the manner and time that it did. The complexities of an adequate causal analysis are formidable but they do not gainsay the truth that all intelligent discussion of policy, past or present, assumes that we can rationally say not only what might have been, and sometimes even what would have been but also what might be and sometimes what will be. If we can never say this, then we can never explain anything.

The issue has more than theoretical importance. For if we cannot intelligibly raise questions and intelligently answer them, how can we ever learn from the past? It may be that history is so discontinuous that we cannot learn anything about the past except, as Hegel put it, that we cannot learn from the past. But we can learn more than that. Among the things we can learn are the probable costs and consequences of forcibly attempting to introduce socialism in underdeveloped countries.

Like any historian who accepts some form of determinism, Marx was not wrong in denying that all things are possible in history. Nor was he wrong in predicting that socialism as he understood it could not be developed in a country that lacked the economic and cultural prerequisites for it. He was wrong in not predicting that the attempt would be made, and that a new type of society, neither capitalist nor socialist, would result from it. Among the many merits of Professor Cohen's study of Bukharin and the Russian Revolution is that its scholarly findings leave in the sensitive reader the same impression that he will gather with an immeasurably stronger force from reading Solzhenitsyn. It is that if our choice were restricted—as happily it is not—between present-day democratic capitalist welfare states with all their many imperfections and any society like that of the Soviet Union regardless of whether Stalin was one of the regnant deities within it—the Communist option would be shudderingly rejected.

ADDENDUM: A DIALOGUE WITH AN "UNOFFICIAL" SOVIET RUSSIAN DELEGATION

Late in May of 1967 I was invited among others to meet a visiting Soviet Russian delegation for a free and frank discussion of matters of mutual interest. The delegation was returning the visit made to the Soviet Union a few years ago by a delegation of unofficial Americans, most of whom were out of sympathy with current American foreign policy. I was told that the Russians had enjoyed the American visit immensely and in the spirit of reciprocity had offered to send a delegation of unofficial Soviet citizens to the United States to talk to plain folks like themselves in the arts and professions. The State Department approved the visit but left its organization completely in the hands of the American hosts, the USSR Committee, among whom was Mr. Robert Gilmore, well known for his activity in peace organizations, whose Chairman was George A. Beebe, formerly Director of the Institute for International Order.

There were seven persons in the unofficial Russian delegation but three of them were diverted to a dinner meeting with Norman Cousins and Philip Mosely after our own dinner appointment had been set up. I was asked to find three other Americans for a dinner meeting at very short notice—less than a day. I was able to induce Dr. Norman Jacobs, Director of Program Materials of the Foreign Policy Research Center, Dr. Milton Fried, Research Economist of the Amalgamated Clothing Workers Union, and Mr. Moshe Decter, Director of the Committee for Democracy in the Near East, to join me. The four Russians were Messrs. Vitali Korionov, Igór Sokolov, Constantine Geyvendov, and Vladimir Makarov. Since it seemed likely that the conversations would be more intimate and fruitful if the spirit of a political meeting were avoided, I suggested that we dine at two separate tables. Dr. Fried and I paired off with Mr. Korionov, whose card identified him as a Political Observer for *Pravda,* and with Mr. Makarov, who introduced himself as secretary of a youth organization, and who translated for Korionov. Sokolov and Geyvendov, who were fluent in English, shared a table with Dr. Jacobs and Mr. Decter.

I shall try to reproduce my colloquy with Korionov as accurately as I can. I cannot guarantee that every word I here write was uttered, but the spirit and meaning of the exchange are faithfully reproduced. My impression was that none of the Russians had been briefed about our political views. Although they were told of our professional associations they seemed unaware at the outset that we were in any way different from the run-of-the-mill unofficial Americans whom they had previously met and whom Korionov, at one point toward the close of the evening, referred to as "people of good will, fortunately not interested in old questions of history." (I presumed upon the fact that Dr. Fried was an old student of mine to begin the discussion. At several points Dr. Fried tried to reverse the course of the discussion from the apparently historical to the explicitly contemporaneous but was rebuffed by Korionov, who seemed nettled by some of my questions and wanted "to finish me off" quickly before turning to other measures.)

I began by asking Korionov what a "political observer" was and whether his role was comparable to that of our political commentators or columnists. I shall run together his answers to a variety of questions on related themes.

"No, a 'political observer' has a much more important role. He doesn't merely comment on the news or interpret news but makes news in virtue of the depth of his analysis. . . . No one tells him when and about what to write. He has to have a good nose for the important developments. He doesn't have to wait for events to break before discussing important problems. He often anticipates events. . . . There are four political observers on *Pravda*. [One of them accompanied Kosygin on his trip to the United States.] They are part of the editorial staff. Although *Pravda* is the Communist Party newspaper it is independent in the sense that no one tells the editors what to print or what line to take on anything. A daily session is held at which the chief editor presides and in which collective decisions are taken about what stories to feature and how to handle them."

"What happens," I asked, "if the editorial staff reaches a con-

clusion or position which is different from that of the Central
Committee or Politbureau of the Communist Party?"

"This is out of the question. The editors are all party people.
They know how the Politbureau thinks. So there is no difference."

"But surely the Politbureau doesn't sit in continuous session.
How can the editors of *Pravda* know what the party line will be on
the many complex issues which arise? Isn't there someone from
the Politbureau or a Publication Committee of the Central Committee to whom the editors of *Pravda* are responsible, and who
gives them their directives?"

"No. We already know how the party thinks, and simply go by
that. In all my many years on *Pravda*, I know of no case in which
any difference existed between the position taken by the editors
and that of the party."

"But sometimes the line of *Pravda* changes, for example,
toward Tito or to the Chinese or on the domestic cultural front.
Does *Pravda* follow the lead of the party or does the party follow
the lead of the editor of *Pravda?* Or do they simultaneously
change their positions without any intervention by party
bureaucrats?"

"These are idle questions. No one follows the lead of anyone.
From the same premises, the same conclusions follow. I repeat,
the editors of *Pravda* are solely responsible for what is published;
and what is more, all the editors, I among the others, have equal
voice and vote in deciding what is to be printed."

"How do you explain then, that *Pravda* did not print Khrushchev's speech against Stalin and the cult of personality at the
Twentieth Congress of the Party?"

"It was a closed meeting."

"But the matter was of such momentous importance. Surely the
editors of *Pravda* must have realized how important Khrushchev's speech was to the whole country."

"It was no one's business but that of the Communist Party. . . .
No, the speech has not been published in the Soviet Union . . . but
it was read at the local meetings of the Communist Party units
held after the Twentieth Congress."

"Did the revelations of Khrushchev about Stalin's crimes come
as a shock to the members of the Communist Party?"

"Some knew about them. Some did not. . . . Particularly those who saw some trusted comrades disappear whom they knew to be loyal Communists knew about Stalin's violations of Soviet legality in the last years of his life. They were not surprised."

"Did the editors of *Pravda* know about Stalin's crimes and were they free to write about them?"

"This is a long and complicated story, and although I am willing to talk about such things I do not find these historical questions interesting."

"Forgive me if I have asked embarrassing questions but my concern is not at all historical. Like many other students of Soviet theory and practice, and especially as a scholar of Marxism, I have been profoundly puzzled by Khrushchev's speech and the Soviet reaction to it. It is a Marxist commonplace that neither good men nor bad men make history as much as the development of social institutions. If all the horrible crimes, the purges, the shootings, the concentration camps, and terror without limit described by Khrushchev are to be laid at Stalin's door, must not one hold the social system, which made the emergence of Stalin's dictatorial power possible, responsible? The same Constitution, the same set of institutions which enabled Stalin to build up the cult of personality are substantially in existence today, too. There is no independent press or judiciary, etc. As much as you may deplore the cult of personality, in the absence of institutional changes that prevent the existence of arbitrary dictatorships, how do you know that the future may not restore the cult of personality in another form and with different names? Surely those who call themselves Marxists or Leninists, as Soviet theoreticians proudly do, must face this problem. I shall be very grateful to you if you can illumine this difficulty, for in all frankness I have found not a single Soviet explanation even remotely plausible. Either everything is blamed on Stalin, as if he had no assistants in crime, or the whole bloody history of the Stalin era is presented as historically inevitable. One suspects that if Stalin had lived on until today, the cult of personality would still be flourishing."

"You have asked a lot of questions. But they can all be easily answered. You must have patience and hear me through without interruptions and more questions. Stalin despite his violations of legality in his last years was a great man. First of all, you must not forget that the Soviet Union was encircled on all sides by countries that wanted to destroy it. The United States also invaded. We owe the defeat of the imperialist powers to Stalin. But it was not only the external enemy we had to fear. The internal class enemy was even more dangerous, and here Stalin deserves credit for being watchful and increasingly stern as the enemies of the Soviet Union pretended to be loyal. But Stalin could not be everywhere, and see everything for himself. He had to rely on his advisors. And some of them put their own interests above that of the party and the Soviet Union. It was they who misled him, and the worst of all was Beria. As a Georgian, Beria knew what special fears and suspicions of Stalin to play on, and he inflamed Stalin's mind against many who were faithful. It was Beria who undermined Stalin's confidence in Yagoda and Yezhov. During this period and even somewhat later whenever he could find out the facts, Stalin was able to do justice properly. The trouble is he had too much confidence in Beria. Khrushchev relates that once when a leading Ukrainian comrade was falsely accused of being 'an enemy of the people,' he, Khrushchev, went to Stalin to plead his cause. After looking at some documents Stalin asked Khrushchev: 'Who will guarantee the accused's loyalty?' Khrushchev replied: 'I will.' Thereupon Stalin ordered that all those who made the charges against Khrushchev's protégé should be immediately shot. It cannot be denied that Stalin became overconfident and made many mistakes. This was particularly true at the time of Hitler's invasion of the Soviet Union in 1941. But don't forget that despite these mistakes we won the war against Hitler and for this Stalin must receive great credit. The cult of personality became greatly exaggerated after the war and it was in these years toward the end of his life that Stalin violated the norms of Soviet legality. What you say of the absence of institutional changes to prevent the emergence of another Stalin is completely false. We do not fear the rebirth of the cult of the individual. Khrushchev was moving in that direction when he was removed. I am not finished but I shall conclude by repeating that not everything that Stalin did was bad even if it is true that toward the end of his life he did many things that were not good.

"Please excuse me but I am even more bewildered by your explanation than I was before. In one breath you seem to apologize for Stalin and defend his actions as necessary; and in the next you condemn him. I also begin to see why you are not interested in history."

"What's wrong with my history?"

"Many things. But I mention briefly two points. You condemn only the actions of Stalin's late years as violations of Soviet legality. But the greatest crimes in number and degree occurred from 1934–39 and even Khrushchev cites them against Stalin. You also claim that Stalin was misled during those and subsequent years. But the evidence is overwhelming that Stalin personally directed the tortures during these years and right up to the time of the alleged Jewish Doctors' plot. Second, you make it appear that Stalin's internal terror was necessary to save the country from invasion. But during the invasions when Lenin was alive there was more relative freedom than after 1924 when all was peaceful under Stalin who claimed that the stronger the Soviet State became the greater the necessity for terror."

"You cannot tell what condition a country is in by reading about it. I wouldn't tell you about conditions in the United States, because you live here and I don't. So you can't tell me about conditions in the Soviet Union.

"It is not your experience I am questioning. I am wondering about your interpretation of the experience. I spent three months in Moscow in 1929 at the Marx-Engels Institute at the invitation of Riazanov, who was subsequently purged, and discussed conditions with many persons, both party and non-party. Nobody feared an invasion then. Nor were there obvious food shortages."

"Nineteen-twenty-nine was a good year, yes, but the internal enemies were growing stronger, opposing industrialization and collectivization. Stalin defeated them."

"Well, a case can be made that Stalin created his own enemies by his program. Before, you said that Stalin deserves the credit for the Soviet defeat of Hitler, but it was Stalin's policies, especially his theory of social-fascism, which helped bring Hitler to power. Similarly the enforced pace of industrialization and collectivization of agriculture created an objective class-enemy which certainly was not until that time *actively* hostile to the régime."

"This is the way things may appear to capitalist eyes."

"No, the criticism I have just made, including the absence of workers democracy, comes from socialists."

"What socialists?"

"Criticism of the absence of Soviet democracy from many socialists, beginning with Rosa Luxemburg. The criticism of Stalin's industrialization and collectivization program, together with criticism of his policy in Germany, has been made by Leon Trotsky."

"What, you call Trotsky a socialist! This is ridiculous. Trotsky was an embittered enemy of the Soviet Union. He was no socialist at all."

"I was under the impression that Trotsky was one of the leading architects of the October Revolution. Lenin must have regarded him as a socialist. Surely you know the 'testament' in which Lenin urged that Stalin be dropped and Trotsky cherished. I speak as a critic of Trotsky. I am no Bolshevik. But I am curious to learn why you deny that Trotsky was a socialist."

"Trotsky led a demonstration against the Soviet Union on November 7, 1927. It really is nonsense to call him a socialist."

"I was under the impression it was a demonstration against Stalin's violation of internal party democracy, not against the Soviet Union. And even if he was wrong why does that make him *not* a socialist?"

"Because he was disloyal, because he didn't accept defeat, because he came out against Stalin's program."

"You have confused things. His original criticism was against Stalin's violation of party democracy. His criticism of Stalin's program came later when he accused Stalin, after defeating Bukharin, of adopting the program of the left-opposition, raising its goals to absurd lengths and using force rather than example and persuasion in relation to the peasants."

"You must be a wonderful joke-maker. When I return to the Soviet Union and tell people I met an American professor who believes that Stalin borrowed any part of his program from Trotsky, I shall create an epidemic of death by laughter."

"This can easily be settled by consulting the record. If the

Soviet régime would print Trotsky's works, you and your friends could easily establish the facts for yourselves."

"Another joke! Why should the Soviet Union print Trotsky's works? Nobody wants to read the works of a counterrevolutionary in the Soviet Union."

"How do you know they don't, if you refuse to print them?"

"This is getting funnier and funnier. Before long you will be proposing that we print Hitler's works, too?"

"Why not? People would learn about the dangers and menace of racism and anti-Semitism. Actually if the Soviet citizens had read *Mein Kampf* in the 1930s, a book in which Hitler declares his intention of attacking and dismembering the Soviet Union, Stalin might not have been able to get away with the Soviet-Nazi Pact of 1939 which precipitated World War II."

"In the Soviet Union we can read anything we want to, by anybody about anything. But we don't want to. . . ."

"This surprises me. I have just spoken to a friend who has returned from a month's visit to the Soviet Union. She reports that the only foreign newspapers available are Communist ones. She originally hailed from Kiev and speaks Russian like a native."

"Your friend is mistaken. She didn't know where to go to get them. (Incidentally we tried to buy a recent issue of *Pravda* on 42nd Street and all we could find was one that was weeks old.)" [The sentence in parentheses was contributed by the translator.]

"I didn't know that you had freedom of the press in the Soviet Union."

"Yes, just like here."

"Is Brodsky, the poet, sentenced for social parasitism, still in exile?"

"I never heard of him. [To the translator, "Did you?" Translator: "No."]

Dr. Milton Fried then asked some searching questions about contemporary matters. I hope he writes his conversation up.

Toward the end I turned toward the twenty-six-year-old translator and asked him whether the point of view of his generation was the same as Korionov's.

"No, we don't care so much about history and ideology."

"But have you no interest in the subjects Korionov and I have been discussing?"

"To tell the truth, and to use one of your expressions, I don't give a f--- about history, about Trotsky or Stalin. . . ."

"Does that go for Lenin, too, and Marx and all the other historical figures of the past?"

"You ask too many questions."

"But, seriously, when you read Khrushchev's speech, if you have read it, or even if you read the novel *One Day in the Life of Ivan Denisovich* by Solzhenitsyn have you no feeling of moral indignation at the brutality and tortures used against innocent men and women?"

"Yes, of course, of course, there is hardly any one among my friends who has not had a relative in the camps. My grandfather died in one. . . . We don't want any of that back again."

"Wouldn't it help prevent bringing those conditions back if there were genuine freedom of the press? My Russian friends in Moscow in 1929 were convinced that Trotsky had voluntarily left the Soviet Union for the fleshpots of capitalism instead of being literally carried by force over the border by Soviet officials. *Pravda* was their source."

"You can rely on *Pravda* today."

"Can you? Including what *Pravda* says about Sinyavsky and Daniel? What about freedom of press for them?"

"Not for those bastards! Prison is too good for them. I disagree with the government about how they should be treated. They should have been kicked out of the country, exiled for life. To run down their own people and nation with lies and negative criticism. . . ."

"Couldn't they be answered with the truth? What is wrong about negative criticism? We permit plenty of it and the republic still stands."

"Sinyavsky and Daniel have no right to use freedom of the press to tell lies."

"But if the government has the right to determine what is true or false then there is no freedom of the press."

"How would you feel if American writers told lies about the United States?"

"Many do, but that's the price one pays for freedom of the press."

"Well, we won't stand for it."

At this point Decter, who had finished with an even more animated conversation at his table and was listening to us interposed with the remark, "Why not try it and see what happens?" Korionov meanwhile had broken off while we were talking with the young translator and was excitedly conversing with Sokolov and Geyvendov. Judging by a few words I caught he was giving them an account of what we discussed.

The evening concluded with some pleasantries. I asked whether the standpoint of an official delegation would be different on the matters we discussed from that of an unofficial delegation. Substantially not, I was told, because both would be true. I told Korionov the impression I got from him was that although Stalin and Khrushchev could err, the party could do no wrong. He replied with a grin that this was indeed his view, that it was not an accident that he was born in 1917, and that his fiftieth birthday would coincide with the fiftieth anniversary of the Soviet Union. "I am a real child of the Revolution." He was one child the Revolution had not devoured.

Although the Russians may have regretted the evening, I found it extremely instructive. And even hopeful. For despite the obvious attempt to limit de-Stalinization to the minimum entailed by the calamitous mistake of permitting Khrushchev's speech, it was clear that the questions I had raised about the Moscow Trials, the purges, the struggles within the Russian Party, and others that affected the entire theory and practice of Leninism could not help but rise in the mind of every intelligent Soviet citizen. There is no guarantee that the old Bolsheviks will be rehabilitated and even less that the liberal and socialist victims of the old Bolsheviks will be restored to a place of honor in popular consciousness. But unless the memory of Khrushchev's speech is obliterated, this prospect will remain.

One thing, finally, seems clear. If Korionov is typical of the ruling bureaucracy in the Soviet Union today, one may infer that although it would not like to have Stalin back, the patterns of thought and judgment engrained during his rule still remain.

CHAPTER NINE

The Ideology of Violence

Wars, it has been said, begin in the minds of men. It is a truth that makes the education of a country, the ideals of its school system and its underlying ideology, not a purely domestic matter but a subject of international concern. It becomes not less true when we acknowledge that the minds of men are molded by the history, culture, and institutions in which they have developed. The conflicts of interest *in* any given society and *between* different societies will inescapably reflect themselves in the minds of those who live in them.

So long as men remain men conflicts of interest are likely to remain integral to the human condition. That is why the perspective of peace cannot be guaranteed merely by establishing agreement or unity in the minds of men independently of the social institutions in which they have been nurtured. That is why no purely internal transvaluation of values can bring peace in society and among nations of different societies unless accompanied by profound institutional change. Even a common interest in survival, without some institutional means of resolving conflicts among other interests, will not guarantee peace.

One of the perennial illusions of human thought is the supremacy of human thought isolated from its institutional matrix. It expresses itself in myriad ways—sometimes in the belief that a common ideology is a sufficient condition or even a necessary condition of peace. Sometimes the chief weight is placed on a common tradition or a common language on which the hopes for peace hang. Yet we know that some of the fiercest wars have been fought among those who have shared the same fundamental *Weltanschauung,* for example, in the great wars of religion. The greatest military conflict in world history up to that time was waged during the American Civil War between the North and South whose basic traditions and language were common. Spain, Korea, and Viet Nam reinforce the point.

On the other hand, we know that nations can and have lived in peace with different ideologies, different traditions, different languages. If world peace depended upon the establishment of a unitary world outlook, whether religious or secular, or a common language—different histories make a common tradition unattainable— prospects of attaining it would be dim indeed. The existence of diversity and plurality of world outlooks, traditions, languages is for many reasons highly desirable, aside from the intrinsic value of the variety of delightful experiences it makes possible. Fortunately it is not required to sacrifice them in order to reduce the likelihood of war between nations and within nations.

Granted, then, that the hope of peace and peaceful social change depends more upon the institutional ways of resolving differences of interest than upon common beliefs or rationalizations—in both senses of the word. Still, there are some views about the nature of man and society, some more or less systematically articulated doctrines and attitudes which make more difficult the achievement of the institutional changes required for peace and peaceful change. The mind of man, culturally determined though it be, is not merely a passive resultant of social forces. It cannot be reduced without remainder either to the Objective Mind of Hegel or to the neural impulses of physiological psychology. It reacts selectively upon its conditions and often redetermines, by virtue of its beliefs, the direction of its own development. Thinking makes a difference, and sometimes a crucial difference, when genuine alternatives of action open up before us. To recognize the conditions out of which ideas arise is not incompatible with recognizing the great impact they may have on events. It is because of their impact that we sometimes seek to understand their origin and validity. Knowledge could never be power unless ideas made a difference. Any intelligent form of Marxism that acknowledges that "men make their own history" acknowledges therewith that ideas count. Otherwise what would be the point of trying to convert people to Marxism? To deny this would be to deny the importance of consciousness.

It is not only true beliefs but false beliefs, not only valid attitudes but invalid attitudes, however they be defined, that affect behavior. With respect to the prospects of peace among nations and peaceful social change within nations, I believe it is indisputable that Nationalism and Racism are prejudicial to their furtherance. By nationalism I mean not patriotism, understood in Santayana's phrase as "natural piety for the sources of our being" but the glorification of the nation-state as privileged above others or exempt from principles of political morality in its relation to other states. By "racism" I mean not the belief that there are inherent genetic differences in capacities between ethnic groups which is still an open scientific question—but the belief that to the extent that there are, this justifies invidious distinctions in their social treatment, and an abandonment of the postulate of the moral equality of all persons in the democratic community. There are entire libraries devoted to the evil effects of the ideologies of nationalism and racism. It is significant that except for a handful of fanatics all representatives of these ideologies today seek to justify them defensively as nothing more than claims for compensatory inequalities to redress historic grievances.

More threatening today to world and especially domestic peace is the growth of a family of doctrines that I call the Ideologies of Violence. These ideologies have developed on the peripheries of movements of social protest originally fired by an idealism opposed to war and oppression. Gradually, however, they have acquired a programmatic character of their own. They assert that, to quote one writer,

> The threat of violence, and the occasional outbreak of real violence (which gives the threat credibility) are essential elements in conflict resolution not only in international but also national communities.[1]

Some go further and assert that violence and the threat of violence are necessary and useful in achieving social reforms. The criticism of the use of violence is denounced as hypocritical, as a way of playing the game of the Establishment, as a reaching for a cowardly peace with it. I cannot recall any period in American history in which there has been so much extenuation and glorification of the use of violence not as episodic forays of symbolic character to call attention to shocking evils but as a legitimate strategy in social, political—and even educational reform. (It will be recalled that even John Brown and most of those who rallied to his defense after the raid at Harper's Ferry denied that his original intention was violence against persons or destruction of property, insurrection or murder but only a design to free the slaves and lead them to Canada. Up to the Civil War, the leading abolitionists were pacifists.)

Until recently those who defended the role of violence in social change did so in the main from a revolutionary perspective that forthrightly repudiated democracy as a political system either as a sham, covering up class rule, or as an inadequate institutional expression of self-government. The only question that faced the revolutionist when the question of violence was posed was an instrumental one—the relative cost, effectiveness, and consequences of extraparliamentary means of opposition compared

1. H. L. Nieberg, "The Uses of Violence," *Journal of Conflict Resolution* (1963), vol. 7, no. 1, p. 43.

with the legal means when they were available. Marxists, as a rule, have been opposed to *individual* acts of terror, to the "propaganda of the deed" as a senseless policy that plays into the hands of reaction. They recognize and condone *class* violence. The violence of class against class is to them only an acute form of the inescapable class struggle. Daniel De Leon is the only orthodox Marxist I know who expressly declared that a constitutional victory for socialism without any violence was *preferable* because its legality represented a triumph for the principle of civilization. Marx himself declared that in the case of England, United States, and Holland peaceful transition to socialism was "possible." They were exceptions to the perspective of forcible overthrow. Lenin canceled the exceptions and proclaimed the inevitability of war between the Communist and non-Communist world in the inevitable triumph of the Communist system. Lenin's disciples, especially Stalin, echoed him on this matter to the last syllable. It was Khrushchev, reluctantly convinced of the lethal possibilities of nuclear weapons, who had the courage to modify Leninist doctrine. He asserted that the victory of world communism was still inevitable but not inevitably through war. War was still possible, wars of national liberation very probable, but Armageddon was not necessary. For tactical purposes some national Communist parties have cautiously put forward the non-Leninist idea that they may conquer political power without violence—especially if their opponents are accommodating enough to surrender.

I shall not pursue the analysis of the Communist theory and practice of violence and its divagations from Lenin to the present because it is so frankly opportunist in character that the real intent of Communists can only be construed, not from their words, but from the constellation of forces in which they find themselves at the moment. Simple justice, however, requires the recognition that they too sometimes find the ideologists of violence in some countries somewhat of an embarrassment.

What is comparatively novel in our time is the defense of violence by those who are not prepared openly to abandon the standpoint of democracy but who, out of design or confusion, contend that a "healthy" or "just" or "progressive" democratic society will tolerate violence, recognize its productive, even creative role, and eschew any strategy for the control of violence by resort to the force of the civil authorities or to police power.

A Report of one of the Task Forces of the "National Commission on the Causes and Prevention of Violence" *(The Politics of Protest)* concludes by repudiating the conventional wisdom of the so-called "two-pronged approach" to violence. The first prong of this approach seeks to control or restrain the violence. The second prong attempts to meet genuine grievances by appropriate reform and remedies. Apparently the use of "controlled force to protect civil order," while efforts are organized to cope adequately with the underlying grievances, is unacceptable to Prof. Skolnick's Task Force. On this view once the demands made by those who are violent are distinguished from the causes of the violence, the major effort must go into meeting the demands, into reforming society, not into curbing violence. Society itself must accept the burden of guilt for the violence. Those who initiate the violence must be considered victims not malefactors.

It goes almost without saying that this sympathetic approach to manifestations of violence is limited only to particular groups and to special causes. It is not generalized to hold for all public violence, especially violence *against* good causes. It is not brought to bear on the public violence of groups enraged by the violence of the partisans of "good" causes. We are therefore not dealing with general principles of social action whose validity can be tested by universalizing them to assess their consistency and social consequences. We are dealing with a proposed strategy in a struggle for power—a strategy that appears to me both arbitrary and shortsighted.

There are certain common sense objections that are flagrantly overlooked in this rejection of the "two-pronged approach." First of all, to urge that we treat only the *causes* of violence, and not divide our energies by efforts to curb violence overlooks the obvious fact that we do not always know what the causes of violence are when the facts of violence are quite manifest. Second, even if we believe we *know* what the causes are—treating them properly, remedying the evils, changing the behavior patterns necessary to change the situation, may require time. For example, if the existence of slums is regarded as the chief cause of urban violence (something not really established), rebuilding the city ghetto or dispersing it cannot take place overnight. If violence meanwhile is not curbed more buildings may be burned than can be constructed in the same time period. To be sure *promises* to reform the city can be easily made. And it is true that it is not certain that these promises will be kept once the danger of arson and violence is contained. But neither is it certain that violence, arson, and looting will expedite the redemption of promises of reform. To this very day the scarred, desolate streets of our riot-torn cities are a gaunt and painful reminder of the ineffectuality of violence. Is it not possible that the fear inspired by the violence and confrontation instead of spurring on reforms or strengthening the desire for reform may set off a counterviolence? Why is it assumed that violence will result in the mutual accommodation of interests rather than in further provocation and escalation of violence?

Thirdly, let us suppose we escape this danger and violence does not call into existence its own Nemesis. Is there nothing illegitimate and blameworthy about the action even if it turns out successfully? Is there no socially deleterious effect of violence upon the delicate fabric of confidence and trust, so essential to a civilized society, if it can be rudely torn whenever violence pays?

I shall return to these questions. I raise them here only to indicate the degree to which violence and incitement to violence are acquiring today a respectable status. They have become *salon-fähig*. They are assumed to have a legitimate, in some quarters, an essential role in the process by which consensus, even democratic consensus, is established.

One of the most frequent confusions in the apologetic literature of violence is the identification of force and violence. Since all government and law rest ultimately—although not exclusively—upon force, the universality of the actual or potential exercise of force prepares the ground for a slide to the view that violence, too, is universal and therefore an inescapable facet of all social life. Those who condemn resort to violence in a democracy are then denounced as themselves confused or hypocritical.

The differing connotations of the words "force" and "violence," the fact that in actual usage there is something strained in substituting one expression for another in all contexts, suggests that they refer to different situations or types of experience. Violence is not physical force *simpliciter* but the "illegal" or "immoral" use of physical force. That is why the term "violence" has a negative and disparaging association except when it anticipates a more acceptable state of affairs, political or moral, in behalf of which physical force is used, i.e., when "revolutionary violence" is approved.

"Force" is normatively neutral in meaning. It cannot be renounced without making ideals that encounter resistance ineffectual. Only absolute pacifists can consistently condemn the use of physical force under all circumstances. And their argument can be shown to be self-defeating or irrational, for it is apparent that the very values on behalf of which the use of force is foresworn—the preservation of life, the absence of cruelty, the avoidance of indignity—under some circumstances can be furthered only by the use of force. Force is necessary to sustain or enforce legal rights wherever they are threatened—and human rights, too, which have a moral authority of their own to justify them. Otherwise they are no more than aspirations or pious hopes. When James Meredith was denied the right to study at the University of Mississippi, when Negro women and children were prevented from attending school at Little Rock, after the U. S. Supreme's Court's first school desegregation decision, it was force that protected and redeemed their right against the violence and the threat of violence of the Southern mob.

Whatever rules of the political game are established in order to resolve human conflicts, personal or group, force must ultimately defend or enforce the rules if they are attacked. Where a party resorts to violence in order to breach those rules, to disrupt or destroy the game, it cannot justifiably *equate* its violence with the force used to sustain the rules so long as it professes allegiance to the political system defined by those rules. That is why it makes little sense to discuss the questions of force and violence in the abstract independently of the political context. What holds true for the use and limits of violence in a despotism is not true for the use and limits of violence in a democracy.

One of the most powerful justifications of democracy is that it more readily permits the resolution of human conflicts by argument, persuasion, and debate than is the case under anarchy or despotism. Under anarchy the chaos of recurrent violence defeats the possibility of consensus. Under despotism the appearance of consensus is achieved by terror—the unrestrained and unrestricted use of force. When violence breaks out in a democracy, to that extent it marks the failure or the weakness of the system. Some have therefore concluded that democracy is too noble and rational an ideal to be serviceable to man. Others resign themselves to the suicide of democracy by inactivity in the face of violence. But these do not exhaust the alternatives. A democracy has the moral right to protect itself. Its legitimate use of force to preserve the rules of a democratic society, to enforce the rights without which democracy cannot function, may be wise or unwise, judicious or injudicious. But such use cannot sensibly be classified as violence on par with the violence it seeks to repress. The democratic system ideally seeks to make the use of force in human affairs responsible to those who are governed, and to reduce the occasions, frequency, and intensity with which physical force is actually employed. In so far as it expresses a moral ideal, independently of the political mechanisms instrumental to its realization, it is that the reduction of human suffering, the elimination of pain, the avoidance of bloodshed, and the right to collective self-government are desirable. There is much wider agreement among men on the validity of these ideals than on the best way to achieve them. And despite all the theoretical disagreements and uncertainties about the proper analysis of the meanings of "good" and "better" it does not affect their substantial agreement in many situations on what is specifically good or better. Few reflective persons will deny the proposition that "a divorce is better than a murder"—or when conflict arises in social life, whether in trade unions, political organizations, or the life of nations—the proposition that "separation is better than extermination," if these are the only alternatives.

The importance of considering the question of violence in a *political* context is apparent when we examine some typical syndromes of apologetic justification for violence.

1. The first was exhibited by Mr. Rap Brown, the Black Power militant, in his now classic observation in defending urban riots that "Violence is as American as cherry pie." This piece of wisdom actually is the gist of the findings of several task forces of the National Commission on the Causes and Prevention of Violence (the most notable of which has been Skolnick's *Politics of Protest* to which I have already referred). They gravely inform us that violence is customary in American life—as if that were news, as if that made violence more acceptable, as if the prevalence of violence proved anything more than that the democratic process in America had often broken down in the past, as if the relevant question concerned the past rather than the present and future of the democratic political process, as if the fact that something is authentically American necessarily made it as praiseworthy as cherry pie. Certainly lynching is as American as cherry pie but hardly a cause for boasting!

2. A second popular syndrome of apologetic justification for violence may be called the Boston Tea Party syndrome. Since our patriotic American forebears dumped valuable property into the harbor and engaged in other acts of violence, why is it wrong, we are asked, for present-day rebels to follow suit? Here, too, it is shocking to observe both the source and the frequency of this response to criticism of violence. The *SDS* invoked the Boston Tea Party in their legal defense of their violence at Columbia University and elsewhere. In their case the exuberance and ignorance of youth may perhaps be pleaded in extenuation. But what shall we say of the adults who in a special foreword to *The Politics of Protest* wrote:

> We take the position that the growth of this country has occurred around a series of violent upheavals and that each one has thrust the nation forward. The Boston Tea Party was

an attempt by a few to alter an oppressive system of taxation without representation. The validation of these men rested on their attempts to effect needed social change. If the Boston Tea Party is viewed historically as a legitimate method of producing such change, then present day militancy [*i.e.,* violence] whether by blacks or students, can claim a similar legitimacy. (Greer and Cobb, *The Politics of Protest,* p. xi)

This total disregard of the fact that the American colonists had no means of remedying their grievances by peaceful constitutional change is symptomatic of the grossly unhistorical approach to problems of social change. It is reinforced by the cool disregard of peaceful changes under our constitutional system of extending representation. Further, what is morally and politically permissible to a democrat struggling for freedom under despotic political conditions is not permissible to him once the mechanisms of democratic consent have been established. What makes the Boston Tea Party morally legitimate is the absence of an established procedure of peacefully redressing grievances. When reforms open up the political democratic process to Negroes and make possible the election of black mayors, senators, and other representatives, the tactics of the Boston Tea Party become historically illegitimate. As well argue that because the assassination of tyrants under some circumstances is morally defensible, this legitimizes the assassination of a chief of state who has been democratically elected.

Democracy cannot function if political decisions are to be made not through political process but by actions of street mobs, no matter how originally well-intentioned. To be sure, democratic institutions work slowly and, like all institutions, imperfectly. That is the price of democracy which the democrat cheerfully pays because he knows on the basis of history and psychology that the price of any other political alternative is much higher. The democrat who pins his faith on democracy knows that the majority can be wrong but he will not therefore accept the rule of a minority because it occasionally may be right. The integrity of the process by which a minority may peacefully become or win a majority is all-important to him. If the democratic process functions in such a way as to violate the basic moral values of any group of citizens, they have a right to attempt to overthrow it by revolution but they cannot justifiably do so in the name of democracy. And it is open to others to counter these efforts on the basis of their own revolutionary or counterrevolutionary mandate from heaven.[2]

3. The third syndrome challenges the contention that a principled democrat cannot reform an existing democracy by violence without abandoning democratic first principles. This position asserts that existing means of dissent are inadequate, that the wells of public knowledge are poisoned, that the majority has been misled by its education, corrupted by affluence or enslaved by its passions. Allowing for certain changes in time and idiom this indictment against democracy is as old as the Platonic critique. (But Plato did not pretend to be a democrat.) That the institutional life and mechanisms of American democracy are inadequate is undeniable. But just as undeniable is the fact that in many respects they are more adequate today than they have ever been in the past, that dissent has a voice, a platform, a resonance greater than ever before. The issue is, however, this: Does a democrat, dissatisfied with the workings of a democracy, strive to make them more adequate by resorting to violence or by appealing with all the arts of persuasion at his command, from an unenlightened majority to an enlightened one? And what is the test of the inadequacy of existing democratic mechanisms to

2. Disregard of these considerations is only one of the failings in the scandalous piece of propaganda for violence which appears under the auspices of the National Commission on the Causes and Prevention of Violence. Of Skolnick's *Politics of Protest,* Professor Milton R. Konvitz of Cornell University, a genuine civil libertarian, outstanding for his compassion and scrupulous sense of fairness, writes: "The main thrust of the book is to validate political violence in America. There is very little in the body of the work that would tend to dispel the myth of violent progress and that would make the value of a constitutional democracy credible—not in some utopian society but in the United States" *(Saturday Review,* 15 November 1969).

remedy grievances? That the minority has failed to persuade the majority? This is like saying that a democrat will be convinced that elections are truly democratic only when *he* wins them. Having failed to persuade the majority by democratic and constitutional means, the minority claims the right in the name of a hypothetical, future majority to impose its opinions and rule by violence on the present majority. And by a series of semantic outrages it calls this a democratic method of reforming democracy!

It is easy enough to expose this when it is—as it has often been in the past—a stratagem in the propaganda offensive of totalitarian groups. But the difficulty is greater when these contentions are put forward by individuals who sincerely believe themselves committed to democracy. What they are really saying in their sincere confusion is that in any democratic society that falls short of perfection—that is, in any democratic society in which they fall short of winning a majority—they have a democratic right to resort to violence—which is absurd. Unfortunately, as Cicero once observed, there is no absurdity to which some human beings will not resort to defend another absurdity.

4. The fourth syndrome in the contemporary apologetic literature of violence is the justification of the tactics of violent disruption and confrontation on the ground that the state itself employs force, and sometimes makes an unwise use of it either in war or in preserving domestic peace. Who has not heard militants of the New Left, not only students but their professorial allies, countering rebukes of their irresponsible resort to violence with the cry: "But the Government uses force! Therefore it cannot be wrong for us to use it. . . ." Only an anarchist who does not recognize any state authority can consistently make this kind of retort—and even anarchists are not likely to be much impressed by it if it were to be mouthed by raiding parties of the Ku Klux Klan and similar groups. In any society, democratic or not, where the state does not have a monopoly of physical force to which all other sanctions are ultimately subordinate, we face incipient civil war.

Nor is the situation any different when the state embarks upon actions that offend the moral sensibilities of some of its citizens. In debates with spokesmen for student disruption, I have often been asked: "How can you reasonably protest against the comparatively limited use of violence by the *SDS* at Columbia University and elsewhere in view of the massive use of violence by the United States in Viet Nam?" It is a retort frequently heard when student and Black militant violence is condemned. Many who make this retort are great admirers of A. J. Muste, the late revolutionary pacifist leader. I find it ironical that the questions they asked me are the same kind of question hurled at Muste by members of the Communist Party in the 1930s in rejoinder to Muste's protests against the violent disruption of the meetings of the American Workers Party of which, together with others, we were the founders. They said to Muste: "How can you bring yourself to protest against the inconsequential and largely symbolic violence of Young Communists in breaking up your meetings while Hitler is mobilizing all the violence of Fascist reaction against the European working class? *That* is the violence you must protest against, not ours." One would never have guessed from Muste's language at these junctures that he was a clergyman!

For one thing these rhetorical questions overlook the obvious fact that one can be opposed *both* to student violence on campus and to the American involvement in Viet Nam just as one could bitterly resist *both* the Stalinist goon squads and Hitler's terrorists who were to clasp arms in fraternal consent a few years later. And even if this were not the case, as we easily can conceive it by changing the illustrations, the comparison is specious and question-begging to boot. Because we disapprove of violence in one context (say, when extremists organize a riot to prevent a dialogue from taking place), we do not have to disapprove of it in another (say, when those who believe in freedom fight to overthrow their oppressors). The assumption that all of these contexts are necessarily involved with each other will not stand examination for a minute.

The objection to violence in a democratic polity stems from various sources—not all of them narrowly political.

The first reflects the civilized and humane belief that the amount of physical coercion of men over other men can be reduced although it cannot ever be eliminated. Even those who are wedded to violence as a strategy of social change profess to believe that their actions will produce a world that ultimately will be less violent. This is extremely unlikely although not inconceivable either theoretically or practically. Tolstoy to the contrary notwithstanding, we *can* sometimes fight fire with fire and touch pitch without being defiled. But because of the interrelationship of means and ends, because the ends achieved depend not on the ends proclaimed but on the consequences of the means used, a very careful assessment of the probabilities is required before embarking on a course that entails much physical coercion. Those who choose the democratic option, whose institutions permit the minority peacefully to become the majority, have presumably calculated the probabilities. Without accepting the argument of absolute pacifism, they recognize the pacifist insight that in using coercive force against the violent domestic and even foreign enemies of a democracy, there is always a danger that we may become like them. But there is no world without its dangers, and the dangers of the triumph of evil through nonresistance or even passive resistance to evil are much greater than that physical resistance to evil will necessarily reinstate the evil to as great an extent.

Another source of opposition to violence is the desire of men for continuity and predictability in their social life within the limits of what is humanly sufferable. It is the *certainty* of the law, the knowledge of what can be relied on as we go about arranging our affairs and tying them into the future, rather than our expectation that the delicate balance of justice will be precisely achieved in human relations, that is its chief desideratum. Violence, especially chronic violence, upsets the normal expectations of orderly procedure. Unless a new pattern of stability is quickly reached, an atmosphere of impending chaos and catastrophe is generated that prepares the ground for the growth and tolerance of despotism. Despotism is not easily or freely chosen. It is accepted more readily when men become fearful of anarchy.

It is in the light of these considerations that we must examine what seems to be the most pervasive as well as the most persuasive argument for violence. This maintains that the threat of violence, and its actuality which is necessary to make the threat credible, are the most effective means of achieving reforms, that without the violent extremist the moderate reformer has no chance to implement his program, that the prospects of reform are always enhanced by the fear generated through the threat of violence and its sporadic outbreaks. *"Kill, burn, ravage!"* exhorts the extremist leader. *"Deal with me, or else face the irresponsibles,"* warns the moderate or reformist leader. His proposed compromises and concessions seem sweetly reasonable against the background mob's shrill cries. On this view it is only because of the multitudinous threats of violence emanating from plural pressure groups that keep each other in check that the democratic system works peacefully *on the whole.* But episodically and fitfully there must be outbreaks of violence to reinforce the readiness to be reasonable, to soften if not to dissolve the stubborn recalcitrance dug in to defend the sacred principles of the Establishment.

Without doubt there is some truth to this view. But it is a half-truth and a dangerous half-truth at that. From the abstract proposition that the threat of exercise of violence *may* facilitate enlightened social change or policy, it is the sheerest dogmatism to assume that in any particular situation, violence or its threat will in fact serve a beneficial purpose. It may just as likely set up a cycle of escalating violence and counterviolence that will be more costly and undesirable than the reforms subsequently instituted. It all depends upon the case.

The theoretical basis of this position is purely Hobbesian with all its limitations. As one defender of this view puts it:

In an important sense, all individuals, groups or nations desire "to rule the world" but are constrained to collaborate with others on less desirable terms because of the objective limits of their own power. (H. L. Nieberg, "Uses of Violence". *loc.*cot.)

In other words, the chief, if not the only, reason we bargain, tolerate, cooperate, "live-and-let-live" with others is that we are not powerful enough to kill or enslave them. This is false not only for individuals but even for some states in some areas and in some periods of the world. Otherwise we could hardly explain the existence of small, relatively defenseless powers. And even Hobbes recognizes (as some of his modern descendants do not) that, despite the hypothetical and largely mythical "natural state of anarchy," once a community is established, a binding commitment to resolve differences by due political process arises. For who would enter into a compact to surrender his powers and abide by certain rules if every party to the compact added to it a rider that whenever it was strong enough to violate the rules with impunity, it would do so? If violence always (or even in most cases) "paid," no social life could continue. It was realization of this that accounts for Hobbes's third law of nature—"that men perform their covenants made."

That they do not always and in every circumstance perform their covenants does not negate recognition of the authority and validity of the covenant, especially when freely entered into, any more than the fact that we sometimes do not tell the truth impugns the validity of the rule or principle which enjoins truth-telling. The validity of a covenant or promise may sometimes be overriden by a stronger moral imperative.

Turn from the dialectic of theory to the record of history.

Is it true that the historical record proves that the fear or the actual outbreak of violence has been the sole or even the most important cause of reform? It would be a fantastic misreading of European and American history to assert this. Vast amounts of social welfare legislation for women, children, the aged, the sick and handicapped, the unemployed, cannot be explained in terms of fear of violence. The motives and causes for their adoption are mixed but among them an expanded social consciousness and sense of responsibility rank high. No one, in our own times, rioted for social security or unemployment insurance or Medicare relief or for consideration by the Federal government of the potentially revolutionary principle of a minimum family income-wage payment. Tremendous advances have been made on both sides of the Atlantic in the defense and extension of civil rights and liberties, in judicial and penal practice, in the liberalization of laws relating to marriage, divorce, birth control, and abortion. All of these measures—and many more—have been adopted in the absence of any credible threats of violence. Not a single one of the great landmark decisions of the U. S. Supreme Court (including its outlawing of school segregation in 1954 and mandatory state political reapportionment a decade later) was made under the threat of the gun, the mob, or the torch. It was not to violence or the threat of violence that we owe their enactment but to the growth of enlightenment, the enlargement of imagination, and the development of the democratic idea.

The view that violence and the threat of violence are always effective in preparing the minds of men for change is in a sense worse than false. It is thoroughly confused. It does not distinguish between the effect of the fear that violence *may* break out, and the effect of the actual violence *after* it has broken out, between the anticipatory fear and the consequential fear. There is no need to deny that fear of violence, but certainly not fear alone, does often have an influence upon the willingness to reform conditions. And up to a point it is altogether reasonable that it should have an influence. Every society rests upon some shared values that determine acceptable and unacceptable, approved and disapproved norms of conduct. Basic in the hierarchy of such values is a shared interest in survival. Where conditions are so oppressive that those who live under them are tempted to a revolt that may encompass our common doom, self-interest legitimately reinforces the weight of ideals and human sympathy in motivating necessary reforms. R. L. Stevenson once observed that "If we were all seated at the same table, no one would go hungry"—and, I add, not because of *fear* but in virtue of the compassion that quickens the perception of need in others. We are indeed seated at the same table but there are so many and they are so far away from us that those out of sight are out of mind. Our imaginations are often too weak and uncultivated to close the gap. Where vision falters, common sense or intelligent fear may suggest a sensible course of conduct. If consideration for others does not lead to our extending to them the courtesy of the road, prudent fear for our own safety should. If the deficiencies of our imagination and moral feeling make us insensitive or indifferent to the plague, the poverty, the crime and degradation that flourish beyond our narrow horizons, then chill fear—born of the realization that these contagious evils, these diseases of body and spirit could strike down our own children—may shake us out of our torpor into taking remedial action. Under such circumstances intelligent fear, including fear that basic human needs long frustrated may erupt in violence, furthers cooperative effort.

Although *fear* of violence is often a persuasive reason among others for initiating reforms, this is not true to the same extent of overt, repeated *threats* of violence. And least persuasive of all is the brute outbreak of violence that imperils security of life, of one's home and property. For the consequence of such violence is the generation of hysteria and panic among its victims and all elements of the population who identify empathetically with them. This is particularly true when women and children are in the path of the violence.

Mass hysteria and panic are blind. They mistake fantasy for reality and breed unreasoning, not intelligent, fear and hate. If enough people among the majority are swept up in these emotions a reaction sets in, all the more intense for being delayed, that makes reforms more difficult to achieve, not less. It not only can stop the movement toward reform—it sometimes reverses it.

Whoever, then, calculates on the educational value of violence for the community, who anticipates that violence will strengthen the influence of moderates and expedite reform is taking a considerable risk—a foolish risk, and in the absence of compelling evidence that no other way is possible, a criminally irresponsible risk. He risks provoking a backlash, risks the hardening of opposition to further reforms, risks a counterviolence that as it escalates moves the conflict toward civil war, the cruellest form of all wars. In short, violence more often drowns out the voice of moderation than it succeeds in getting a hearing for it otherwise denied. It narrows options, destroys the center, and polarizes the community into extremes.

We may cite the Irish and Israeli-Arab conflicts in support of our view but the American Civil War is the best case in point. It did not solve the Negro question. We are still suffering from its legacy of hate and fear which left the Negro politically disfranchised (despite his legal emancipation as a war measure in 1863), economically in peonage, and socially and educationally victimized by a Jim Crow system. It is still a moot question among historians whether at one time Lincoln's original plan of liberation of the slaves by purchase at a far lesser cost in life, money, suffering, and paranoic hatred would not have integrated the Negroes into American life more quickly and more effectively than did the Civil War. The prospects for the adoption of Lincoln's plan diminished to the vanishing point as the fanatics of violence on both sides heated regional consciousness with its passionate loyalties to the boiling point.

What is not moot at all is the fact that since the Civil War the greatest gains in the condition of the Negroes in the United States were won not in consequence of violence or the threat of violence but by the use of democratic administrative and legal processes fortified in recent times by the nonviolent civil rights movement headed by Dr. Martin Luther King. Civil (i.e., nonviolent) disturbance has a place in a democratic community as a means of bearing testimony and reeducating the majority. Uncivil (i.e., violent) disturbance has no place whatsoever. The ghetto riots that periodically swept cities during the first three decades of this century brought no substantial reforms despite great loss of life. Anyone who recalls the state of the USA before World War I and today will testify to the remarkable progress made—granted, of course, that this progress has still far to go to achieve the substantial equality to which all groups are entitled in a democratic community.

Mr. Roy Wilkins in defending the impressive record of the NAACP in its unremitting militant but nonviolent struggle for Negro rights recently reminded a group of black extremists, impatient with its methods, that the victories won by the NAACP and other organizations of the Negro people had changed the political picture of the country, provided the opportunities for the extremists to be heard and to survive, and had laid the basis for still greater victories. He charged that white racism was responsible for the emergence of black racism; but he warned that black racism would result only in a stronger and subtler form of white racism. And he pleaded for the abolition of every form of racism in human relations.

Those who approve of violence as the most effective instrument of achieving reform, because of its intimidating effect, discount the weight of Mr. Wilkins's testimony. They usually seize upon some impressive reform or piece of social legislation that has been won in the teeth of formidable resistance and insist that it has been wrung from the opposition only in virtue of the shock and fear induced by the preceding or accompanying violence. For example, it has been claimed that the Open Housing Bill of 1968 was adopted only after the assassination of Dr. Martin Luther King and the riots to which it gave rise. A hard look at the evidence shows actually that a majority of the Congress had been lined up before the tragic occurrences.[3] Although the majority vote may have been swelled by some sympathetic reactions that followed the slaying of Dr. King, some votes may have been lost in consequence of a backlash to the urban disorders it precipitated.

What holds for the relationship between violence and reform with respect to the Negro citizens of the United States holds true even more obviously for the relationship between student violence and university reform. Some apologists for student violence maintain that it led to necessary and healthy curricular and administrative reforms in the university. The wisdom of such reforms remains problematic where they were adopted not on the basis of sound educational inquiry but (as was frankly proclaimed in many institutions) as a means of keeping the campus quiet, of

3. Cf. *Congressional Quarterly*, April 24, 1968, "Open Housing Bill Credited to [Clarence] Mitchell's Lobbying."

bringing peace to embroiled institutions. This is an extraordinary criterion by which to determine the validity of an educational curriculum.

Where the educational reforms mark essential improvements in instruction and administration, the crucial question to be decided is whether they would have been adopted if students had persistently agitated for them through the customary forms of dissent without threatening to tear the university apart or burn it down. The most significant feature of the student rebellion at Berkeley, at Columbia, at Harvard, and elsewhere is that the grievances were not in the first instance connected with the students' own educational experience but with issues unrelated to curricular matters. Subsequently educational issues were moved to the forefront from the far periphery of student interest to outflank the devastating criticism of student irrationality in holding the university responsible for social and political in-volvements altogether beyond its sphere of competence and authority.

That *some* good results from violence does not justify the violence unless it can be proved that the good so achieved was necessary, could not have been achieved more effectively and at a lesser cost in other ways, and did not result in evil that outweighed the good. It is notorious that wars accomplish (or, rather, result in) some good—e.g., a great many advances in science, technology, and medicine have resulted from war. But only someone seriously deficient in compassion and imagination would therefore justify war. The truth of the matter is that most educational reforms in most institutions have come about *without* a show of force, where arguments have been the only weapons, where dissenters and protesters have evinced not only zeal but persistence in a good cause. Where violence has been used, a grievous wound has been inflicted on the fabric of university community life. It may take a generation to heal it. For the commitment of the university, even more so than of the democratic community, has been to the processes of deliberation and to the authority of reason.

Some faculty apologists for the student rebels have sought to play down the enormity of the offenses against intellectual and academic freedom by dismissing them as inconsequential. "Just a few buildings burned," they say—"some machines destroyed, a handful of classes disrupted, a dozen or so administrators and professors manhandled. . . ." This is as if one were to extenuate the corruption of justice by the numbers of magistrates not bribed, the desecration of a temple by the unusual character of the defilement, lynchings by their infrequency. The sober fact is that violence has reached such proportions on the campuses today that the whole atmosphere of American—and not a few European (not to mention Japanese)—universities has been transformed. The appeal to reason is no longer sufficient to resolve problems or even to keep the peace. In order to make itself heard in some of our most prestigious institutions, the appeal to reason must finally appeal to the courts and to the police.

Violence in the academy is an outgrowth of violence in the streets and cities of the country. That is where the gravest current danger lies. Were violence confined to the universities alone its evils could not long continue if only because the state and society on whose support the universities ultimately depend would restrict and perhaps cancel their precarious autonomy. This could easily be done under the currently fashionable slogans of "community control" and "participatory democracy" in educational institutions.

In the democratic community at large the resort to violence, instead of reliance upon the due political process of a self-governing republic, attacks that community at its foundations. And this regardless of the merit of the cause or the sincerity and self-righteousness of the *engagés* and the *enragés*. For every such outbreak of violence makes other outbreaks of violence more likely by serving as a model or precedent to some, or as a provocation to others—in either case escalating the violence.

In this connection Alexander Hamilton was truly prophetic. In the *Federalist Papers* he warned us of this:

> . . . every breach of the fundamental law, though dictated by necessity, impairs that sacred reverence which ought to be maintained in the breast of rulers [who in a self-governing

republic are all the people] towards the Constitution of the country, and forms a precedent for other breaches, where the same plea of necessity does not exist at all, or is less urgent and palpable.

Hamilton unerringly cited, on the basis of evidence from the past, the great danger of situations of this kind—the likelihood that citizens "to be more safe . . . at length become more willing to run the risk of becoming less free."

In the end, then, the great paradox and the great truth is that in a democratic society freedom, which is often invoked to justify violence, is itself imperiled by the exercise of violence. The ideologists of violence in a democracy are the sappers and miners of the forces of despotism, the gravediggers, willing or unwilling, of the precious heritage of freedom.

CHAPTER TEN

Democracy and Social Protest: Neither Blind Obedience Nor Uncivil Disobedience

In times of moral crisis what has been accepted as common-place truth sometimes appears questionable and problematic. We have all been nurtured in the humanistic belief that in a democracy citizens are free to disagree with a law but that so long as it remains in force they have a *prima facie* obligation to obey it. The belief is justified on the ground that this procedure enables us to escape the twin evils of tyranny and anarchy. Tyranny is avoided by virtue of the freedom and power of dissent to win the uncoerced consent of the community. Anarchy is avoided by reliance on due process, the recognition that there is a right way to correct a wrong, and a wrong way to secure a right. To the extent that anything is demonstrable in human affairs, we have held that democracy as a political system is not viable if members systematically refuse to obey laws whose wisdom or morality they dispute.

242

Nonetheless, during the past decade of tension and turmoil in American life there has developed a mass phenomenon of civil disobedience even among those who profess devotion to democratic ideals and institutions. This phenomenon has assumed a character similar to a tidal wave which has not yet reached its crest. It has swept from the field of race relations to the campuses of some universities, subtly altering the connotation of the term "academic." It is being systematically developed as an instrument for influencing foreign policy. It is leaving its mark on popular culture. I am told it is not only a theme of comic books but that children in our more sophisticated families no longer resort to tantrums in defying parental discipline—they go limp!

More seriously, in the wake of civil disobedience there has occasionally developed *uncivil* disobedience, sometimes as a natural psychological development, and often because of the failure of law enforcement agencies especially in the South to respect and defend legitimate expressions of social protest. The line between civil and uncivil disobedience is not only an uncertain and wavering one in practice, it has become so in theory. A recent prophet of the philosophy of the absurd in recommending civil disobedience as a form of creative disorder in a democracy cited Shay's Rebellion as an illustration. This Rebellion was uncivil to the point of bloodshed. Indeed, some of the techniques of protesting American involvement in Vietnam have departed so far from traditional ways of civil disobedience as to make it likely that they are inspired by the same confusion between civil and uncivil disobedience.

All this has made focal the perennial problems of the nature and limits of the citizen's obligation to obey the law, of the relation between the authority of conscience and the authority of the state, of the rights and duties of a democratic moral man in an immoral democratic society. The classical writings on these questions—Socrates's argument in the *Crito;* the confrontation between Antigone and Creon in Sophocles's *Antigone;* the writings of Rousseau, Thoreau, Garrison, Tolstoy, Gandhi, and their critics—have acquired a burning relevance to the political condition of man today. I propose briefly to clarify some of these problems.

To begin with I wish to stress the point that there is no problem concerning "social protest" as such in a democracy. Our Bill of Rights was adopted not only to make protest possible but to encourage it. The political logic, the very ethos of any democracy that professes to rest, no matter how indirectly, upon freely given consent *requires* that social protest be permitted—and not only permitted but *protected* from interference by those opposed to the protest, which means protected by agencies of law enforcement.

Not social protest but *illegal* social protest constitutes our problem. It raises the question: "When, if ever, is illegal protest justified in a democratic society?" It is of the first importance to bear in mind that we are raising the question as principled democrats and humanists in a democratic society. To urge that illegal social protests motivated by exalted ideals are sanctified in a democratic society by precedents like the Boston Tea Party is a lapse into political illiteracy. Such actions occurred in societies in which those affected by unjust laws had no power peacefully to change them. As a democrat, I am in favor of any social protest, legal or illegal, peaceful or violent, in any nondemocratic society that is likely to free human beings from oppression or lessen the pitch of such oppression, without exposing them to serious risks of greater evils at the time.

Further, many actions dubbed civilly disobedient by local authorities, strictly speaking, are not such at all. An action launched in violation of a local law or ordinance, and undertaken to test it, on the ground that the law itself violates state or federal law, or launched in violation of a state law in the sincerely held belief that the state law outrages the Constitution, the supreme law of the land, is not civilly disobedient. In large measure the early sympathy with which the original sit-ins were received, especially the Freedom Rides, marches and demonstrations that flouted local Southern laws, was due to the conviction that they were constitutionally justified, in accordance with the heritage of freedom, enshrined in the Amendments and enjoyed in other regions of the country. Practically everything the marchers did was sanctioned by the phrase of the First Amendment which upholds "the right of the people peaceably to assemble and to petition the Government for a redress of grievances." Actions of this kind may be wise or unwise, timely or untimely, but they are not civilly disobedient.

They become civilly disobedient when they are in deliberate violation of laws that have been sustained by the highest legislative and judicial bodies of the nation, e.g., income tax laws, conscription laws, laws forbidding segregation in education, and discrimination in public accommodations and employment. Another class of examples consists of illegal social protest against local and state laws that clearly do not conflict with Federal Law. An act of civil disobedience is not only deliberate and nonviolent but public. Were it not public, it would be pointless and hard to distinguish from a criminally evasive action for personal gain.

Once we grasp the proper issue, the question is asked with deceptive clarity: "Are we under an obligation in a democratic community always to obey an unjust law?" To this question Abraham Lincoln is supposed to have made the classic answer in an eloquent address on "The Perpetuation of Our Political Institution," calling for absolute and religious obedience until the unjust law is repealed. Said Lincoln: "Bad laws if they exist should be repealed as soon as possible, still while they continue in force, they should be religiously observed." This sentiment was echoed by President Kennedy. Said Kennedy: "Americans are free to disagree with the law but not to disobey it. For in a government of laws, no man, however powerful or prominent, and no mob, however unruly or boisterous, is entitled to defy a court of law."

I said that this question is asked with deceptive clarity because Lincoln, judging by his other writings and the pragmatic cast of his basic philosophy, could never have subscribed to this absolutism or meant what he seemed literally to have said. Not only are we under no moral obligation *always* to obey unjust laws, we are under no moral obligation *always* to obey a just law. One can put it more strongly: sometimes it may be necessary in the interests of the greater good to violate a just or sensible law. A man who refused to violate a sensible traffic law if it were necessary to do so to avoid a probably fatal accident would be a moral idiot.

There are other values in the world besides legality or even justice, and sometimes they may be of overriding concern and weight. Everyone can imagine some situation in which the violation of some existing law is the lesser moral evil, but this does not invalidate recognition of our obligation to obey just laws.

There is a difference between disobeying a law which one approves of in general but whose application in a specific case seems wrong, and disobeying a law in protest against the injustice of the law itself. In the latter case the disobedience is open and public; in the former, not. But if the grounds of disobedience in both cases are moral considerations, there is only a difference in degree between them. The rejection, therefore, of legal absolutism or the fetishism of legality—that one is never justified in violating any law in any circumstances—is a matter of common sense.

The implications drawn from this moral commonplace by some ritualistic liberals are clearly absurd. For they have substituted for the absolutism of law, something very close to the absolutism of individual conscience. Properly rejecting the view that the law, no matter how unjust, must be obeyed in all circumstances, they have taken the view that the law is to be obeyed only when the individual deems it just or when it does not outrage his conscience. Fantastic comparisons are made between those who do not act on the dictates of their conscience and those who accepted and obeyed Hitler's laws. These comparisons completely disregard the systems of law involved, the presence of alternatives of action, the differences in the behavior commanded, in degrees of complicity of guilt, in the moral costs and personal consequences of compliance, and other relevant matters.

It is commendable to recognize the primacy of morality to law, but unless we recognize the centrality of intelligence to morality we stumble with blind self-righteousness into moral disaster. Because, Kant to the contrary notwithstanding, it is not wrong sometimes to lie to save a human life, because it is not wrong sometimes to kill in defense to save many more from being killed, it does not follow that the moral principles: "Do not lie!" "Do not kill!" are invalid. When more than one valid principle bears on a problem of moral experience, the very fact of their conflict means that not all of them can hold unqualifiedly. One of them must be denied. The point is that such negation or violation entails upon us the obligation of justifying it, and moral justification is a matter of reasons not of conscience. The burden of proof rests on the person violating the rules. Normally, we don't have to justify telling the truth. We do have to justify *not* telling the truth. Similarly, with respect to the moral obligation of a democrat who breaches his political obligation to obey the laws of a democratic community. The resort to conscience is not enough. There must always be reasonable justification.

This is all the more true because just as we can, if challenged, give powerful reasons for the moral principle of truth-telling, so we can offer morally persuasive grounds for the obligation of a democrat to obey the laws of a democracy. The grounds are many and they can be amplified beyond the passing mention we give here. It is a matter of fairness, of not being a free-loader, i.e., profiting from the political system that one professes to reject or refuses to support, of social utility, of peace, or ordered progress, of redeeming an implicit commitment.

There is one point, however, which has a particular relevance to the claims of those who counterpose to legal absolutism the absolutism of conscience. There is the empirically observable tendency for public disobedience to law to spread from those who occupy high moral ground to those who dwell on low moral ground with consequent growth of disorder and insecurity.

Conscience by itself is not the measure of high or low moral ground. This is the work of reason. Where it functions properly the democratic process permits this resort to reason. If the man of conscience loses in the court of reason, why should he assume that the decision or the law is mistaken rather than the deliverances of his conscience?

The voice of conscience may sound loud and clear. But it may conflict at times not only with the law but with another man's conscience. Every conscientious objector to a law knows that at least one man's conscience is wrong, viz., the conscience of the man who asserts that *his* conscience tells him that he must not tolerate conscientious objectors. From this if he is reasonable he should conclude that when he hears the voice of conscience he is hearing not the voice of God, but the voice of a finite, limited man in this time and in this place, and that conscience is neither a special nor an infallible organ of apprehending moral truth, that conscience without conscientiousness, conscience which does not cap the process of critical reflective morality, is likely to be prejudice masquerading as a First Principle or a Mandate from Heaven.

The mark of an enlightened democracy is, as far as is possible with its security, to respect the religious commitment of a citizen who believes, on grounds of conscience or any other ground, that his relation to God involves duties superior to those arising from any human relation. It, therefore, exempts him from his duty as a citizen to protect his country. However, the mark of the genuine conscientious objector in a democracy who professes belief in a democracy as morally preferable to any realistic alternative at the time, is to respect the democratic process. He does not use his exemption as a political weapon to coerce where he has failed to convince or persuade. Having failed to influence national policy by rational means within the law, in the political processes open to him in a free society, he cannot justifiably try to defeat that policy by resorting to obstructive techniques outside the law *and still remain a democrat.*

It is one thing on grounds of conscience or religion to plead exemption from the duty of serving one's country when drafted. It is quite another to adopt harassing techniques to prevent others from volunteering or responding to the call of duty. It is one thing to oppose American involvement in Vietnam by teach-ins, petitions, electoral activity. It is quite another to attempt to stop troop trains: to take possession of the premises of draft boards where policies are not made; to urge recruits to sabotage their assignments and feign illness to win discharge. The first class of actions falls within the sphere of legitimate social protest; the second class is implicitly insurrectionary since it is directed against the authority of a democratic government which it seeks to overthrow not by argument and discussion but by resistance—albeit passive resistance.

Nonetheless since we have rejected legal absolutism we must face the possibility that in protest on ethical grounds individuals may refuse to obey some law which they regard as uncommonly immoral or uncommonly foolish. If they profess to be democrats, their behavior must scrupulously respect the following conditions:

First, it must be truly nonviolent—peaceful not only in form but in actuality. After all, the protesters are seeking to dramatize a great evil that the community allegedly has been unable to overcome because of complacency or moral weakness. Therefore, they must avoid the guilt of imposing hardship or harm on others who in the nature of the case can hardly be responsible for the situation under protest. Passive resistance should not be utilized merely as a safer or more effective strategy than active resistance in imposing their wills on others. And nonviolence must be judged by the consequences of the allegedly nonviolent action, not by whether physical force is dramatically employed. To cut off a person's food or water, or to deny him access to them, is an act of violence which, if prolonged, may be more cruel than cutting off his head. It is almost always counterproductive. Uncivil or violent disobedience evokes a fear in the general population of either an incipiently revolutionary movement directed against the existing political and legal system or of chaos and anarchy whose potential evils dwarf any existing one.

Second, resort to civil disobedience is never morally legitimate where other methods of remedying the evil complained of are available. Existing grievance procedures should be used. No grievance procedures were available to the southern Negroes. The courts often shared the prejudices of the community and offered no relief, not even minimal protection. But such procedures *are* available in the areas of industry and education. For example, where charges against students are being heard such procedures may result in the dismissal of the charges not the students. Or the faculty on appeal may decide to suspend the rules rather than the students. To jump the gun to civil disobedience in bypassing these procedures is telltale evidence that those who are calling the shots are after other game than preserving the rights of students. This was the case when students of the FSM at the University of California at Berkeley in 1964, in response to a request that four of their leaders appear for a hearing before the Faculty Committee on Student Conduct to answer charges that they had engaged in acts of illegal physical violence, seized possession of Sproul Hall, the administrative building.[1]

Third, those who resort to civil disobedience are duty bound to accept the legal sanctions and punishments imposed by the laws. Attempts to evade and escape them involve not only a betrayal of the community, but they erode the moral foundations of civil disobedience itself. Socrates's argument in the *Crito* is valid only on democratic premises. The rationale of the protesters is the hope that the pain and hurt and indignity they voluntarily accept will stir their fellow citizens to compassion, open their minds to second thoughts, and move them to undertake the necessary healing action. When however, we observe the heroics of defiance being followed by the dialectics of legal evasion, we question the sincerity of the action.

Fourth, civil disobedience is unjustified if a major moral issue is not clearly at stake. Differences about negotiable details that can easily be settled with a little patience should not be fanned into a blaze of illegal opposition.

Fifth, where intelligent men of good will and character differ on large and complex moral issues discussion and agitation are more appropriate than civilly disobedient action. Those who feel strongly about animal rights and regard the consumption of animal flesh as food as morally evil would have a just cause for civil disobedience if *their* freedom to obtain other food was threatened. They would have no moral right to resort to similar action to

---

1. See my "Second Thoughts on Berkeley," *Teachers College Record,* 1965, reprinted as an appendix in my *Academic Freedom and Academic Anarchy* (New York, 1969).

prevent their fellow-citizens from consuming meat. Similarly, with fluoridation.

Sixth, where civil disobedience is undertaken, there must be some rhyme and reason in the time, place, and targets selected. If one is convinced, as I am not, that the Board of Education of New York City is remiss in its policy of desegregation, what is the point of dumping garbage on bridges to produce traffic jams that seriously discomfort commuters who have not the remotest connection with educational policies in New York? Such action can only obstruct the progress of desegregation in the communities of Long Island. Gandhi, who inspired the civil disobedience movement in the twentieth century, was a better tactician than many who invoke his name but ignore his teachings. When he organized his campaign of civil disobedience against the Salt Tax, he marched with his followers to the sea to make salt. He did not hold up food trains or tie up traffic.

Finally, there is such a thing as historical timing. Democrats who resort to civil disobedience must ask themselves whether the cumulative consequences of their action may in the existing climate of opinion undermine the peace and order on which the effective exercise of other human rights depend. This is a cost which one may be willing to pay but which must be taken into the reckoning.

These observations in the eyes of some defenders of the philosophy of civil disobedience are far from persuasive. They regard them as evading the political realities. The political realities, it is asserted, do not provide meaningful channels for the legitimate expression of dissent. The Establishment is too powerful or indifferent to be moved. Administrations are voted into office that are not bound by their election pledges. The right to form minority parties is hampered by unconstitutional voting laws. What does even "the right of the people to present petitions for the redress of grievances" amount to if it does not carry with it the right to have those petitions paid attention to, at least to have them read, if not acted upon?

No, the opposing argument runs on. Genuine progress does not come by enactment of laws, by appeals to the good will or conscience of one's fellow citizens, but only by obstructions which interfere with the functioning of the system itself, by actions whose nuisance value is so high that the Establishment finds it easier to be decent and yield to demands than to be obdurate and oppose them. The time comes, as one student leader of the civilly disobedient Berkeley students advised, "when it is necessary for you to throw your bodies upon the wheels and gears and levers and bring the machine to a grinding halt." When one objects that such obstruction, as a principle of political action, is almost sure to produce chaos, and that it is unnecessary and undesirable in a democracy, the retort is made: "Amen, if only this were a democracy, how glad we would be to stop!"

It is characteristic of those who argue this way to define the presence or absence of the democratic process by whether or not *they* get their political way, and not by the presence or absence of democratic institutional processes. The rules of the game exist to enable them to win and if they lose that's sufficient proof the game is rigged and dishonest. The sincerity with which the position is held is no evidence whatsoever of its coherence. The right to petition does not carry with it the right to be heard if that means successfully influencing those to whom it is addressed. What would they do if they received incompatible petitions from two different and hostile groups of petitioning citizens? The right of petition gives one a chance to persuade, and the persuasion must rest on the power of words, on the effective appeal to emotion, sympathy, reason, and logic. Petitions are weapons of criticism, and their failure does not justify appeal to the criticism of weapons. Some groups that have resorted both to civil and uncivil disobedience justify themselves by claiming that the authorities did not listen to their demands on the ground that their demands were not granted. This begs all the questions about the legitimacy and the cogency of the demands.

It is quite true that some local election laws do hamper minority groups in the organization of political parties; but there is always the right of appeal to the courts. Even if this fails there is a possibility of influencing other political parties. It is difficult, but so long as one is free to publish and speak it can be done. If a group is unsuccessful in moving a majority by the weapons of criticism, in a democracy it may resort to peaceful measures of obstruction, provided it is willing to accept punishment for its obstructionist behavior. But these objections are usually a preface to some form of élitism or moral snobbery which is incompatible with the very grounds given in defending the right of civil disobedience on the part of democrats in a democracy.

All of the seven considerations listed above are cautionary, not categorical. We have ruled out only two positions—blind obedience to any and all laws in a democracy, and unreflective violation of laws at the behest of individual consciences. Between these two obviously unacceptable extremes, there is a spectrum of views which shade into each other. Intelligent persons can differ on their application to specific situations. These differences will reflect different assessments of the historical mood of a culture, of the proper timing of protest and acquiescence, of the extent to which the procedures of democratic decision obtain in practice or are being violated and of what the most desirable emphasis and direction of our teaching should be in order to extend "the blessings of liberty" as we preserve "domestic tranquillity."

Without essaying the role of a prophet, here is my reading of the needs of the present. It seems to me that the Civil Rights Acts of 1964 and the Voting Acts of 1965 mark a watershed in the history of social and civil protest in the United States. Upon their enforcement a great many things we hold dear depend, especially those causes in behalf of which in the last decade so many movements of social protest were launched. We must recall that it was the emasculation of the 15th Amendment in the South which kept the Southern Negro in a state of virtual peonage. The prospect of enforcement of the new civil rights legislation is a function of many factors—most notably the law-abiding behavior of the hitherto recalcitrant elements in the southern white communities. Their *uncivil,* violent disobedience has proved unavailing. We need not fear this so much as that they will adopt the strategies and techniques of the civil disobedience itself in their opposition to long-delayed and decent legislation to make the ideals of American democracy a greater reality.

On the other hand, I think the movement of civil disobedience, as distinct from legal protest, in regions of the country in which Negroes have made slow but substantial advances are not likely to make new gains commensurate with the risks. Those risks are that what is begun as civil disobedience will be perverted by extremists into uncivil disobedience, and alienate large numbers who have firmly supported the cause of freedom.

One of the unintended consequences of the two world wars is that in many ways they strengthened the position of the Negroes and all other minorities in American political life. We do not need another, a third world war, to continue the process of liberation. We can do it in peace—without war and without civil war. The Civil Rights and Voting Acts of 1964 and 1965 are far in advance of the actual situation in the country where discrimination is so rife. Our present task is to bring home and reinforce popular consciousness of the fact that those who violate their provisions are violating the highest law of the land, and that their actions are outside the law. Therefore, our goal must *now* be to build up and strengthen a mood of respect for the law, for civil obedience to laws, even by those who deem them unwise or who opposed them in the past. Our hope is that those who abide by the laws outlawing segregation may learn not only to tolerate them but, in time, as their fruits develop, to accept them. To have the positive law on the side of right and justice is to have a powerful weapon that makes for voluntary compliance—but only if the *reasonableness* of the *prima facie* obligation to obey the law is recognized.

To one observer at least, that reasonableness is being more and more disregarded in this country. The current mood is one of growing indifference to and disregard of even the reasonable legalities. The year's headlines from New York to California tell the story. I am not referring to the crime rate which has made frightening strides, nor to the fact that some of our metropolitan centers have become dangerous jungles. I refer to a growing mood toward law generally, something comparable to the attitude toward the Volstead Act during the Prohibition era. The mood is more diffuse today. To be law-abiding in some circles is to be "a square."

In part, the community itself has been responsible for the emergence of this mood. This is especially true in those states which have failed to abolish the *unreasonable* legalities, particularly in the fields of marriage, divorce, birth control, sex behavior, therapeutic abortion, voluntary euthanasia, and other intrusions on the right of privacy. The failure to repeal foolish laws, which makes morally upright individuals legal offenders, tends to generate skepticism and indifference toward observing the reasonable legalities.

This mood must change if the promise of recent civil rights legislation is to be realized. Respect for law today can give momentum to the liberal upswing of the political and social pendulum in American life. In a democracy we cannot make an absolute of obedience to law or to anything else except "the moral obligation to be intelligent," but more than ever we must stress that dissent and opposition—the oxygen of free society—be combined with civic obedience, and that on moral grounds it express itself as legal dissent and legal opposition.

ADDENDUM: SOME THESES ON THE NATURE AND SOURCES OF CONSCIENCE

1. The term "conscience" is used ambiguously:
   a) sometimes it refers to a power or faculty that enables a person to determine what his *duty* is;
   b) sometimes it refers to a distinctively moral sense that discloses the presence of good or bad in human conduct;
   c) sometimes it is identified as "a still, small voice" of regret, remorse, or guilt expressing a *negative* judgment on what has been done or is about to be done;
   d) infrequently it refers to an emotion or feeling of approval that allays anxiety over the rightness or wrongness of an action already performed or contemplated.
2. The objective reference of these terms, whether considered as a power, faculty, emotion, or disposition is a psychological reality.

3. Whatever its source or origin, the most important question we can ask about conscience is its moral authority.
4. This moral *authority* cannot be derived from the psychological experience itself. Seeing is not believing; nor is moral sight *ipso facto* warranted belief.
5. The moral authority of conscience cannot be derived from any religious source without obvious question begging: If the voice of conscience is the voice of God, how can we know we have heard the genuine voice of God rather than the tempting, deceptive voice of Satan without antecedent knowledge of the goodness or rightness of what God commands? For example, Feuerbach versus Kierkegaard: "Men build their gods in their own image."
6. The deliverances of conscience cannot all be infallible since every person who invokes his conscience must in principle believe that the deliverance of any other consciences declaring him to be an imposter is mistaken.
7. There are other reasons for doubting the moral authority of deliverances of conscience:
   a) The consciences of past generations led to actions which in the perspective of later times seemed needlessly cruel. "Thou shalt not permit a witch to live."
   b) The consciences of present generations rarely speak up in many kinds of situations in which conduct is clearly morally wrong. For example, customs, income tax, the imposition of unnecessary suffering on sentient creatures consumed as food (vegetarianism).
   c) The multiplicity of complex moral problems—housing patterns, bussing, punishment, the rights and limits of privacy—on which conscience speaks either not at all or with an uncertain voice.
8. There is no reason to invoke any transcendental or supernaturalistic element in accounting for the existence and operation of conscience.
9. Among the natural causes that enter into the development of conscience and the expression of its edicts are:

a) the internalization through growth of habits of the norms of behavior of society, family, school, peer groups;
b) fear of detection of violation of accepted norms and of consequent sanctions, physical and social.

10. Most explanations of the origin of conscience explain plausibly why conscience speaks whenever an action is proposed or committed that violates an accepted social norm. They do not explain when and why conscience will manifest itself by condemning what the social norm approves—
   a) Jeremiah, Socrates—John Brown
   b) What distinguishes the prophet from the crackpot?

11. Conscience acquires authority only as the outcome of conscientiousness, or conscientious reflection.
   a) Where the edict of conscience is taken as an unalterable moral datum, conscientiousness is merely rationalization, i.e., the quest for "good reasons" (rather than valid ones) and refusal to uncover the "real reasons" (actually "causes") of bias.

12. No genuine moral problem, therefore, in which good conflicts with good and right with right can be solved by reliance on conscience which in its immediacy can only reflect the strength of the initial dispositions associated with the conflict of values.

13. This analysis of conscience does not invalidate "conscientious objection" when it is an attitude toward a specific law resulting from the use of discriminating intelligence in tracing the consequences of the relative alternatives of action open to the moral agent.

14. This analysis of conscience calls into question the validity of any deliverance that claims to be final or ultimate or infallible, or "absolute," for example, absolute pacifism.

15. It recognizes as the overriding obligation of moral life the obligation to be intelligent (Erskine's phrase) and to take into account the consequences of individual action upon the public welfare or common good.

CHAPTER ELEVEN

Bureaucracy and Human Freedom

For centuries desperate citizens have watched government and industrial bureaucracies grow in size and complexity like throbbing globs of protoplasm determined to swallow up the whole world, but it was not until a few years ago that a brilliant young professor of history, C. Northcote Parkinson, put his finger on the forces here at work and summed it up with a mathematical quip. In his masterwork, *Parkinson's Law,* he reduced the problem of "staff accumulation" to a simple mathematical expression

$$x = \frac{2k^m + l}{n}$$

where x stands for the number of new staff required each year; k, the number of staff seeking promotion through the appointment of subordinates; l, the difference between the ages of appointment and retirement; m, the number of man-hours devoted to answering memos within the department; and n, the number of effective units being administered. Instead of dividing by *n,* one should perhaps multiply.

The full implications of Parkinson's discovery and mathematical pleasantry lie beyond the scope of this analysis, but we feel its suggestive nature best if we appreciate that on the basis of Parkinson's Law we can illumine such a phenomenon as this: in 1914 the Royal Navy had a strength of 146,000 officers and men, 3,249 dockyard officials and clerks, 57,000 dockyard workmen, 62 capital ships; in 1928 there were 100,000 officers and men, 62,439 workmen, 20 capital ships, and 4,558 *dockyard officials and clerks.* The equation does not, of course, recommend what to do with all these clerks, but it may suggest another aid in halting recessions.

Now, a bureaucrat is not just a *k* in a formula whose special pleasure it is to harass patient taxpayers. A bureaucrat is an administrator. When we are dissatisfied with the way an administrator behaves we call him a bureaucrat. In this sense, bureaucracy is a disease of administration. All organizations are subject to it—whether government, business, union, church, or university.

The problems of bureaucracy are as old as human organization. They are accentuated today by four contemporary factors. First, there is the problem of hugeness in the size of institutions. This interferes with intimacy and face-to-face relationships. Second, there is the specialization of skills and knowledge. This makes us more and more dependent upon trained administrative personnel. Third, there is the interlocking character of the chains of command in various institutions. This makes it difficult to counterpose one bureaucratic power against another in order to limit excesses of power. Fourth, there are external dangers to the security of the state, sometimes from without, sometimes from within. This gives policymakers and administrators great authority in the interests of defense. "Weapons of criticism are laid aside when criticism by weapons begins"—at least for the time being. If all this is true, we must be careful to avoid easy denunciations of bureaucracy. In fact, we ought never to overlook the human being in the bureaucrat and the potential bureaucrat in ourselves.

Administration is like government. It always takes away some individual freedom, but its justification must be sought in the fact that it makes possible more of the desired kinds of freedom than would be possible in its absence. Without the operation of our present complex administrative procedures of licensing, regulating, inspecting, and controlling the use of automobiles, for example, who in his senses would maintain that he could have the same individual freedom to use his car in our highly populated cities as he presently has? The situation is grim enough today despite existing controls but would we get to our destinations more quickly and safely without them, and without the potential of enforcement behind them? Every anarchist who drives a car in traffic owes his life to the very institution he would abolish.

Nonetheless, there is good and sufficient reason for scrutinizing carefully the entire machinery of administration in the light of new developments. There is first the tendency exhibited by all bureaucracies, whether in government or outside it, to expand their personnel and needlessly to proliferate their functions. A "healthy" officialdom is apparently an expanding one, and this irrespective of function. The story is told that in a large American university a special messenger service was introduced to expedite the sending of dissertations and important documents from office to office. As the years went by the messenger service became more extended until the campus swarmed with messengers, scurrying to and fro. A new president intent on economy looked at this department with a jaundiced eye and wanted to eliminate it. In a desperate effort to justify the messenger service its head asked: "Why, all sorts of things come up. Just suppose a million-dollar check came in tomorrow. How would we get it to the bank?" "I'd take it to the bank myself," the president replied, and he got rid of the messenger bureau.

Bureaucratic growth and deformation occur even when the function is originally justified. The bureaucratic machine keeps on growing even when the need for it has disappeared. During the last war the Office of War Information set up a radio monitoring service to keep a check on enemy propaganda. Efficient routines were established and a steady content-analysis of enemy propaganda flowed from the relevant OWI offices. Toward the end of the war the enemy radio stations in Italy were captured by the Allies and used for Allied propaganda. An OWI executive in Washington discovered that the monitoring service was still making a content-analysis of these stations even though they were issuing not enemy propaganda but Allied propaganda. When this was called to the attention of the staff members responsible, they justified their procedure on the ground that the content-analysis was useful to the other staffs still monitoring German and Japanese stations. This naturally was confirmed by these staffs in turn, who were wondering what would be their fate when Allied troops took over the German and Japanese radio stations.

Everyone can tell his own story about bureaucratic ineptitudes. Yet I do not believe this is the central point. No group or individual has a monopoly on human stupidity. The cure of bad administration is better administration, not no administration. The more important question to ask is: what are the justifying values of administration or bureaucracy? And how can we improve it and check its excesses in their light? We may agree with Woodrow Wilson that "it is better to be untrained and free than to be servile and systematic," but surely, as he was well aware, these are not the only alternatives.

After all, how an administrator becomes a bureaucrat is what concerns us. Analysis of this key question depends upon the values we take as fundamental and upon our conception of the best process by which these values are to be achieved. Here we come to conflicting views of the proper role of administration. One view is familiar to us in the Platonic conception of the rule of the philosopher-king or, in modern idiom, the rule of the expert. The second is the democratic view, which takes its chances with inefficiency but insists on diffusing power and yet making it more responsive and responsible.

The first view is based on the assumption that the expert, the man who has specialized knowledge, training, and experience, knows the genuine interests of those whose welfare he administers better than the masses affected by his decisions. Just as the physician knows better than the patient what constitutes good health and the best means of achieving it, so the experts, the physicians of state, so to speak, are supposed to know better than the citizens in what the public welfare consists. This view crops up in all sorts of organizations, public and private. Those who administer service organizations sometimes assert that they know the interests of their clients better than the latter do themselves. Leaders of trade unions often insist that they can achieve greater benefits for their members by paternalistic guidance than by permitting the spontaneous expressions of preference which too often reflect the influence of loud and demagogic voices. All this is urged in defense of proposals to restrict the processes of decision-making to the expert and informed: i.e., by definition, to the administrator and the bureaucrat.

The democratic view to which most Americans are committed in theory, although our practice does not always reflect it, challenges this position. It asserts that, by and large, adult human beings who have access to relevant sources of information are better judges of their own interests than any group of administrators, bureaucrats, or experts. The most relevant source of information for most people is their own experience and their reflection upon that experience. In the basic affairs of life this is obvious and can be denied only by paternalists who believe that the human estate is one of perennial childhood.

After all, those who wear the shoes know best where they pinch. The expert may know best how to correct shoes that pinch, but the criterion of proper correction is set by the consumer. It cannot be set by the planner of the "ideal" shoe, who would force people's feet into perfect footwear and charge them with sabotage or "reactionarism" when they cry out in distress. (Plato had a glimpse of this in the tenth book of the *Republic* in the report Er brings back of the inept choices the denizens of the ideal commonwealth make when they are free of the tutelage of the philosopher-kings. But he did not grasp its implications. For it threatens the principle on which his "Republic" rests.)

We take it as axiomatic that we have the right to change our political shoes in the light of experience. Although we may seek advice, take it, or reject it, in the end the responsibility is ours. We cannot forego this responsibility without admitting that others are better judges than we ourselves of our own true interests. From this it follows that delegation of power to officials or administrators presupposes that the proper exercise of their function will involve periodic consultation with those affected by their decisions, awareness of their needs and desires, the exchange of relevant information, and the multiplication of opportunities for participation of ordinary citizens (or rank-and-file members) in the processes of decision-making.

A common retort to suggestions of this sort is that it hampers efficiency. And it is undeniable that consultation, the give-and-take of argument, the establishing of a consensus take time. Measured by time spent or wasted, it is more efficient to entrust *one* person with policy decisions. Yet sometimes it is possible to pay too high a price in human dignity for such efficiency. Furthermore, there are many kinds of efficiency—defined in terms of plural satisfactions or defined in terms of a single narrow goal of production. The efficiency of an army is determined differently from the efficiency of a trade union or a university. Even in cases where production is taken as an index of efficiency, it may turn out that production is in turn dependent upon employee morale, satisfaction, *esprit de corps* resulting from a consciousness of effective participation, of co-responsibility for operations of the enterprise. In affairs of the mind, however, where creativity not efficiency is the final good, the graver danger comes from mediocrity not bureaucracy. Here quality not numbers must rule.

It is sometimes protested that this attitude leads to the invasion of the province of administration, and subjects the expert to the judgment of those who are not expert. Here we must make a distinction. There is of course a danger that untrained individuals will presume to talk about what they do not know and about what they are not competent to assess. But one does not have to be an expert in order to judge the handiwork of experts. Surely, I can judge whether the soup is good even though I cannot prepare it. No chef can intimidate a man who knows what he likes into abandoning his judgment because he does not possess the chef's culinary prowess. We don't have to be a general to know who is a good general, a watchmaker to tell a good timepiece from a poor one, a pilot to know who brings his passengers safely to port. A wise use of things depends upon knowledge of them, but not all knowledge of things leads to a wise use of them. For wisdom is an affair of values. It rests on a knowledge of what we really want, what we are prepared to give up for what we want, its price or cost not only in terms of pain but in the alternatives of other goods which are excluded by our choice. In this sense, for free men there are no experts in wisdom even though some men are obviously wiser than others. Whoever deprives us of our responsibility for choosing—for choosing even unwisely—deprives us of our freedom. That is why, as Jefferson saw, the defense of freedom in a democracy ultimately lies in a legislature responsible to the people, not in a supreme court responsible only to itself, and certainly not in untrammeled executive power.

There is some weighty historical evidence which reinforces natural skepticism of those who are convinced that their expertness gives them the "right to manage" the affairs of men. For bureaucracies acquire power not so much by usurpation as by gradual use and wont. Nor do they always succumb to the specific temptation of furthering their material interests. James Marshall's observation: "When the few govern, they govern in the interests of the few" is largely true but sometimes false. Not infrequently it is the desire to get things done quickly which exercises the corrupting influence. There is a type whom we can identify as the managerial autocrat who enjoys driving himself as much as others even when his material rewards are not disproportionately higher than others. He may even exhibit a certain self-righteousness about his sacrifices and dedication. And all this may be abetted by the indifference of the ordinary citizen or member. The consequences of benevolent autocracy and popular apathy may be very grave. In some trade unions, the individual member possesses fewer rights with respect to his own organization, especially if he opposes or agitates against official policy, than he possesses as a citizen with respect to his government.

History, however, cuts two ways, and those of us who defend the democratic variant of administration must face the contention of a formidable school of Italian thinkers—Michels, Pareto, and Mosca—who assert that all institutions require organization, all organization hierarchy, and all hierarchy the operating rule of a minority. This is the so-called "iron law of oligarchy," or rule of the élite. It may be formulated in various ways, but for present purposes it can be characterized as the view that democrats may be victorious, democracy never, and that a bureaucracy can indeed be overthrown or tamed but only by a movement which supplantś the old bureaucracy with a new one. According to this view, behind all the grandiose ideology and rhetoric, one underlying law allegedly dominates social life. In every system and at all times there is a class which commands and a class which is commanded. The first class is always smaller, smarter, stronger and, when they call themselves democrats, more unctuous and hypocritical than the second class. You can do anything to the ruling class, they tell us, but you can never get it off the backs of the masses until you have another ruling class to take its place.

It would take us too far afield to do justice to all phases of this view. It makes sense only when counterposed to the nonsense which interprets democracy as if it were *the direct rule* of the majority. But democracy never is the direct rule of a majority because it never can be. All democratic life depends upon the delegation of power and all delegation must be to a minority. This is the veriest tautology. The significant question is how this minority is selected, whether it is responsible and to whom, whether it has a monopoly of power, whether it is subject to law, whether it rests on uncoerced consent or whether the consent is elicited by the judicious use of bread, circuses, and force.

The iron law of oligarchy puts us on our guard against the myriads of ways in which by smooth manipulation of the rules of the game minorities in power can frustrate the needs and defeat the aspirations of those who are the source of sovereignty in democratic communities. But the fact that it allegedly holds both for the régimes of Hitler and Stalin, and those, say of Roosevelt and Churchill, for trade unions headed by Hoffa and Beck as well as those headed by Reuther and Dubinsky, shows we are dealing not with a law but with a tendency that can be managed. Whether the "law" be made of iron or not, it can be bent by the strength of our knowledge of human frailty and temptation, and by our passion for human freedom and justice, into a pattern which does not bind or constrict the will of the majority so tightly that it cannot get rid of the ruling minority. The majority cannot rule directly since even in an ideal democracy it must delegate authority to those who apply and enforce the laws; and the life of the law lies in its application and enforcement. But wherever mechanisms and institutions exist which enable the majority freely to replace one minority of bureaucrats by another democracy exists.

Democracy and democratically functioning administrators are therefore possible but they are difficult. They are difficult because our goals often conflict and must be reconciled, sometimes by emphasizing one value, sometimes another. All of our administrative mechanisms must be applied in concrete situations in which we confront conflicting claims to security and freedom, efficiency and happiness, safety and adventure, greater profit and greater service.

One of the great dangers of organization is that it inhibits spontaneity. There are areas of human experience, especially personal relations, in which there can be no compensation for the loss of spontaneity, of fresh, natural response. Even educational institutions may be overorganized to a point where the mastery of the syllabus becomes more important than cultivation of the power of independent judgment and the capacity for self-education. But there are other areas of common activity in which we cannot safely rely on spontaneity and must prepare in advance the mechanisms to channel spontaneity. For example, whoever would wait for an enemy attack before establishing a civil-defense organization overlooks the fact that panic, blind spontaneous panic, is a more likely response to great disaster than cooperative effort.

The number of persons in the world, their quest for plenty and leisure, their unangelic nature, and the necessity for just distribution in a technological age compel us to conclude that the multiplication of organizations in society is inescapable. Repining will not reverse the trend. There are some who see in this the eclipse of individual freedom and justice which they seek to avoid or attenuate by setting up still other organizations which in time exhibit the disease they would combat. I make so bold as to contend that by and large, so far as the great masses of individuals are concerned, our world of giant organization, despite its bureaucratic deformations, has more effectively widened the scope of individual freedom, the freedom to develop one's powers and talents, the freedom to move, the freedom to learn, to think, and to dissent than was possible in the world of smaller organizations it has replaced. Those who glorify the past freedoms of the ordinary man and woman do not know the past very well. This is subject, of course, to some important qualifications, but I think it is wrong to say or imply that the individual has become helpless in the face of huge aggregates of power, a creature utterly dependent upon forces beyond control or modification, and that he can survive only by becoming a compliant "organization man." We err in underestimating what one man or woman can still do, at least in initiating great movements of change and reform, in our corporate world. Even if one cannot organize or participate in a movement, one *can* be a person in a bureaucratic age. It requires courage, but it always required courage to be a person, a courage which in the past, because of the absence of appropriate means and conditions, was not sufficient except for the privileged.

What does it mean to be a person in a bureaucratic age as distinct from being a number, a unit, a member of a crowd, a working bee in a communal hive? It means to have knowledge—knowledge of the world we live in, physical and social, its possibilities and its dangers. It means to have knowledge of *ourselves*, what we really want in the light of our capacities and limitations. It means the courage to make our own choices in the basic decisions of love, vocation, friendship, political life, and religious communion. Although all alternatives are not open to us, the more we seek them the more often we will find them. It means a willingness to risk something in behalf of our ideals and our sense of justice. It means a refusal to play it so safe that personal experience loses its zest and tang; a refusal to make mere survival the be-all and the end-all of life and politics. It means a commitment to a social order whose institutions make it possible for more and more people to become persons. It means, finally, the absence of fanaticism—the recognition that good often conflicts with good, that there are no total solutions, that the test of ends is to be found in the actual or probable consequences of the means used to achieve them. This entails the view that the ultimate authority in resolving all conflicts among men is not the authority of institutions, traditions, or men but the authority of rational method, of intelligence which must not be confused with a sweet reasonableness or posture of appeasement unable to see the face of evil when it shows itself.

No one can be a complete person except perhaps a divine being. And even the divine beings of myth and religion fall short of perfection. But although we cannot be gods, we can still live like men in a community of persons. When we put organizations, administrations, or bureaucracies on trial our verdict ultimately must rest on whether they help or hurt persons.

CHAPTER   TWELVE

Human Rights and
Social Justice

This year * there will be a universal celebration of the twentieth
anniversary of the adoption of the UN Declaration of Human
Rights. There is a certain irony and fatuity in the fact that in many
countries which have subscribed to the Declaration, the human
rights promulgated by our Declaration of Independence and the
French Declaration of the Rights of Man and Citizen are completely disregarded and often openly violated by their governments. This raises a number of interesting questions about political semantics and political sincerity that cannot be pursued here.

In our own country the celebration of the Declaration on
Human Rights comes at a time when there is increasing concern
about social justice. In the past, declarations about the rights of
man focused primarily on political and civil rights. Today, however, in official documents and declarations bearing on human
rights we find specific references to whole clusters of social,

* This essay was composed in 1965 and slightly modified to reflect
recent developments.

economic, educational, and cultural rights. In some areas of the world, this emphasis upon social and economic rights has become the justifying ground—in the eyes of some observers, the pretext or rationalization—for sacrificing existing political and civic rights of dissent or for postponing their introduction to a time in the future when war will be among the institutions studied in the museums of antiquity. Unfortunately, this may be a long time to wait.

What I propose to do is to explore some problems which grow out of the tensions, paradoxes, and indeed "conflicts" among the complex of human rights that enter into that comprehensive and controversial expression, "social justice."

I shall not spend much time on the difficult questions of definition. When we speak of human rights we are speaking of rights that are broader than legal rights and narrower than the morally right. Human rights are more inclusive—perhaps broader or more fundamental—than legal rights because they serve as criteria of what should or should not be the basic legal rights enforced by the state. And, obviously, there are many legal rights, like the right to sue for damages or for specific performance if a contract has been breached, that will not be found on any list of human rights. On the other hand, there are many things that are morally right to do, like helping someone in distress or telling the truth, which would hardly appear on a schedule of human rights. By and large, when we use the expression "human rights" we mean by it a justifiable claim to certain powers or goods and services, to certain modes of treatment, especially freedom from interference, which upon reflection we acknowledge we have an obligation or duty to respect. And this irrespective of whether they are enshrined in a constitution or not.

Why these claims are justified is a very difficult question to which philosophers have given incompatible answers—religious, metaphysical, and psychological. I shall not discuss these justifications, save peripherally, because it is clear that most human beings are much more convinced, e.g., that men have a right to a fair trial, to worship God according to their conscience, to freedom of speech, to property, to educational opportunity, etc., than they are about the justifications of these rights. This is analogous to the fact that we are more convinced that "proposition x is truer than y," that "policy a is better than b," than we are of any definition of "truth" or "good." Indeed, we test the adequacy of any definition in terms of its conformity to the usage of the terms "true" and "good" as revealed in our pragmatic, reflective commonsense judgments. All knowledgeable persons will admit the truth of the statement "Bread is more nourishing to humans than stones" but they will quarrel about the meaning of "truth." All sensible persons will grant that "a divorce is better (or a lesser evil) than a murder," but it is not likely they will agree about the meaning of "good" and "bad."

There is one characteristic of schedules of human rights that is noteworthy. They vary from age to age. And in the same age different rights receive different emphasis. This proves not, as some skeptics assert, that they are nonexistent or arbitrary expressions of individual wish but that they are *historical,* to be understood in the context of their time and place, and rooted in what is experienced as an urgent need, signifying either distress or hope for better things, and crying out for remedy, reform or, if improvisation fails, revolution. This emphasis upon the importance of historical considerations is essential if we are to avoid fanaticism in the pursuit of human rights and social justice.

If the phrase "human rights" is ambiguous, the expression "social justice" is even more so. The evidence for this lies at hand: everyone asserts that he believes in social justice even though the conceptions of social justice vary so widely. At one end of the spectrum is the view that society or the state should do nothing but set down and enforce fair rules to regulate the universal quest for welfare or happiness. At the other, is the view that the state or society should do everything it can to guarantee that in the race for welfare or happiness everyone is a winner. But it is obvious that these views are also ambiguous. What are *fair* rules of a race? Does this mean that all start from scratch—the halt, the maimed, and blind as well as the healthy and vigorous? Or, to be fair, must we give handicaps to the handicapped? And on what basis? Do fair rules in the distribution of educational opportunity require that we spend more on the dull than on the bright? Why? And if we sincerely desire that the community do what is necessary for everyone to come in a winner—what shall we do when not everyone can win? Does it really make sense to speak of a winner without there also being losers?

To think of human beings as losers, in a life they did not choose and in a world they never made, may offend our moral sensibilities. Abandon then the very conception of social life as a race for victory or struggle for survival! Excellent! But the problem remains no matter how we conceive of society, to wit, *Where there does not exist more than enough of everything in the way of desirable goods, services, and opportunities that can be made available to everyone at the same time, by what rule shall we distribute them?*

Regardless of the ambiguities in the conceptions of "human rights" and "social justice" two characterizations of them are obviously valid. They presuppose that we are dealing with social relations, that where a man lives by and for *himself* alone, it is senseless to talk of human rights and/or social justice. Secondly, whenever we discuss these concepts we are committed to a belief in *equality* of some sort. Every pronouncement in favor of human rights stresses some principle of equality. Every proposal to do justice to a person is a proposal to treat him with equality in some respect. F. H. Bradley and some other philosophers define justice as the impartial application of a rule to all cases that fall within its jurisdiction. As we shall see, these notions are necessary but not sufficient to understanding justice. After all, it would take considerable hardihood to declare that any rule, whatever its character, if impartially applied, was just.

Actually, there is another expression not synonymous with "social justice" that nonetheless has a bearing on it, and suggests that there is something else that must be taken into consideration. We sometimes speak of "natural justice," more often of "natural injustice" when, through no fault of their own, human beings suffer pain and misfortune from physical evils. Sometimes this is referred to especially in the writings of Dostoevski, as "cosmic injustice." From time immemorial one can hear mingled with the cries for social justice cries for cosmic justice or surcease from cosmic injustice. It can be heard in the Indian Upanishads, in the chorus of Sophocles's *Oedipus Coloneus,* in the Book of Job—in the laments of anyone born blind or crippled or ugly or in any natural state which is the source of human anguish. There is a sense of "unfair" intimately related to being "unlucky." One curses the time in which he is born: bemoans the fate of being thrust into the world in a condition of servitude or in a benighted country or in an impoverished and loveless family There is a saying attributed to an Eastern sage who proclaimed: "Only a few enjoy the high privilege of not being born." That life itself is a sentence of punishment from which death is a welcome release is suggested by Socrates's last words in the *Phaedo* enjoining his disciple, Crito, to sacrifice a cock to Aesculapius, the Greek God of medicine. (How strange that the philistine-genius Hegel should have interpreted this as a reminder by an honest man on his death bed of a debt he owed a neighbor!)

Behind *this* cosmic lament on every level and at all times is the experience of suffering, pain or agony, spiritual humiliation, in the sense of an evil *imposed* without justification, discriminatory because not shared universally, and therefore an ever present source of resentment. A *universal* calamity seems more easily endurable to most human beings than a merely *personal* one even if the totality of suffering is greater in the first. These cosmic or natural injustices are indirectly taken note of by all theories of social justice in a manner that suggests the recognition of the fact that "equality" does not exhaust its meaning, that another dimension is involved. For every theory of social justice makes special provision for, or extends special consideration to, the "victims" of natural injustice, for those who are handicapped or disadvantaged at birth or by accident. It is as if in applying the rules of social justice we wish to compensate for the privations and hardships that, but for the grace of God, or Chance, or Accident (name it what you will!), might have befallen us. It is as if we were trying to do something to *equalize* or diminish the burden of discomfort or suffering in giving differential privileges to the handicapped and deprived not out of philanthropic zeal or compassion but as if it were their due.

That is why it is not enough to define social justice as equal treatment or equality before the law or the impartial application of a rule to its domain. It is not enough because of the difference between saying: "Justice consists in *treating* everyone equally" and "Justice consists in *mistreating* everyone equally." The diffnce goes to the heart of our conception of social justice—as distinct from legal justice. It is recognized in the spontaneous judgments mature adults make in humorous as well as tragic situations. The child who startles her pious mother, when taken to the museum to see the well-known picture of the Christian martyrs thrown to the lions, with her exclamation: "Look, Mummy, there's one poor lion who has no Christian!" has taken too literally the principle of equality as a sufficient guide in determining just treatment. The invader who in retribution orders every tenth hostage shot is not acting less unjustly but more so, when on reflection, to avoid the reproach of not being fair, he orders all the hostages to be shot.

What I am saying is that there is a built-in demand either for the diminution of acute human suffering or for the expansion of human welfare in the very demand for social justice. Sometimes there is a conflict between the components of equality and welfare—but not for long when great human suffering may be avoided by sacrificing or modifying the *formal* rules of equality. When it is not a question of great human suffering, short of a reflective analysis of the whole situation and a consideration of the consequences of alternative possibilities of action, decision is difficult. I know of no one rule or one value that can guide us in making this decision.

Let us recognize at the outset, although this means we can offer no clean, clear-cut solutions to difficulties, that in the concept of social justice two notions are involved (but not fused)—equality and human welfare.

It is necessary now to look at the concept of equality more carefully. It is a commonplace that no one can take literally the phrases in the great historic documents that state or imply that all men are created or are born equal. Even when this is acknowledged, we often find a desperate and subtle search for some property, apparent or recondite, natural or supernatural, which is presumably common to all men, and therefore can serve as a basis or justification for the equality of treatment that is due men if they are to be treated justly. Sometimes it is said that all men *have* intrinsic dignity or a spark of divinity in them or a common fate of mortality or some other basic attribute. And further, that unless they possessed this common attribute, the whole notion of justice as equality of treatment would be fatuous or even senseless.

It seems to me that this approach is profoundly mistaken. I am not convinced that there is any trait which is equally common to all men. It is obvious that if there were any such trait, you could not deduce from it any specific mode of equality of treatment. (One could release all the hostages or destroy them all.) This is true also of alleged nonnatural traits possessed by men. Even if all men are equal in the sight of the Lord, equally sinners or beloved children, this would be compatible both with the belief in, and practice of, the divine right of kings to rule on earth, and with the equal democratic right of sinners to participate in a government based on consent. Be the natural or supernatural constitution of man what anyone believes it to be, what makes one method of treatment wiser or better or more desirable than another is the upshot or fruits of the differential treatment. Put another way, the justification for treating human beings in relevant circumstances equally is not to be found in the possession of some antecedent trait but in the *consequences* of treating them equally contrasted with the *consequences* of not treating them equally.

What does it mean, however, to treat human beings equally or justly—aside from the question of whether all human beings possess an inherent equality? How shall we characterize the policy or proposal of equality of treatment, granted that we are not presenting it as a description of equality?

The first response made to this question is misleading because we sometimes confuse the equal with the uniform, the equal with the identical. The demand, for example, for "equality before the law" is one of the oldest expressions of the demand for human rights. Assume an incorruptible judge. Is it just to impose equal punishment on a youthful stripling and a mature adult both apprehended committing the same crime? Is it just to mete out the same sentence to a first offender and a fourth offender even if both are mature adults? Shall we hold all offenders charged with the same offense in equal bail—even if it means that the wealthy man walks free and the poor man must languish in jail until trial? Shall we fine the millionaire and the driver of the Good-Humor truck the same amount for going through the traffic light?

What is a just tax bill? A flat tax for everyone? That would be absurd because it would not lead to *equality of burdens*. Shall it be a percentage tax? But Engel's law shows the poor may have to do without necessities if they pay the same percentage of their income as their wealthier brethren because they spend a larger percentage of their income on food, clothing, and shelter. A progressive income tax? How do you know when you have equalized the burdens?

Consider situations not related to taxation or courts but in which I want to be fair, e.g., in teaching.

Shall I assign the best teacher to the best students (or class) or to the poorest students?

Shall I address myself in my class to the dullest? the brightest, or to the mediocre?

Actually isn't the best or ideal teaching situation one in which I adjust the teaching to the individual needs of the individual student—the tailor-made curriculum?

This individualization means, of course, *not* treating everyone alike but differently.

Doesn't justice also require, because of the different histories of the defendants at the bar and their different capacities for suffering, etc., individualization of punishment? Similarly for medicine.

Where then does this leave us? We started out by saying that justice consists in treating individuals under a rule *alike*. Now we are saying it consists in treating them *differently*.

Well, we correct ourself. We say that justice consists in treating everyone in identical circumstances equally. Who is really in *identical* circumstances? We must modify that to read in *similar* circumstances. But even that isn't enough. The similar circumstances must be *relevant.*

Now we are getting closer to the nature of social justice. But it is obvious that what is relevant depends upon the *situation* in which a rule is being adopted and the *purpose* of the rule. *Treating people justly in relevant circumstances does not require that we treat them uniformly but only that we must have a good reason for treating them differently, for making exceptions. These good reasons are derived from our desire to increase human weal and avoid human woe, to diminish suffering and to maximize welfare.*

We follow the rule of equality but we know that there can be legitimate and illegitimate grounds for *discriminating.* Many illustrations come to mind. In cases of great distress and scarcity rationing of supplies by the community is adopted, but often we make—and should make—special allowance for the *aged* or for the *infant* or for the *sick* but not for those whose religion or race or creed or friends are like ours.

We speak of equal rights for women but we have social welfare laws which forbid the employment of women in some kinds of hazardous work like mining, etc. *Sex* may then be a ground for fairly excluding some from work—but race may not be a ground. If the Equal Rights Amendment becomes law social welfare legislation in behalf of women may be abolished, but it is not likely that sex differences will be altogether disregarded in the administration of laws. Except in some special cases men will not be granted paternity leave from work comparable to the maternity leave extended to women.

Perhaps the best illustration of equality of treatment which is compatible with *justified differences* of treatment is found in the behavior of a dedicated physician toward his patients. Not only does he treat his patients differently when he gives them equal medical consideration—in a crisis situation he may give a patient in an acute condition or on verge of death *more* consideration than others, and we understand why and accept it.

Even more apt is the illustration of parents who treat their children with an *equality of concern* that does not, of course, presuppose an equality of talent among the children. What parent on the basis of the discovery that the children range in I.Q. from 80 to 140 would therefore conclude that this justified denial of food, clothing, decent shelter, and medical treatment to any of his or her children?

This provides an analogue for our approach to the organization of society. Assuming that there is an equality of concern on the part of the community for all its citizens to develop to their fullest growth as persons—which is the cardinal ethical belief of democracy as a way of life—then what is wrong is not inequality of treatment but unwarranted or unreasonable inequality. The democratic task in a society whose history reflects the inescapable heritage of class societies of the past is to replace inequalities of treatment which are unreasonable by those which are reasonable. It must replace *discriminations* that are irrelevant to the tasks in hand by discriminations that are relevant. (If, e.g., the task is to construct a great symphony orchestra, it must select musicians not by their color or religion or creed but by their ear, their sense of pitch, and their related skills.)

So far our considerations have been abstract. I want to bring them to bear upon some of the concrete problems of American life. I can only touch briefly on them because detailed analysis is impossible in short compass. What I have been saying is not unrelated to the commitments which the United States as a nation has made in its historic documentary professions of faith. We have rejected all the historic notions of an élite society and are committed to the political institutions of a self-governing community. We have prided ourselves that the democratic political and legal rules of the game have permitted the possibility of an equality of opportunity for all citizens to live the life of free men in it in accordance with their capacities. It was the philosopher-statesmen of the American Republic, particularly Thomas Jefferson and James Madison, who realized long before Karl Marx how difficult it was to preserve effective freedom for all in the face of great disparities in wealth. Where property is power, and where insufficiency of power deprives the masses of independence, the freedom of political institutions is imperiled.

What Jefferson and Madison failed to see was that the disparities produced by the concentration and centralization of wealth could not be controlled without the government interventions they feared, and that the preservation of the mechanisms of freedom depended upon a healthy economic and social organism.

When one analyzes the concept of "equality of opportunity" one discovers that if it is taken seriously it is a truly revolutionary principle which would require the remolding of social institutions to a point where we could speak of the *revolution en permanence.* Actually it was Plato who first realized how revolutionary the principle of "equality of opportunity" was because he argued that children could be provided with equality of opportunity to develop their best talents and personality only if they were brought up by the best possible fathers and mothers. He therefore proposed to wipe out the family and have all children educated by those who had a professional genius for parenthood. Not all who are biologically fit to be parents are educationally, morally, or socially fit—a proposition no one can reasonably doubt.

However, one need not go so far as Plato (or even Freud) in this analysis of the family as an institution which makes for *inequality* of opportunity to recognize that where no provision is made for decent housing, adequate schooling, readily available health facilities, and, above all, proper nourishment and subsistence, there can be no meaningful talk about equality of opportunity. And today it is commonly recognized that those who *inherit* poverty and its consequent social deprivations are the victims of social injustice even if we dispute about the causes. This is certainly true of the *children* of those of whom we may be tempted to say that they deserve their misfortune. Even conservative thinkers acknowledge that there is a floor or level of subsistence below which we regard it as unseemly for a human being to sink. The principle of a negative income tax advocated by proponents of free enterprise like Professor Milton Friedman is testimony to the strength of the common conviction that where there exists sufficient affluence to distribute to those in want, justice as well as prudence requires that their basic needs be met, independently of merit or desert. This seems to be particularly true when there is a superfluity of goods and potential resources that go to waste or remain unused unless distributed. There is even talk of a guaranteed income as a floor with a rising slope depending upon the development of technology.

In the area of public health we are recognizing to an increasing degree that the same principle which justifies the extension of police protection to citizens independently of their worth or merit or ability to pay, also justifies the extension of medical protection, both preventive and remedial. If all citizens have a right to protection against human agents who threaten their safety and survival—whether on the grounds of equality of opportunity to live freely or to reduce insecurity or human suffering—why have they not a right to protection against the natural, nonhuman agents of destruction that threaten their health and life? A child who is ill or hungry certainly does not possess opportunities to develop himself equal to those normally enjoyed by his healthy and well-fed fellows. Why should people be expected to pauperize themselves before receiving medical protection any more than when they receive police protection? Of course where there are insufficient resources to make either police or medical services available to all, certain costs may be imposed.

This principle of equality of concern for all citizens in a democracy to develop themselves to their fullest as persons enables us to find a guide—if only roughly—in determining the locus and limits of permissible and impermissible discrimination—a theme about which so many individuals are confused today. Essential to the notion of a free man or free person is the right to choose, the freedom to develop his taste, his judgment, and the overall patterns of his life. Consequently in those domains of experience that are inherently or predominantly personal—friendship, family, cultural pursuits,—we must be free to discriminate, and legally protected in that freedom, even when our moral judgments are insensitive, capricious, or defective. For freedom to develop carries with it the right to err and to impoverish oneself.

Where, however, in fields in which discrimination prevents the development of personality in *others,* or erodes and undermines equality of opportunity, it is morally blameworthy and should be legally enjoined. Discrimination cannot therefore be tolerated in any of the public institutions that exist to serve the purposes of the governed, or in the domains of citizenship, housing, vocation, schooling, etc., since they grossly obstruct or interfere with the right and power of the person to live his own life.

Granting, however, that we are motivated by an equality of concern for all persons to lead the best life of which they are capable, there still remains the question of what *specific* rules to follow in the distribution of the social product in a given society at a given time. Granted that the distribution of goods and services cannot be literally or absolutely equal, except in limiting cases of extreme scarcity, but only *proportionately* equal. What should be the yardstick or criterion of the proportionate distribution? Many canons of distribution have been proposed. Merit or desert, basic needs, effort or willingness to work, etc. And if we take merit or desert as a criterion, what should be the measure of a man's desert? The *price* his services command in a free market? The *value* of the product determined by other than market considerations—say the quantity and quality of what is produced? Or its contribution to what is regarded as of greater social usefulness at the moment, whether it be a great symphony or medical discovery or inventions to guarantee national security against an atomic Pearl Harbor?

I do not believe there is any one canon of distribution for all types of situations. In an effort to achieve an overall equality it may be necessary to recognize the desirability of short-run inequalities of reward for highly skilled work or dangerous work or sacrificial work required to meet an emergency. If we are awarding *prizes* in a competition, what other criterion for the award can we follow except merit—at least as a necessary condition? After merit has been considered, we may assess as relevant the magnitude and urgency of economic need. Once minimal criteria of merit have been met, there is no one overriding principle that can guide us in all situations.

It is clear that in every situation where there is a scarcity of goods and services, over and above those necessary to preserve life and health, some principle of differential reward must be adopted. Necessities may be distributed on the basis of need or lot or chance but what about "luxuries"—using the word in the comparative or relative sense?

There are some who argue with Locke that in all situations natural justice requires that a man has a right to what he *produces* or to the full *product* of his labor—whether he be baker, tailor, farmer, sailor, or teacher. But the very enumeration of these professions—and the difficulty of determining *what* they produce, shows the inapplicability of any principle of natural justice. Take Locke's own illustration of the *loaf of bread* whose value is produced by labor. Whose labor? By the baker's labor, of course! But not by his labor alone! There is the labor of the miller and the farmer who produced the flour and the labor of the journeymen who made the things that entered into the gathering, storing, and transporting of the crop; and the services of the soldiers and sailors and others who prevented the country and crop from being despoiled; and not only these, but the labor of a long line of others who invented the ovens, and discovered the techniques of baking. The upshot of this line of inquiry is that in a sense *the whole of society produced that loaf of bread and not the unaided effort of one man however worthy.* Indeed, it is hardly an exaggeration to say that the debt of any individual to society in terms of what he receives from it, as a rule, is far greater than he can ever discharge by his own contributions to it.

To be sure, one may retort, it is true in some farfetched sense to say that society produces the loaf of bread and everything else in the society but it is also true that not all elements of society produce it or anything else *to the same extent.* Some produce more than others both quantitatively and qualitatively, and therefore justice requires that more be given to them than to others. Does this mean that whoever takes this position is committed to the view that it is just to enjoy the social privileges or rewards that result from the possession of natural inequalities of strength, intelligence, beauty, or what not? This conception of justice may be challenged. Why should some individuals be rewarded *socially* for the natural luck or grace of being born better endowed than others? Why should others be penalized for their natural infirmities of strength or intelligence? If people are to be socially rewarded over and above the satisfaction and pleasure of enjoying the unearned *natural privilege of talent*, why not reward human beings for being born more beautiful than others? But that is precisely what we do! Think of the rewards we shower on the beautiful! Yes—but who would undertake to defend this differential treatment of a beautiful woman on the ground of *injustice?* A better case could be made perhaps for the justice of rewarding the woman's less-beautiful sisters. "To them who hath shall be given—and from them who hath not, shall be taken away" is certainly a fact of life! But only a cynic will say that it is a rule of justice! It may be that the natural distribution of talents for which no one is responsible should be regarded as a matter of luck rather than of justice, assuming that there is no God whom we can praise or blame for it. The compensation for those who are victims of bad luck, natural or social, may be justified either on grounds of compassion or of some insurance principle.

My point is not that differential performance or merit should never be rewarded but that when we do so the justification must be found in some other principle than that of the natural fact of inequality itself. Even those who espouse an extreme egalitarianism of treatment must recognize that in some situations there may be good and sufficient reasons in terms of overall utility and individual advantage to accept as a supplementary principle— differential rewards.

Assume a situation in which all members of a group are receiving equal shares of the total social product for whose output they are responsible with equal dedication and zeal. Assume that an individual hits upon an idea or invention that would enable the group to more than triple its total output. The inventor refuses to disclose his new technique unless he receives considerably more payment than anyone else. And this despite the fact that he owes his scientific education to the community, to its cumulative traditions, to its legacy of skills, and that he would have honor enough for his discovery even if he did not receive a differential natural reward. If your choice were between one scheme of distribution in which all would share *equally* in poverty without the benefit of the invention, and another in which all except one, the inventor, would share an affluence, and that one, the inventor, enjoying a greater affluence than all the others, which scheme of distribution would you choose? I think wisdom would dictate the choice of the second scheme. Only a conception of justice rooted *exclusively* in envy and resentment would prefer a literal or mechanical equality of deprivation to one of differential distribution after a minimal acceptable standard for each individual has been met.

When individuals prefer that everyone go without rather than some enjoy more than others, it is only because the differential distribution becomes the source of invidious and patronizing judgments. There is a sense of rejection, inferiority, lack of status—as in children's response to comparable situations. But where the individual is convinced that he is as much an object of care and concern as anyone else, inequality loses its sting and bite. It requires sensitivity, intelligence, tact, empathy, and sympathy to apply policies so that licit inequalities of treatment are not misunderstood but are properly construed as flowing from an equality of concern. But as difficult as it is to implement this policy, which is central to the conception of social justice, it indicates the direction in which we must go—if social justice is a genuine goal.

So far I have been discussing the requirements of social justice without using high level abstractions like "capitalism" or "socialism." My experience has been that once these terms are introduced they block fresh thought because so many individuals react viscerally to them. I am confident that we can get greater agreement if we avoid large terms like "capitalism" and "socialism" and concentrate on a pragmatic approach to specific problems. These problems may require large scale changes like that of a guaranteed annual wage or unemployment insurance for all who are willing and able to work. We should be able to count on a much firmer commitment to human rights and social justice than to any economic theory.

The problem of implementing our analysis is very difficult

because there are so many different agencies concerned on so many different levels with the task of removing the obstacles to equality of opportunity for all American citizens to lead a good life. There is need for coordination of energies. Although much remains to be done on local levels, the Federal government must shoulder the main responsibility.

I said earlier that questions of social justice are historical because we never begin with problems from scratch or as they were at the Garden of Eden but always in *this* time and in *this* place. When we tackle *present* problems we must face up to *present* alternatives. And when we do this we must disregard even if we cannot forget the historical evils of the past, and not try to punish the living for the failure of moral responsibilities, alleged and real, of the dead. There is a curious attitude developing among those who think they are repudiating liberal blandness for radical sincerity which sees the problem of social justice today bound up with *historical* justice, conceived as undoing, or compensating for, the evils of the past. Because a great many wrongs in the past have been done to the Indians in this country, to the Negroes, to Mexicans, and other ethnic groups, it is argued that the white race must *today* atone for it, and be punished for the evils of the past. One priestess of the new politics of absurdity, Miss Susan Sontag, has declared that "the white race is the cancer of human history." She does not say whether the cancer should be cauterized by flame or knife but leaves little doubt that she approves a violent solution to problems of social justice as they affect the descendants of those presumably guilty of American "genocide." Fortunately, the American Indians today who are probably more numerous than they ever were in the past, despite the many problems they still face, have no truck with Miss Susan Sontag's irresponsibility. Unfortunately, however, something of her mood has infected some highly articulate but hardly representative members of the Negro community who have been abetted in these sentiments by the so-called New Left. Thus at the historic Chicago National Conference on New Politics held not so long ago, the ultimatum of the Black Caucus was adopted as the official program of the Conference. One of the thirteen demands of the ultimatum reads: "Make immediate reparation for the historical, physical, sexual, mental and economic exploitation of Black people."

Edmund Burke found it difficult to draw up an indictment against a whole people. Contemporary rhetoricians of violence find it easy to draw up an indictment of a whole race. They accept without qualms the very doctrines of collective guilt and guilt by association that have done so much mischief in the past. They fail to see that morally human beings are guilty only for those consequences which *their* actions or failure to act have caused. Whatever the crimes in the past may have been; they do *not* justify any crimes in the present. Otherwise we may as well hang a man today because his grandfather was a horse thief! No nation, no people, no race is free of guilt in the perspective of the past. But this is not relevant to the present.

The prospects for the achievement of some progress in coping with the difficult problems of social justice are difficult enough without prejudicing them with invitations to violence in the name of historical right. No historical injustice of the past can be remedied by violating the rights of individuals in the present, without compounding another injustice which by the same illogic of reprisal for reprisal generates an historical feud that continues until it ends in a mutual destruction of all parties.

Whatever social justice is in this world it can never achieve absolute justice. We must recognize that even when we attempt rectification of evils, absolute justice is unattainable. Its pursuit and persistent refusal to settle for anything less may lead to wrecking the possibilities of getting more and better results here and now. The whole loaf in human affairs can never be achieved.

The program of social reconstruction to be achieved in order to further the equality of human concern essential to the commitment to social justice is vast. It requires large-scale and small-scale, piecemeal and yet bold, planning. But success depends upon the continuous exercise of those political and civic freedoms which are integral to the democratic community.

That is why despite the attempt to downgrade the importance of political rights among the schedules of modern human rights, I regard the political rights of a free society as of paramount importance. There is no such thing as "two kinds of democracy"—political democracy in contrast with economic democracy or any other kind—but only a more complete and less complete form. Social justice is a completer form of democracy than one in which only political rights are recognized and guaranteed. For in the absence of social justice, the expression of political rights is often blunted and frustrated. But social justice without political democracy is impossible, since the greatest injustice of all is to impose rules upon adult human beings without their consent.

Index

289